Cochrane Shipbuilders
Vol 2 : 1915 - 1939

by

Gilbert Mayes and Michael Thompson

*Front cover : The **Admiral Drake** (yard number 1154).*

(Authors' collection)

*Back cover : A splendid image of work being done on the **Beachflower** (yard number 1098) as the vessel nears completion.*

(Cochrane shipyard collection)

*Above : A splendid view of the **Silvertown** (yard number 1207) passing the Tower of London.*

(Cochrane shipyard collection)

FOREWORD

To compile the history of a shipyard as prolific and diverse as Cochrane's has taken the authors many years of research. Numerous people have come forward to assist in the work including shipping historians, enthusiasts, archivists and librarians. To illustrate the book, photographs have been obtained from several notable collections. Representations are included of the house flags and funnels of prominent owners.

Volume Two takes the reader from the beginning of the Great War to the start of World War 2 and includes details of vessels taken into Admiralty service. The book provides an insight into the advances in design which trawler owners were constantly seeking in order to improve the catching ability of their fleets.

The shipyard had to cope with many problems during the period covered by this volume. Obviously there was the Great War itself and its need for troops. It also had to deal with the requirements of the Admiralty. The gradual recovery of the nation after the war soon gave way to recession and then the increasing threat of another war. Just as we noted in Volume 1 that the Cochrane yard had to move from sail-powered vessels to steam, so in this volume we see the change from steam to motor power. We shall also note an increase in the number of tugs, coasters and other vessels being constructed.

Michael Thompson, Hull, June 2014

ACKNOWLEDGEMENTS

Firstly, we would like to acknowledge the work done by Tony Lofthouse and David Newton; two of the original authors who worked hard on the first draft of this project and have supported it going forward and being improved.

The staff of the Hull History Centre for their invaluable assistance with this project. Documents used include: Hull Shipping Registers, fishing registers, voyage books, Hull Trawler Owners' Minute books, ledgers, journals and printed material, Admiralty papers involving trawler owners, local newspapers and publications.

Anne Cowne: Information Administrator, Information Services, Corporate Communications at Lloyd's Register, London.

Arthur Credland: former Keeper of Hull Maritime Museum who organised the Cochrane Archive and assembled the outline history of the company.

Jonathan Grobler (Grimsby trawler photographs); Paul Whiting (George Scales' photographs); Peter Bass (tug photographs). Suppliers of other photographs are named in the credit beneath their images.

Jack Daussy, Fécamp: Reference to French Grand Bankers from his book *Les Chalutiers Morutiers Fécampois*.

Jim Porter (fleetwood-trawlers.info); Barry Johnson (milfordtrawlers.org.uk); Andy Hall (grantontrawlers.com); Chris Petherbridge (hulltrawler.net); Barry Banham; Roger Griffiths; Peter Bell; William Blow; George Westwood; David Slinger; Birgir Thorisson; Maurice Voss; Jan Harteveld and Douglas Paterson.

Last and certainly not least, the authors wish to thank Short Run Press for the splendid printing.

Published by Bernard McCall, 400 Nore Road, Portishead, Bristol, BS20 8EZ, England.
Website : www.coastalshipping.co.uk.   Telephone/fax : 01275 846178. Email : bernard@coastalshipping.co.uk.
All distribution enquiries should be addressed to the publisher.

Printed by Short Run Press, 25 Bittern Road, Exeter, EX2 7LW.
Telephone : 01392 211909.   Fax: 01392 444134.   Email: info@shortrunpress.co.uk.

ISBN : 978-1-902953-65-6

The Cochrane Shipyard, 1914-1939

Following the outbreak of WW1 all trawlers that were in build at Selby were requisitioned by the Admiralty for war service as they were completed. By the middle of 1916 it was realised that so many trawlers and drifters had been requisitioned it was not possible to take any more without jeopardising the supply of fish to the nation. In consequence the Admiralty selected three trawler types which, with some modification, could carry additional naval equipment without detriment to stability. The Selby yard **Lord Mersey** (yard no. 647) design was chosen as one prototype and following successful inclining of **Lord Reading** (yard no. 648) at Newcastle, the design was developed as the 'Mersey' class, suitably armed for naval tasks including minesweeping, anti submarine and patrol duties. Further it was envisaged that these standard trawlers, once hostilities ceased, would be sold and quickly converted for fishing, compensating to some extent for war losses. All three classes of Admiralty standard trawlers took their names from the crew muster roles of HM Ships **Victory** and **Royal Sovereign** at the Battle of Trafalgar.

Cochranes were the lead yard and supplied plans and expertise to other clients of His Majesty's Government building this class. At some 325 tons gross and 138ft 4in long, they were built on ten berths (five pairs) and launched two at a time at the spring tides, about two vessels a fortnight. The main trades spent a fortnight on each pair, in sequence: the first pair - framing; the second - inside work; the third - plating; fourth - riveting; and fifth pair - caulking and riveting [1]. From laying the keel to readiness for towing down the river took a total of about three months. There was a fifty mile journey on the Ouse and Humber to Hull; the shell would be towed as soon as it lifted from the mud on the flood tide, the tugs preferring to tow against the tide, at some 4-5 knots, in the upper reaches of the river. Some two hours would see the craft at Drax, where the power station now is, and they would tie up and await the next tide within the old railway bridge on the Hull and Barnsley line. Again on the flood tide they would move when the tow lifted, and reach Blacktoft after another 1½ to 2 hours and another similar period to Hull, but they would have to wait to lock into Humber dock on arrival. Skelton railway bridge was difficult when the tide was starting to change, pushing the tow down into the tug with increasing speed. A total time of 5-6 hours over three tides was usual but clearly the much bigger craft reaching the size limit of the yard might have problems when tides were at neap and also when the water flow in the rivers was reduced during the summer. The vessels finally arrived at Queens Dock for installation of machinery and general finishing.

Andrew Cochrane the founder was aging and his son of the same name needed help to run the yard. The latter's eldest son, Andrew Lewis Cochrane (1892-1965), born in Hull and educated in Leeds, spent a short period in the drawing office, mould loft and some of the 'outside' departments at Selby before moving in 1911 to the shipyard at Grangemouth on the Firth of Forth where he gained experience in the drawing office. He returned to Selby three years later and after enlisting in the East Yorks Regiment he was directed back to the shipyard by the Admiralty in September 1915. As Assistant Yard Manager, his job was to supervise vital war time contracts and he was responsible for the fitting-out and trials of more than 100 craft for the Royal Navy. Later A L Cochrane became manager and was elected to the board in 1917. Donald McGill Cochrane (d.1962), the second son, joined his brother at the yard in 1915. Family members always played their part in the community and Donald took a seat on the Selby Urban District Council, and from 1937 until 1947 was Chairman of this Council.

In 1917 alone, 44 trawlers were launched, a total of 14,013 tons. Electricity was installed in the same year; electrification of industrial sites was widespread at this time and the King George V Dock at Hull (opened in 1914) was the first in the country to be completely provided with electric power.

The Admiralty realised they needed a vessel that was faster and cheaper to construct than the Admiralty design trawlers of the Mersey, Strath and Castle types which could manage 10 knots. Designs were submitted by six shipbuilding companies and orders were eventually placed for 85 vessels of the new Kil class to the design of Smiths Dock Co, Middlesbrough. Construction of each hull cost between £18,000 and £20,000 and machinery a further £19,600 and these patrol vessels were capable of 13 knots. Few were completed before hostilities ended, 11 vessels were adapted for minesweeping, while HMS **Kilmun** was briefly a Q ship and was then retained by the Royal Navy for harbour cable duties. A total of 37 ships were built at various yards and 36 quickly put up for sale; some Empire navies acquired a small number but most were converted for mercantile use as coasters [2].

*HMS **Kilfree** (859)*

(Cochrane shipyard collection)

NAME Official No. Port letters/numbers	Yard No. Launched Delivered	Registered Gross tons Net Tons	Length (feet) Breadth (feet) Depth (feet)	Engine builder Horse power Registered speed	Owner (built for)
WELBECK 137020 Steam trawler GY455	627 19.01.1915 31.03.1915	302 157	135.0 23.5 12.3	C D Holmes 84 rhp 3-cyl 10.5 knots	E C Grant, Grimsby

20.03.1915: Registered at Grimsby (GY455).   05.1915: Requisitioned for war service as a minelayer (1-6pdr HA) (P.No. N.4A, then N.8A). Based Portsmouth.   03.1919: Required for post-war service.   1920: Returned.   01.08.1916: Sold to Welbeck Steam Fishing Co Ltd, Grimsby.   07.02.1919: Sold to Yarborough Steam Fishing Co Ltd, Grimsby.   12.1919: Sold to F & T Ross Ltd, Hull. 20.12.1919: Grimsby registry closed.   02.01.1920: Registered at Hull (H128).   21.02.1920: Registered at Hull as **OHM** (H128). 25.08.1929: A large fire destroyed No.2 Hull Fish Market. Seven trawlers which were on the landing stage caught fire, three **OHM**, **MARCONI** (H488) (see yard no.656) and **LORD DERAMORE** (H461) (see yard no.1026) were burned out. All were repaired and returned to service.   08.1939: Requisitioned for war service as a minesweeper (P.No.FY.561); hire rate £83.1.0d per month.   Based Aberdeen with M/S Group 37.   02.1940: Inspected by Her Majesty The Queen at Aberdeen.   10.1940: Employed on miscellaneous naval duties.   1941: Transferred to Ardrossan. Based Ardrossan with M/S Group 37.   1942: Based Grimsby with M/S Group 57. 22.12.1945: Laid up.   31.05.1946: Returned.   16.03.1946: Sold to Westward Trawlers Ltd, Milford Haven.   10.04.1946: Hull registry closed.   20.04.1946: Registered at Milford as **WESTCAR** (M110).   22.07.1960: Sold to Haulbowline Industries Ltd, Passage West, Co Cork, for breaking up.   27.07.1960: Arrived Passage West.   10.08.1960: Milford registry closed.

| **VERESIS**
137027 Steam trawler
GY483 | 628
19.01.1915
14.04.1915 | 302
157 | 135.0
23.5
12.3 | C D Holmes
84 rhp 3-cyl
10.5 knots | Atlas Steam Fishing
Co Ltd,
Grimsby |

14.04.1915: Registered at Grimsby (GY483).   04.1915: Requisitioned for war service (1-6pdr) (Ad.No.1616). Based Egypt. Post 12.03.1919: Returned.   08.06.1931: Stood by steam trawler GAMBRI (GY99) (349grt/1929) 100 miles NW of Hoy Head with bunkers on fire and proceeding to Stromness.   16.01.1932: Left Icelandic grounds for Grimsby.   16.01.1932: In hurricane, swept clean by seas and lost wheelhouse and two compasses.   19.01.1932: Made radio contact and monitored by trawler MERISIA (FD153); requested any vessel to give bearing and supply a compass. Dodging for 36 hours, believed in vicinity of Faroe Islands and then steering by wind.   20.01.1932: Contact made with LUNE (FD59) which supplied bearing and confirmed crew safe and no assistance required.   20.01.1932: Arrived Scrabster at 1.20pm. Took compass and food and sailed 4.10pm for Grimsby. 22.01.1932: Arrived Grimsby.   22.11.1933: Reported stranded at Hoholmen, south Sandnessjøen, Norway. Salvage steamer PARAT (135g/1905) in attendance.   25.11.1933: Refloated with assistance of PARAT. Checked, tight and proceeded. 09.1936: Sold to Earl Steam Fishing Co Ltd, Grimsby.   20.04.1937: Registered at Grimsby as **WYOMING** (GY483). 04.1940: Employed on Fishery Protection based at Grimsby.   02.06.1940: Requisitioned for war service as an auxiliary patrol vessel; hire rate £83.1.0d per month. Based North Shields.   12.1940: Sold Sir Alec Black, Bart, Grimsby.   06.1941: Fitted out as a minesweeper (P.No.FY.1862). Based Ipswich with M/S Group 78.   22.04.1942: Sold to Active Steam Fishing Co Ltd, Fleetwood, for £8,100.   20.05.1944: Mined near 54 Buoy, 20 miles ENE of Harwich. Five crew lost.   1944: Grimsby registry closed.

| **CALVIA**
137024 Steam trawler
GY476 | 629
03.02.1915
01.05.1915 | 304
158 | 136.9
23.5
12.5 | Great Central Co-op
80 rhp 3-cyl
10.5 knots | Grimsby Alliance Steam
Fishing Co Ltd,
Grimsby |

06.04.1915: Registered at Grimsby (GY476).   05.1915: Requisitioned for war service as a minesweeper (1-12pdr, 1-7.5" A/S Howitzer) (Ad.No.852). Southern Patrol.   Post 12.03.1919: Returned.   03.1918: Sold to John L Green Ltd, Grimsby.   1923: Sold to owners in Portugal.   12.11.1923: Grimsby registry closed. Registered at Lisbon as **ESTRELLA POLAR**.   11.1923: Wrecked N of Peniche whilst on passage Grimsby towards Lisbon.

| **FRASCATI**
137006 Steam trawler
GY315 | 630
25.08.1914
08.10.1914 | 220
98 | 120.2
21.5
11.5 | Great Central Co-op
70 rhp 3-cyl
10.5 knots | Strand Steam Fishing
Co Ltd,
Grimsby |

02.10.1914: Registered at Grimsby (GY315).   11.1914: Requisitioned for war service as a minesweeper (1-12pdr) (Ad.No.49). Based Taranto.   By 12.03.1919: Returned.   23.10.1933: Sold to Harry Markham Cook, London.   18.11.1933: Sold to Aldred Fishing Co Ltd, Grimsby.   30.09.1941: Sold to J Bennett (Wholesale) Ltd, London. Fishing from Fleetwood.   1943: Working Icelandic grounds.   13.08.1945: Sold to British & American Salmon Curing Co Ltd, London.   29.10.1947: Sold to Elkington Estates Ltd, Grimsby.   04.1952: Sold to Thomas Young & Sons (Shipbreakers) Ltd, Sunderland, for breaking up.   19.04.1952: Delivered to Sunderland.   21.05.1952: Grimsby registry closed.

| **ST CYR**
136235 Steam trawler
H257 | 631
05.12.1914
11.03.1915 | 315
126 | 135.3
23.5
12.6 | C D Holmes
84 rhp 3-cyl
11.0 knots | Thomas Hamling
& Co Ltd,
Hull |

05.03.1915: Registered at Hull (H257).   06.1915: Requisitioned for war service as a minesweeper (1-12pdr) (Ad.No.1527). Special Services based Portsmouth.   By 12.03.1919: Returned.   05.07.1918: Sold to William G Allnut & Joseph W Debnam, Grimsby. 15.07.1918: Hull registry closed.   16.07.1918: Registered at Grimsby (GY1157).   01.02.1919: Sold to Audrey V Cole, Cleeve Hill, Cheltenham. Fishing from Scarborough.   04.1920: Sold to James Johnson, Scarborough.   08.04.1920: Grimsby registry closed. 04.1920: Registered at Scarborough (SH300).   30.05.1924: Sold to Sir Henry Samman Bt, Hull.   06.1924: Scarborough registry closed.   11.06.1924: Registered at Hull (H22).   03.06.1924: Sold to Munro Steam Trawling Co Ltd, Hull.   11.10.1926: Sold to Walter Crampin, Grimsby.   11.1926: Sold to Pêcheries à Vapeur S A, Ostend.   07.12.1926: Hull registry closed. 12.1926: Registered at Ostend as **DUCHESSE DE BRABANT** (O80).   16.04.1937: Stranded at Sumbo, Sydero Island, Faroe Islands. All crew saved. Ostend registry closed.

AISNE 136257 Steam trawler H257	632 03.04.1915 06.07.1915	315 126	135.3 23.5 12.6	C D Holmes 84 rhp 3-cyl 11.0 knots	East Riding Steam Fishing Co Ltd, Hull

01.07.1915: Registered at Hull (H343).   29.05.1917: Requisitioned for Fishery Reserve.   1919: Released.   24.05.1921: Hull registry closed.   25.05.1921: Sold to Viuda de Canosa – Cierto, Barcelona, Spain.   05.1921: Registered at Barcelona as **CIERTO**. Re-measured to 316grt, 168net.   1952: Sold to Benita Gutierrez Diaz, Barcelona.   1955: Sold to Ramon Canosa & Hermanos, Barcelona. Converted to burn oil fuel.   1967: Removed from Lloyd's Register of Shipping.

MANX QUEEN 137029 Steam trawler GY491	633 16.02.1915 29.05.1915	234 115	120.3 22.2 11.5	C D Holmes 65 rhp 3-cyl 10.0 knots	William H Beeley, Grimsby

10.05.1915: Registered at Grimsby (GY491).   06.1915: Requisitioned as a minesweeper (1-6pdr) (Ad.No.1529).
01.03.1916: Stranded on Filey Brigg.   31.03.1916: Grimsby registry closed - "Wrecked".

JACINTA 139206 Steam trawler FD235	634 17.07.1915 14.12.1915	289 115	130.2 23.5 12.8	C D Holmes 84 rhp 3-cyl 10.5 knots	J Marr & Son Ltd, Fleetwood

02.11.1915: Registered at Fleetwood (FD235). Requisitioned from the builders and fitted out as a minesweeper (1-6pdr, 1-7.75" A/S Howitzer) (Ad.No.1976). Based Moray Command.   23.10.1918: Re-registered at Fleetwood (FD235).   1920: Returned.
14.10.1932: In the early hours, struck submerged rock 8 miles off Rathlin Island, Co Antrim, losing all blades on her propeller. Taken in tow by DORINDA (FD198) (270grt/1916).   15.10.1932: Arrived Fleetwood.   12.08.1934: On St Kilda ground in collision with steam trawler DAILY CHRONICLE (FD69) (281grt/1917) sustaining damage to starboard side. DAILY CHRONICLE suffered no damage.   04.1940: Employed on Fishery Protection (WA/Fort William/Fleetwood).   27.05.1940: Requisitioned for war service; hire rate £79.9.6d per month.   26.05.1940: 'Operation Dynamo' (Dunkirk evacuation) put into effect.   01.06.1940: With troops onboard bound Ramsgate, stranded on wreck of a steamer near North Goodwin Light Vessel. Steam tug JAVA (128grt/1905-500ihp) attended and took off 150 allied troops and landed them at Ramsgate.   02.07.1940: Found drifting, towed in, repaired and fitted out for auxiliary patrol duties (1-12pdr HA) (P.No.4.138).   10.1941: Fitted out for minesweeping duties.   07.1943: Fitted out for wreck dispersal duties.   06.1944: Assigned to Operation Neptune - Normandy landings; held in readiness at Sheerness.
03.07.1944: Operation Neptune ended.   1944: Sold to Harold Barber Ingram, Fleetwood for £10500.   05.1946: Returned.
09.1953: Sold to BISCO and allocated to Thos W Ward Ltd, Sheffield, for breaking up.   11.09.1953: Delivered Barrow under own power.   09.1953: Fleetwood registry closed.

GAVINA 139207 Steam trawler FD236	635 17.07.1915 06.01.1916	289 115	130.2 23.5 12.8	C D Holmes 84 rhp 3-cyl 10.5 knots	J Marr & Son Ltd, Fleetwood

22.11.1915: Registered at Fleetwood (FD236).   04.1916: Requisitioned from the builders for war service as a minesweeper (1-12pdr HA & W/T) (Ad.No.1995).   23.10.1918: Re-registered at Fleetwood (FD236). Based Falmouth. By 12.03.1919: Returned.
05.10.1921: Outward for west of Ireland fishing grounds in dense fog ran on reef north of Bruce's Castle, Rathlin Island, Co Antrim. Crew launched boat and landed on island. Salvage failed due to extensive bottom damage and vessel declared a total loss. Wreck still visible in position 55.17.50N/06.10W in 6m of water.   17.11.1921: Fleetwood registry closed - "Wrecked 5/10/21".

ARMAGEDDON 136249 Steam trawler H319	636 04.03.1915 13.05.1915	323 129	137.0 23.5 12.9	C D Holmes 87 rhp 3-cyl 10.5 knots	Cargill Steam Fishing Co Ltd, Hull

06.05.1915: Registered at Hull (H319).   09.1915: Requisitioned for war service as a minesweeper (1-6pdr) (Ad.No.1748). Based Stornoway.   13.12.1918: Sold to Wyre Steam Trawling Co Ltd, Fleetwood. By 12.03.1919: Returned.   17.09.1919: Hull registry closed.   22.09.1919: Registered at Fleetwood (FD348).   30.09.1921: Registered at Fleetwood as **DHOON** (FD348).
06.03.1928: Transferred to Hull.   15.03.1928: Fleetwood registry closed.   16.03.1928: Registered at Hull (H396).
07.1929: Transferred to Fleetwood.   09.07.1929: Hull registry closed.   10.07.1929: Registered at Fleetwood (FD54).
18.10.1935: Fishing 50 miles W of St Kilda, at about 10.15pm struck by heavy seas and lost wheelhouse roof and damaged funnel. Heavy seas did further damage and carried away lifeboat injuring three crew members; disabled. Observed by trawler EDWARD WALMSLEY (FD412) (276grt/1919) which hauled gear and proceeded to casualty.   19.10.1935: After twelve hours and seven attempts, connected and proceeded for Fleetwood.   22.10.1935: At 4.20am arrived Fleetwood after difficult tow.   1940: Employed on Fishery Protection (WA/Fort William/Fleetwood).   27.05.1940: Requisitioned for war service and employed on miscellaneous naval duties (1-12pdr) (P.No.4.131); hire rate £88.16.6d per month.   26.05.1940: 'Operation Dynamo' (Dunkirk evacuation) put into effect.   01.06.1940: Carried troops from Dunkirk.   04.1941: Fitted out for minesweeping duties.   1943: Renamed **DHOON GLEN**. Based Yarmouth with M/S Group 83 and Patrol Group.   11.1945: Returned to owner and reverted to **DHOON** (FD54).
06.12.1947: Sailed Fleetwood for Icelandic grounds (Sk Fred Kirby); fourteen crew.   12.12.1947: In heavy swell and fog stranded under the Latrabjarg, west coast of Iceland.   13.12.1947: Farmers from Hvallatur and neighbouring farms descended down cliffs 850 ft to an outcrop called Flaugarnef, 200ft above the shore. Party of four lowered to beach at low water and walked 550 yds to wreck. Shot a line to wreck and with the help of Albert Head, Bosun, recovered twelve survivors. Unable to get the whole group up to Flaugarnef before the tide flooded, a shelter was found under the cliffs for the seven crewmen remaining.   14.12.1947: Rest of group hauled up the cliff and brought to Hvallatur.   15.12.1947: Last members of the party arrived at Hvallatur; three crew members including skipper and mate were lost.   19.12.1947: Survivors arrived Reykjavik in the Icelandic trawler GEIR (RE241) (665grt/1947) for flight to Prestwick.   08.03.1948: Fleetwood registry closed.

CARYSFORT 137762 Steam trawler M32	637 06.03.1915 09.06.1915	243 105 11.7	120.3 21.5	C D Holmes 75 rhp 3-cyl 10.5 knots	David Pettit, Hakin

20.05.1915: Registered at Milford (M32).   06.1915: Requisitioned for war service as a minesweeper (1-6pdr, 1-7.5" A/S Howitzer) (Ad.No.1533). Renamed **CARYSFORT II**. Based Granton.   By 12.03.1919: Returned and reverted to **CARYSFORT** (M32). 27 - 29.01.1922: Stood by Manchester steamer MILLTOWN (1882grt/1908) in southern Irish Sea listing in strong gale and heavy seas after cargo shifted and escorted to Milford Haven.   22.02.1923: Sailed Milford for Small's ground (Sk A Faulker). Seen on the ground but not equipped with WT. Posted missing lost with nine crew.   27.03.1923: Milford registry closed - "Vessel missing".

COTSMUIR 137763 Steam trawler M15	638 17.03.1915 17.06.1915	243 105 11.7	120.3 21.5	C D Holmes 75 rhp 3-cyl 10.5 knots	David Pettit, Hakin

29.05.1915: Registered at Milford (M15).   06.1915: Requisitioned for war service as a minesweeper (1-6pdr HA) (Ad.No.1537). 02.02.1917: Disappeared on passage River Tyne to River Humber. No survivors.   24.01.1919: Milford registry closed - "Vessel Lost".

TRIBUNE 137032 Steam trawler GY563	639 03.04.1915 02.09.1915	302 158 12.3	135.0 23.5	C D Holmes 84 rhp 3-cyl 10.5 knots	Anchor Steam Fishing Co Ltd, Grimsby

06.08.1915: Registered at Grimsby (GY563).   09.1915: Requisitioned for war service as a minesweeper (1-6pdr HA, 1-7.5" A/S Howitzer) (Ad.No.1847).   02.1918: Renamed **TRIBUNE II**.   1920: Returned and reverted to **TRIBUNE** (GY563).   10.1923: Sold to Beacon Steam Fishing Co Ltd, Grimsby.   01.10.1924: Registered at Grimsby as **LORD BEACONSFIELD** (GY563). 08.1928: Sold to Consolidated Fisheries Ltd, Grimsby.   03.1929: Chartered to fish in Canadian waters based at Canso, Nova Scotia, in a training role.   28.03.1929: Grimsby registry closed.   07.07.1930: Registry re opened at Grimsby (GY563). 09.1933: Sold to Martinus A Olesen, Grimsby.   04.1935: Sold to Consolidated Fisheries Ltd, Grimsby.   08.1939: Requisitioned for war service as an auxiliary patrol vessel.   04.09.1939: Returned.   04.06.1940: Requisitioned for war service as a minesweeper (P.No.FY.608); hire rate £83.1.0d per month. Based Harwich with M/S Group 79.   04.1942: Sold to J Bennett (Wholesale) Ltd, London.   17.10.1945: Stranded 1nm SW of Red Head, Auchmithie, Angus.   1945: Grimsby registry closed - "Total Loss".

WILLONYX 137031 Steam trawler GY544	640 15.05.1915 19.08.1915	327 171 12.8	140.4 24.2	C D Holmes 90 rhp 3-cyl 10.5 knots	Orient Steam Fishing Co Ltd, Grimsby

15.07.1915: Registered at Grimsby (GY544).   08.1915: Requisitioned for war service as a minesweeper (1-6pdr, 1-7.5" A/S Howitzer) (Ad.No.1747). Based Portsmouth.   Post 12.03.1919: Returned.   01.1920: Sold to Direct Fish Supplies, London. 23.03.1922: Company in voluntary liquidation.   05.1922: Sold to Francisco Freixas, Barcelona, Spain.   20.05.1922: Grimsby registry closed.   05.1922: Registered at Barcelona as **FRANCISCO**. Re-measured to 328grt, 159net.   1931: Sold to Freixas Hermanos S A, Barcelona.   1946: Sold to José Trullenque Montoro, Valencia.   1957: Sold to Francisco Rey Mendez, Corunna. Barcelona registry closed. Registered at Corunna.   1960: Sold to Spanish shipbreakers and broken up.   1960: Corunna registry closed.

CORRIE ROY 138937 Steam trawler GY635	641 31.05.1915 29.09.1915	327 171 12.8	140.4 24.2	C D Holmes 90 rhp 3-cyl 10.5 knots	Orient Steam Fishing Co Ltd, Grimsby

07.09.1915: Registered at Grimsby (GY635).   11.1915: Requisitioned for war service as a patrol/escort vessel (1-12pdr, 1-7.5" A/S Howitzer) (Ad.No.3218). Based Larne.   By 12.03.1919: Returned.   06.1920: Sold to Direct Fish Supplies, London.   23.03.1922: Company in voluntary liquidation.   10.08.1922: Placed in compulsory liquidation.   10.1922: Sold to Vincenti Galiana S en C, Barcelona, Spain.   11.10.1922: Grimsby registry closed.   10.1922: Registered at Barcelona as **MARIA DOLORES**.   1936: Sold to Galiana Vejarano S en C, Barcelona.   1944: Sold to J Otero Bárcena, Barcelona.   1945: Sold to Eugenio Bravo Muñoa, Barcelona. 26.04.1947:   Stranded on a reef off Cap Ghir, Morocco. Abandoned after salvage attempts failed.   1947: Barcelona registry closed.

GRAND DUKE 138938 Steam trawler GY683	642 31.05.1915 13.10.1915	327 171 12.8	140.4 24.2	C D Holmes 90 rhp 3-cyl 10.5 knots	Frank Barrett, Grimsby

28.09.1915: Registered at Grimsby (GY683).   11.1915: Requisitioned for war service as a minesweeper (1-12pdr) (Ad.No.2512). Based Milford Haven.   Post 12.03.1919: Returned.   01.1920: Sold to Direct Fish Supplies, London.   23.03.1922: Company in voluntary liquidation.   10.08.1922: Placed in compulsory liquidation.   08.1922: Sold to George E J Moody, Grimsby. 25.10.1922: Registered at Grimsby as **NIGHT RIDER** (GY683).   12.1922: Sold to Nocturne Fishing Co Ltd, Grimsby. 10.1939: Sold to Hull Northern Fishing Co Ltd, Hull.   06.10.1939: Grimsby registry closed.   09.10.1939: Registered at Hull (H170). 27.01.1940: Requisitioned for war service as a boom defence vessel (P.No.Z.113); hire rate £89.18.6d per month. Based Granton. 17.02.1941: Sold to Hellyer Bros Ltd, Hull.   23.11.1943: Compulsorily acquired by Ministry of War Transport.   10.02.1944: Hull registry closed.   04.1946: Transferred to Ministry of Transport.   Laid up, placed on disposal list.   02.1947: Sold to L Storhaug & Partners Ltd, UK.   1948: Sold to Storship Salvage Ltd, London. Converted to a salvage tug; tonnages amended to 343grt, 118net. 1949: Sold to Greece. Registered at Piraeus as **KASSOS**. Re-measured to 300grt, 133net.   1951: Converted to motor - 8-cylinder 500bhp oil engine by General Metals Corp, San Francisco.   1954: Sold to Zacharis Bros & M Vassilias & Co, Piraeus.   1958: Sold to Zacharis Bros & Co, Piraeus.   1961: Sold to Goumas Bros, Piraeus.   1963: Sold to Tsitzas Bros & Asterios Belos & Co, Piraeus. 1970: Vessel removed from Lloyd's Register of Shipping.

MAGNETA	643	322	136.2	C D Holmes	F & T Ross Ltd,
139267 Steam trawler	30.06.1915	130	24.0	87 rhp 3-cyl	Hull
H354	17.09.1915		12.9	10.5 knots	

02.09.1915: Registered at Hull (H354).   09.1915: Requisitioned for war service as a minesweeper(1-12pdr, 1-7.5" A/S Howitzer) (Ad.No.1970). Based Galway.   By 12.03.1919: Returned.   31.01.1922: In the early morning fishing about nine miles off the Murmansk coast arrested by a Russian patrol ship; Sk Robert Morgan Geddes and one crewman taken onboard Russian ship and two guards placed on trawler, both vessels proceeded towards Murmansk.   01.02.1922: In storm conditions anchored in cove but cable parted and driven ashore. Ten crew and two Russians lost.   12.09.1922: Hull registry closed - "Wrecked".

KELVIN	644	322	136.2	C D Holmes	F & T Ross Ltd,
139270 Steam trawler	30.06.1915	130	24.0	87 rhp 3-cyl	Hull
H357	21.10.1915		12.9	10.5 knots	

12.10.1915: Registered at Hull (H357).   11.1915: Requisitioned for war service as a minesweeper (1-6pdr HA) (Ad.No.1974). Based Harwich.   07.07.1917: Mined E of Aldeburgh, Suffolk, (mine laid on 29.06.1917 by UC.4). Five crew lost. 21.08.1917: Hull registry closed - "Lost while on Admiralty service."

NIGHT HAWK	645	307	132.0	C D Holmes	Pioneer Steam Fishing
138942 Steam trawler	14.08.1915	150	24.0	89 rhp 3-cyl	Co Ltd,
GY822	03.01.1916		12.8	10.5 knots	Grimsby

01.01.1916: Registered at Grimsby (GY822).   02.1916: Sold to Grimsby Steam Fishing Co Ltd, Grimsby. 03.1916: Requisitioned for war service as a minesweeper (1-6pdr HA) (Ad.No.1936). Employed on escort duties. Based Devonport. By 12.03.1919: Returned.   07.02.1934: On an Icelandic trip off Isafjord sustained damage after striking an ice flow. 01.1939: Sold to Earl Steam Fishing Co Ltd, Grimsby.   01.06.1940: Requisitioned for war service as an auxiliary patrol vessel (P.No.FY.1858); hire rate £86.19.8d per month.   10.1940: Fitted out as a minesweeper. Based Plymouth with M/S Group 76. 08.1941: Sold to North Star Steam Fishing Co Ltd, Aberdeen.   22.09.1941: Grimsby registry closed.   25.09.1941: Registered at Aberdeen (A517).   1944: Employed on auxiliary patrol duties.   13.11.1944: Sold to Parkholme Trawlers Ltd, Fleetwood. Aberdeen registry closed. Registered at Grimsby (GY15).   1945: Sold to Milford Fisheries Ltd, Milford Haven.   08.1946: Returned. 24.08.1948: Landed at Fleetwood (Sk Arthur Harvey) after nine day trip mostly on herring, 1,350 boxes £2,250 gross. 06.1954: Laid up at Milford due to further increase in price of bunker coal.   08.1954: Re-activated.   02.1959: Sold to Jacques Bakker en Zonen, Bruges, for breaking up.   25.02.1959: Last landing at Milford.   28.02.1959: Sailed Milford for Zeebrugge. 02.03.1959: Delivered Bruges.   03.1959: Grimsby registry closed.

DONNA NOOK	646	307	132.0	C D Holmes	Mount Steam Fishing
139209 Steam trawler	14.08.1915	150	24.0	89 rhp 3-cyl	Co Ltd,
FD237	27.01.1916		12.8	10.5 knots	Fleetwood

04.02.1916: Registered at Fleetwood (FD237).   02.1916: Requisitioned for war service as a minesweeper (1-12pdr, 1-3pdr HA & 1-7.5" A/S Howitzer) (Ad.No.1981).   26.09.1916: Re-registered at Fleetwood (FD237). Based Yarmouth.   By 12.03.1919: Returned. 02.11.1920: Picked up sixteen crew members of the Scarborough steam trawler MARY A JOHNSON (SH91) (see yard no.879) which had been abandoned four days previously having struck a reef close to 'Geirfuglasker' rock, SE of Reykanes, Iceland. 03.11.1920: Landed survivors at Reykjavik.   04.1940: Employed on Fishery Protection (WA/Fort William/Fleetwood). 03.06.1940: Requisitioned for war service as an auxiliary patrol vessel (P.No.4.132); hire rate £86.19.8d per month. Based North Shields.   08.1941: Fitted out as a minesweeper (P.No.FY.1559). Based Ipswich with M/S & Patrol Group 78.   25.09.1943: Under attack by E-boats off Shipwash, 12 miles E of Harwich. Foundered following collision with HMT STELLA RIGEL (P.No.FY.657) (418g/1936) when manoeuvring to pick up survivors from HMT FRANC TIREUR (P.No.FY.1560) (GY1041) (see yard no.682) torpedoed by E-boat S.96; crew picked up by STELLA RIGEL.   Fleetwood registry closed.

LORD MERSEY	647	326	138.5	C D Holmes	Pickering & Haldane's
139286 Steam trawler	11.10.1915	134	23.7	93 rhp 3-cyl	Steam Trawling Co Ltd,
H427	15.02.1916		12.8	10.5 knots	Hull

The **LORD MERSEY** design was adopted for the "Mersey" class of Admiralty standard trawlers.
15.02.1916: Registered at Hull (H427).   04.1916: Requisitioned for war service as a minesweeper (1-12pdr, 1-7.5" A/S Howitzer) (Ad.No.1991). Based Kirkwall.   27.11.1917: At Aberdeen fitted with hydrophones.   By 12.03.1919: Returned. 27.04.1928: Sold to Malcolm S McFarlane, London & John A Spilman, Hull.   13.07.1928: Sold to Alan Spilman Ltd, London. 29.08.1928: Registered at Hull as **CASTLETHORPE** (H427).   19.05.1933: Sold to J Marr & Son Ltd, Fleetwood, for £4100. 14.06.1933: Hull registry closed.   16.06.1933: Registered at Fleetwood (FD188).   14.12.1933: Registered at Fleetwood as **ARLITA** (FD188).   20.08.1934: Transferred to Hull, crewed and operated by City Steam Fishing Co Ltd, Hull, on the company acquisition. 11.06.1935: Transferred to Fleetwood.   09.1939: On a trip to St. Kilda grounds (Sk Ernest Christie); twelve crew. 18.09.1939: At 6.48pm. when trawling 22 miles WNW of St. Kilda, stopped by U-boat (U.35) in position 58.09N 09.17W. Advised to follow the submarine in the direction of smoke from two other trawlers. Seized along with trawlers LORD MINTO (FD51) (see yard no.599) and NANCY HAGUE (FD133) (299grt/1911). As boats not considered safe for crew, transferred along with crew of LORD MINTO to NANCY HAGUE. Sunk by gunfire in position 57.51N 09.28W along with LORD MINTO. NANCY HAGUE returned to Fleetwood with survivors.   27.09.1939: Fleetwood registry closed - "Sunk by enemy submarine".

Jacinta (634)

Donna Nook (646)

LORD READING 139287 Steam trawler H429	648 11.10.1915 08.04.1916	326 134	138.5 23.7 12.8	C D Holmes 93 rhp 3-cyl 10.5 knots	Pickering & Haldane's Steam Trawling Co Ltd, Hull

15.02.1916: Registered at Hull (H429). 041916: Requisitioned for war service as a minesweeper (1-12pdr, 1-7.5" A/S Howitzer) (Ad.No.1994). Based Tyne. Post 12.03.1919: Returned. 02.1926: Sold to A/S Tveraa Fiskeriselskab, Trangisvaag (Trongisvágur), Faröe Islands. 16.02.1926: Hull registry closed. Registered at Trangisvaag as **MAGNUS HEINASON** (TG642). 16.07.1927: Sold to John McCann Hull. 16.07.1927: Registered at Hull as **LORD READING**. 08.1927: Sold to Cia Argentina de Nav Angel Gardella Ltda, Buenos Aires, Argentina. 06.08.1927: Hull registry closed. Registered at Buenos Aires. Re-measured to 274grt, 79net. 1927: Registered at Buenos Aires as **BIGUA**. 1939: Sold to Soc Pesquerias Gardella S A (Pesgar S A), Buenos Aires. 1944: Sold to Argentine Government (Flota Mercante del Estado), Buenos Aires. Removed from Lloyd's Register of Shipping.

BELGAUM Steam trawler RE161	649 11.09.1915 10.03.1916	307 150	132.0 24.0 12.8	C D Holmes 93 rhp 3-cyl 10.5 knots	Thorarinn Olgeirsson, Reykjavik

03.1916: Registered at Reykjavik (RE161). 03.1916: Requisitioned from the builders as a minesweeper (1-6pdr HA) (Ad.No.1985). Based Humber. By 12.03.1919: Returned. 09.04.1916: Transferred to H/F Belgaum, Reykjavik. 07.04.1919: Arrived Reykjavik after restoration at Grimsby. 03.02 1921: A number of Icelandic fishermen in open boats were caught by a storm off Snæfellsnes, west coast of Iceland. Three boats with 27 men were picked up and two boats with 20 men by the Grimsby trawler YOKOHAMA (GY1286) (291grt/1909). 1924: Company re-located to Hafnarfjördur, Iceland. Reykjavik registry closed. Registered at Hafnarfjördur (GK161). 25.07.1925: Sold to H/F Fylkir, Reykjavik. Hafnarfjördur registry closed. Registered at Reykjavik (RE153). 21.09.1940: Homeward having landed at Fleetwood, picked up 44 survivors from the Jersey-registered whale factory ship NEW SEVILLA (13,801grt/1900) (Capt Richard B Chisholm) torpedoed by U-boat (U.138) 52 miles NW of Rathlin Island on previous day and foundered under tow 9 miles from Mull of Kintyre. Transferred survivors to Swedish motor vessel INDUSTRIA (1688grt/1940) which already had 215 survivors onboard and all were landed at Belfast. 16.11.1951: Sold to Höfdaborg h/f, Höfdakaupstadur. Reykjavik registry closed. Registered at Höfdakaupstadur as **HÖFDABORG** (HU10). Converted to burn oil fuel. 1952: Laid up. 23.05.1955: Sold to Danish shipbreakers. 27.05.1955: Sailed Reykjavik for Esbjerg, Denmark, in tow of motor tug SIGYN (288grt/1916) along with SKALLAGRIMUR (see yard no.693) and THOROLFUR (see yard no.694) for breaking up. Broken up and registry closed.

ST CUTHBERT 138943 Steam trawler GY824	650 11.09.1915 08.03.1916	311 162	137.0 23.5 12.3	C D Holmes 80 rhp 3-cyl 10.5 knots	Grimsby Victor Steam Fishing Co Ltd, Grimsby

01.01.1916: Registered at Grimsby (GY824). 04.1916: Requisitioned for war service as a minesweeper (1-12pdr, 1-7.5" A/S Howitzer) (Ad.No.1992). 11.1917: Sold to New Docks Steam Trawling Co (Fleetwood) Ltd, Fleetwood. Based Portland. Post 12.03.1919: Returned. 03.04.1919: Grimsby registry closed. 04.04.1919: Registered at Fleetwood (FD137). 16.10.1928: Sold to Capt Gjert Myhre, Halifax, NS, Canada. 12.1928: Sold to Ocean Trawlers Ltd, Halifax, NS. 27.12.1928: Fleetwood registry closed. 01.1929: Registered at Halifax, NS. 1936: Sold to Warren Transportation Co Ltd, Belize, British Honduras, for conversion to dry cargo. Converted to motor with 2-cylinder oil engine by J & C G Bolinders M/V A/B, Stockholm. Re-measured to 311grt, 241net, 508dwt. 1936: Halifax, NS, registry closed. Registered at Belize, British Honduras. 1938: Sold to Motorship St Cuthbert Inc, Tampa, FL. Belize registry closed. Registered at Roatan, Honduras. 1957: Sold to McCormick Shipping Corporation (c/o Eastern Shipping Co, Miami, FL, USA). Roatan registry closed. Registered at Panama. 1986: Removed from Lloyd's Register of Shipping - "Vessel's continued existence in doubt".

FLINTSHIRE 138965 Steam trawler BY875	651 25.10.1915 09.05.1916	215 100	117.3 22.0 11.5	C D Holmes 66 rhp 3-cyl 10.0 knots	North Lincolnshire Steam Fishing Co Ltd, Grimsby

04.05.1916: Registered at Grimsby (GY875). 04.1916: Requisitioned for war service an auxiliary patrol/escort trawler (1-6pdr HA, 1-11" & 1-7.5" A/S Howitzer) (Ad.No.3282). Based Devonport. 11.1919: Sold to the Admiralty, employed on mine clearance in the North Sea. 15.11.1919: Grimsby registry closed. 05.01.1926: Sold to Diamonds Steam Fishing Co Ltd, Grimsby. 08.07.1926: Registered at Grimsby as **TAIPO** (GY389). 11.1939: Requisitioned for war service as a minesweeper (P.No.FY.787); hire rate £63.15.0d per month. Based Grimsby. 1942: Based Dover with M/S Group 126. 04.1944: Converted to a smoke making trawler assigned Operation Neptune - Normandy landings. 08.06.1944: Sailed Bracklesham Bay with Group B1. 09.06.1944: Arrived Mulberry B. Employed smoke making with replenishment at Southampton. 03.07.1944: Operation Neptune ended. Employed as fuel carrier (Esso). 08.11.1944: Returned. 08.1961: Sold to Vereenigde Utrechtse Ijzerhandel, Utrecht, Holland, and broken up at Utrecht. 31.10.1961: Grimsby registry closed.

COLLENA 136904 Steam trawler FD115	652 16.02.1915 01.05.1915	293 116	133.6 23.6 10.7	C D Holmes 84 rhp 3-cyl 10.5 knots	J Marr & Son Ltd, Fleetwood

24.04.1915: Registered at Fleetwood (FD115). 05.1915: Requisitioned from the builders for war service as a minesweeper (1-6pdr HA) (Ad.No.1585). Based Dover. 17.09.1915: At 10.00pm " rendered good service by rescuing the crew of S.S. AFRICA mined in the Downs, 23 in number, who were all in one boat which was on the point of sinking". Based Lerwick. Post 12.03.1919: Returned. 1922: Top port landings - 537.8 tons. 10.10.1929: John Edward Fearnley, bosun, lost overboard and drowned. 1930: Top port landings - 500.3 tons. 31.01.1940: Requisitioned for war service as a boom defence vessel (P.No.Z.151); hire rate £80.11.6d per month. 1942: Sold to Aldred Fishing Co Ltd, Grimsby. 23.11.1943: Compulsorily acquired by Ministry of War Transport. 11.1943: Fleetwood registry closed. 04.1946: Transferred to Ministry of Transport. 07.1946: Sold to Swansea Trawlers Ltd, Mumbles, Swansea. 03.1947: Completed re-build at Appledore, forecastle added. 1947: Registered at Swansea as **SWANSEA BAY** (SA37). 02.1949: Sold to Goodleigh Fisheries Ltd, Milford Haven. 02.1949: Swansea registry closed. 03.03.1949: Registered at Milford (M23). 1950: Registered at Milford as **HOMELEIGH** (M23). 1952: Goodleigh Fisheries Ltd in liquidation. 03.1952: Sold to Ribble Trawlers Ltd, Fleetwood. 19.02.1953: Laid up. 06.1953: Sold to Hermann Westenborg, Milford Haven. 05.10.1953: Sold to Westward Trawlers Ltd, Milford Haven. 10.1953: Registered at Milford as **RUDILAIS** (M23). 1960: Sold to Haulbowline Industries Ltd, Passage West, Co Cork, for breaking up. 22.06.1960: Delivered Passage West. 10.08.1960: Milford registry closed, breaking up completed.

SAURIAN 138966 Steam trawler GY901	653 26.10.1915 20.05.1916	219 102	120.3 21.5 11.5	C D Holmes 67 rhp 3-cyl 10.0 knots	Henry Croft Baker, Grimsby

05.05.1916: Registered at Grimsby (GY901).   07.1916: Requisitioned for war service as a minesweeper (1-12pdr) (Ad.No.3293). Based Falmouth. Post 12.03.1919: Returned.   02.1937: Sold to Sir Thomas Robinson & Son (Grimsby) Ltd, Grimsby. 19.06.1940: Requisitioned for war service as a patrol vessel (P.No.FY.1726); hire rate £62.1.0d per month. Based Invergordon. 11.1945: Returned.   1961: Sold to Van Heyghen Frères, Ghent, Belgium.   03.10.1961: Arrived Bruges for breaking up. 10.1961: Grimsby registry closed.

WIMPOLE 138972 Steam trawler GY923	654 09.11.1915 30.06.1916	320 163	137.0 23.5 12.9	C D Holmes 550 ihp 3-cyl 11.0 knots	Welbeck Steam Fishing Co Ltd, Grimsby

01.07.1916: Registered at Grimsby (GY923).   08.1916: Requisitioned for war service as a minesweeper (1 - 12pdr) (Ad.No.2956). Based Devonport. Later employed on escort duties.   Post 12.03.1919: Returned to owner at Grimsby.   06.02.1919: Sold to Rushworth Steam Fishing Co Ltd, Grimsby.   30.06.1919: Sold to Shaftesbury Steam Trawling Co Ltd, Grimsby.   25.03.1926: Sold to John E Rushworth, Grimsby.   17.08.1931: Sold to J E Rushworth Ltd, Grimsby.   12.03.1935: Sold to Kopanes Steam Fishing Co Ltd, Grimsby.   15.03.1935: Registered at Grimsby as **ANDANES** (GY923).   11.04.1940: Sold to Drangey Steam Fishing Co Ltd, Grimsby.   28.05.1940: Requisitioned for war services as an anti submarine trawler; hire rate £90.13.4d per month.   11.1940: Fitted out for boom defence duties. Based Portland.   22.01.1942: Sold to J Marr & Son Ltd, Fleetwood, for £8000.   23.11.1943: Compulsorily acquired by Ministry of War Transport.   27.01.1944: Grimsby registry closed.   1944: Based Portsmouth.   1945: Laid up pending sale.   04.1946: Transferred to Ministry of Transport.   24.01.1947: Sold to Marine Metals Ltd, London, for breaking up.

ANZAC 139294 Steam trawler H487	655 09.11.1915 26.07.1916	317 127	135.3 23.5 12.6	C D Holmes 84 rhp 3-cyl 11.0 knots	East Riding Steam Fishing Co Ltd, Hull

04.07.1916: Registered at Hull (H487).   08.1916: Requisitioned for war service as a minesweeper (1-6pdr, 1-7.5" A/S Howitzer) (Ad.No.3305).   1917: Fitted with hydrophones.   03.1917: Renamed **ANZAC II**. Based Granton. Post 12.03.1919: Returned and reverted to **ANZAC** (H487).   05.1921: Sold to Viuda de Canosa-Cierto, Barcelona, Spain.   18.05.1921: Hull registry closed. 05.1921: Registered at Barcelona as **CANOSA**.   1952: Sold to Benita Gutierrez Diaz, Barcelona.   1954: Sold to Ramon Canosa, Barcelona.   1955: Sold to Ramon Canosa & Hermanos, Barcelona. Converted to burn oil fuel.   1965: Sold to Ramon Canosa, Gutierrez & Hermanos, Barcelona.   1971: Sold to shipbreakers and broken up. Barcelona registry closed.

MARCONI 139288 Steam trawler H488	656 08.12.1915 10.08.1916	322 131	136.2 24.0 12.9	C D Holmes 86 rhp 3-cyl 10.5 knots	F & T Ross Ltd, Hull

03.08.1916: Registered at Hull.   08.1916: Requisitioned from the builders for war service as a minesweeper (1-12pdr) (Ad.No.3304). Based Kirkwall.   Post 12.03.1919: Returned.   25.08.1929: Burned out in the No.2 Hull Fish Market fire (see yard no.627 for detail). Repaired and returned to service.   02.1940: Requisitioned for war service as a minesweeper (1-12pdr); hire rate £91.4.8d per month. Based Lowestoft with M/S Group 56.   20.09.1941: At anchor near Rough Buoy, E of Harwich, struck by armed trawler LORD BEACONSFIELD (P.No.FY.608) (GY563) (see yard no.639) and started to take in water and settle. Skipper decided to abandon but as this was underway attacked and bombed by German aircraft. Vessel foundered in position 51.54N 01.30E. Ty/Sk G Noble RNR and all crew rescued.   06.01.1947: Hull registry closed - "Vessel sunk after collision with unknown vessel on 20/9/1941."

FARADAY 139291 Steam trawler H490	657 08.12.1915 01.09.1916	322 131	136.2 24.0 12.9	C D Holmes 86 rhp 3-cyl 10.5 knots	F & T Ross Ltd, Hull

03.08.1916: Registered at Hull (H657).   11.1916: Requisitioned for war service as a minesweeper (1-12pdr) (Ad.No.3312). Based Aegean Sea.   Post 12.03.1919: Returned.   09.06.1940: Requisitioned for war service as an auxiliary patrol vessel; hire rate £91.4.8d per month. Renamed **FRANKOLIN**.   05.1941: Fitted out as a minesweeper.   12.11.1941: In North Sea (Ty/Act Sk Lieutenant J Dinwoodie RNR) in company with auxiliary patrol trawler, COMMANDER HOLBROOK (H233) (Chief Sk A S V Jones RNR). Off Happisburgh, Norfolk, attacked and bombed by enemy aircraft, returned fire and shot down aircraft - Dornier Do17, but subsequently foundered. One crewman lost.   06.01.1947: Hull registry closed - "Vessel sunk by enemy aircraft on 12.11.1941"

TRANSVAAL 138979 Steam trawler GY953	658 09.12.1915 15.08.1916	250 119	125.3 22.5 12.0	C D Holmes 88 rhp 3-cyl 10.5 knots	Henry L Taylor, Grimsby

09.08.1916: Registered at Grimsby (GY953).   15.08.1916: Requisitioned for war service from the builders and fitted out as minesweeper (1-12pdr, 1-6pdr HA) (Ad.No.3307). Based Peterhead.   12.07.1917: Arrived on the fishing grounds (Lieutenant W E Dawson RNR), escorting the Fraserburgh fleet. At 6.00pm, heard gunfire and discovered a submarine attacking the sailing drifters SPIDER (BF279) and SURPRISE (BF2008). At 7.10pm, engaged with 12pdr and 6pdr and pursued. Submarine dived and at 7.20pm depth charges dropped. At 8.00pm joined by HM Drifter CLOVER (BF323) (Ad.No.4329) but submarine escaped. By 12.03.1919: Returned.   12.1919: Sold to Henry L Taylor & H G Hopwood, Grimsby.   12.1919: Sold to Melville Steam Trawling Co Ltd, Fleetwood.   26.10.1920: Grimsby registry closed.   27.10.1920: Registered at Fleetwood (FD381).   26.11.1923: Sold to Transvaal Steam Trawling Co Ltd, Fleetwood.   01.12.1939: Requisitioned for war service and designated for minesweeping duties (magnetic); hire rate £70.16.8d per month.   20.01.1940: Returned.   09.06.1941: Sold to Basil A Parkes, Fleetwood. 01.12.1941: Sold to Don Fishing Co Ltd, Aberdeen.   11.08.1942: Requisitioned for war service and fitted out as a fuelling trawler (Esso) (P.No.Y.7.45); hire rate £70.16.8d per month. Mediterranean Command.   06.1944: Operation Neptune - Normandy landings. Assigned as a fuelling trawler to Force O.   03.07.1944: Operation Neptune ended.   18.11.1944: Foundered in English Channel in severe weather conditions. Ty/Sk Thomas Threlfall RNR and all crew lost.   14.12.1945: Fleetwood registry closed.

Collena (652) *as built.*

(Jonathan Grobler collection)

The above vessel was rebuilt in 1947 and renamed **Swansea Bay** *(652).*

(Authors' collection)

Saurian (653)

(Jonathan Grobler collection)

Another view of the **Saurian**.

(George Scales collection)

SAPPHIRE	676	262	121.8		C D Holmes	Kingston Steam Trawling
139320 Steam trawler	28.10.1916	104	22.6		76 rhp 3-cyl	Co Ltd,
H580	04.10.1917		12.2		11.0 knots	Hull

Built to amended design of **ONYX** (see yard no.581). Total cost with all fees, classification and fishing gear - £10,166.15.6d.
10.09.1917: Registered at Hull (H580). 05.12.1917: Requisitioned for war service as a minesweeper. Renamed **SAPLER** (1-12pdr & W/T) (Ad.No.3077). Fitted out as Half Leader. By 01.10.1918: At Falmouth working with Fleet Mine Sweepers. 26.02.1919: At Falmouth for refit and restoration by Cox & Co (Engineers) Ltd at Admiralty expense (£1,085). 31.03.1919: Arrived Hull. Taken off hire and returned. Reverted to **SAPPHIRE** (H580). 11.07.1919: Sold to Lawrence Golding Fenner, Twickenham, en bloc with sister ship **GARNET** (H495) (see yard no.660). 28.07.1919: Sale completed at total cost £45,000. 28.11.1919: Hull registry closed.
29.11.1919: Registered at Fleetwood (FD358). 20.04.1920: Sold to Garnet Steam Trawling Co Ltd, Fleetwood. 28.01.1925: Sold to New Docks Steam Trawling Co (Fleetwood) Ltd, Fleetwood. 03.1925: Sold to Perihelion Steam Fishing Co Ltd, Grimsby. 03.03.1925: Fleetwood registry closed. 05.03.1925: Registered at Grimsby (GY254). 16.08.1928: Transferred to fish out of Aberdeen. 12.1928: Sold to Dublin Trawling, Ice & Cold Storage Co Ltd, Dublin. 17.12.1928: Grimsby registry closed.
01.1929: Registered at Dublin (D18). 01.1935: Sold to A M Morrice, Aberdeen. 01.1935: Dublin registry closed.
09.01.1935: Registered at Aberdeen (A248). 16.05.1935: Registered at Aberdeen as **MARGARET MORRICE** (A248).
1936: Sold to David Dryburgh, Leith (Planet Steam Fishing Co Ltd, Edinburgh). 07.01.1936: Aberdeen registry closed.
01.1936: Registered at Granton as **INVERCAULD** (GN47). 1940: Sold to Carnie & Gibb, Newhaven, Edinburgh.
16.07.1940: Requisitioned for war service as a minesweeper (P.No.FY.1938); hire rate £76.8.4d. 01.01.1941: Based Belfast with M/S Group 144. 1941: Sold to J Bennett (Wholesale) Ltd, London. 1942: Based Belfast with M/S Group 140. 11.1945: Returned to owner. 1947: Sold to Planet Steam Fishing Co Ltd, Edinburgh. 1950: Operating from Aberdeen. 02.10.1950: Sailed Aberdeen for Icelandic grounds (Sk Albert S H Robb); twelve crew. 16.10.1950: While fishing experienced boiler trouble, intended to put into Vestmannaeyjar but damage got progressively worse and decided to make for Reykjavik. 18.10.1950: At 2.10am, Gardskagi Light was abeam and shortly after in calm weather vessel struck the rocks one mile NW from the Light. Icelandic fishing boat transferred the crew to the Lifeguard ship SAEBJORG (64grt/1937) which responded to the distress call. At 7.00am, heavy seas were breaking over the vessel and there was no hope of salvage. 10.1950: Granton registry closed.

VAMBERY	677	316	135.3		C D Holmes	Atlas Steam Fishing
139956 Steam trawler	27.11.1916	127	23.5		84 rhp 3-cyl	Co Ltd,
GY1082	25.07.1917		12.3		11.0 knots	Grimsby

30.07.1917: Registered at Grimsby (GY1082). 07.1917: Requisitioned for war service as a minesweeper and later employed as an escort (1-6pdr, 1-7.5" A/S Howitzer) (Ad.No.1280). Based Milford Haven. 1920: Returned. 08.1936: Sold to Earl Steam Fishing Co, Grimsby. 04.1937: Registered at Grimsby as **SARONTA** (GY1082). 08.06.1940: Requisitioned for war service as an auxiliary patrol vessel; hire rate £92.3.4d per month. 12.1940: Sold to Sir Alec Black, Bart, Grimsby. 01.1941: Fitted out as a minesweeper (P.No.FY.1849). Based Lowestoft with M/S & Patrol Group 9. 22.04.1942: Sold to Active Steam Fishing Co Ltd, Fleetwood (Geoffrey Edwards Marr, manager) for £8500. 07.1945: Sold to Shire Trawlers Ltd, London (William A Bennett, manager) for £14000. 11.1945: Surveyed and restored at Glasgow. 12.1945: Returned. 24.12.1946: Sold to Lord Line Ltd, Hull for £8950.
04.02.1947: Registered at Hull (H390). 17.05.1950: Sold to Associated Fisheries Trawling Co Ltd, Hull for £4500 (T W Boyd, manager). 1952: Laid up. 06.10.1952: Sold to BISCO for £2600 and allocated to Clayton & Davie Ltd, Dunston on Tyne, for breaking up. 18.10.1952: Arrived Tyne.

VENOSTA	678	316	135.3		C D Holmes	Atlas Steam Fishing
139959 Steam trawler	27.11.1916	127	23.5		84 rhp 3-cyl	Co Ltd,
GY1098	12.09.1917		12.3		11.0 knots	Grimsby

08.09.1917: Registered at Grimsby (GY1098). 10.1917: Requisitioned for war service as a minesweeper (1-12pdr, 1-3.5" A/S Howitzer & Hydrophones) (Ad.No.1654). Southern Patrol. By 12.03.1919: Returned. 23.01.1919: Sold to Albert W Green, Grimsby. 02.1920: Sold to Venosta Ltd, Halifax, NS, Canada. 08.11.1923: Fishing from Nova Scotia. Grimsby fishing registry closed 1927: Registered at Halifax, NS. 10.1939: Requisitioned for war service with the Royal Canadian Navy as a minesweeper (1-12pdr). Based Halifax, NS. 06.1941: Employed as a boom gate vessel at Sydney, NS (P.No.J11). 01.1942: Returned. 1946: Sold to National Sea Products Ltd, Halifax, NS. 1948: Converted to motor. 1955: Laid up at Halifax, NS. 1956: Sold to I Verreault, Halifax, NS, for conversion to dry cargo motor vessel with 12-cylinder oil engine by General Motors Inc, Detroit. Registered at Halifax as **REYNELD V**. 1960: Sold to Verreault Navigation Inc, Halifax NS. 1960: Sold to Maritime Agency Inc, Quebec, PQ. Registered at Quebec as **FORT PREVEL**. 1973: Sold to Desgagnés & Perron Inc, St Louis, Isle-aux-Coudres, PQ. Registered at Quebec as **MICHEL P**. 04.1973: Broken up at St Louis, Isle-aux-Coudres, PQ.

AUTOCRAT	679	128	84.5		Earle's Co	Thomas Clarkson Spink,
139262 Steam tug	16.06.1915	-	20.6		66 rhp 3-cyl	Hull
	31.07.1915		9.9		10.5 knots	

07.08.1915: Registered at Hull. 16.02.1916 to 28.11.1916: On hire to the Admiralty. 20.12.1917: Requisitioned for war service as a rescue tug. 09.1918: Allocated P.No.W01. 04.02.1920: Returned. 23.03.1921: Sold to United Towing Co Ltd, Hull.
19.07.1934: With tug SALVAGE (111grt/1908) attending the LMS railway steamer OUSE (1004grt/1911) aground near Whitton, River Humber. On refloating, AUTOCRAT got across the tide and was pulled over and capsized; crew of four rescued. Salved by F Hall & Co, repaired and returned to service. 27.12.1939: Requisitioned for war service under naval control; hire rate £87.10.0d per month.
17.05.1944: Returned. 12.1966: Sold to Van den Bossche, Boom, Belgium for breaking up. 09.01.1967: Arrived at Boom.
09.01.1967: Registry closed.

BUREAUCRAT	680	137	90.0		Shields Eng Co	Thomas Clarkson Spink,
139302	30.08.1916	1.2	21.1		69 rhp 3-cyl	Hull
	07.10.1916		9.1		9.5 knots	

13.11.1916: Registered at Hull. 15.12.1916 to 26.05.1917 and 23.07.1917 to 31.07.1917: On hire to the Admiralty for harbour services. 12.08.1917 to 27.03.1920: On hire to the War Office for service at Calais. 23.03.1921: Sold to United Towing Co Ltd, Hull. 1939-1945: Local towage and salvage work. 12.1966: Sold to Van den Bossche, Boom, Belgium for breaking up.
09.01.1967: Arrived Boom. 09.01.1967: Registry closed.

Autocrat *(679)*

(Stuart Emery collection)

Bureaucrat *(680)*

(World Ship Photo Library - Charles A Hill collection)

FIFINELLA 139942 Steam trawler GY1038	681 20.05.1916 13.07.1917	314 162	137.0 24.0 12.8	Cooper & Greig 87 rhp 3-cyl 11.0 knots	Consolidated Steam Fishing & Ice Co Ltd, Grimsby

25.04.1917: Registered at Grimsby (GY1038).   07.1917: Requisitioned for war service as a minesweeper (1-6pdr) (Ad.No.1279). Northern Patrol.   Post 12.03.1919: Returned.   09.1927: Owners re-styled Consolidated Fisheries Ltd, Grimsby. 04.1937: Sold at Grimsby (£1178) to Metal Industries Ltd, Glasgow.   07.05.1937: Arrived Charlestown, Fife, for breaking up. 02.06.1937: Grimsby registry closed.   14.07.1937: Breaking commenced.

FRANC TIREUR 139945 Steam trawler GY1041	682 20.05.1916 08.06.1917	314 162	137.0 24.0 12.8	Cooper & Greig 87 rhp 3-cyl 11.0 knots	Consolidated Steam Fishing & Ice Co Ltd, Grimsby

26.04.1917: Registered at Grimsby (GY1041).   06.1917: Requisitioned for war service as a minesweeper (1-12pdr) (Ad.No.1270). Based Devonport.   Post 12.03.1919: Returned.   09.1927: Owners re-styled Consolidated Fisheries Ltd, Grimsby. 29.05.1940: Requisitioned for war service as an auxiliary patrol vessel (P.No.4.70); hire rate £88.19.4d per month. Based Grimsby. 05.1941: Fitted out as a minesweeper (1-12pdr HA) (P.No.1560). Based Ipswich with M/S & Patrol Group 78. 04.1942: Sold to J Bennett (Wholesale) Ltd, London.   25.09.1943: Under attack by E-boats off Shipwash, 12 miles east of Harwich (Act/Ty/Lt Cdr L R Greenwood RNVR), torpedoed and sunk by E-boat S-96. Fifteen crew lost. HM Trawler DONNA NOOK (P.No.FY.1559) (FD237) (see yard no.646) foundered following collision with HMT STELLA RIGEL (P.No.FY.657) (418grt/1936) when manoeuvring to pick up survivors. During the action S-96 was rammed by ML.150 and ML.145 and abandoned; two officers and eleven crew were picked up by ML.145 and made prisoner.   10.1943: Grimsby registry closed.

FIAT 139944 Steam trawler GY1040	683 17.06.1916 26.08.1917	314 162	137.0 24.0 12.8	Cooper & Greig 87 rhp 3-cyl 11.0 knots	Consolidated Steam Fishing & Ice Co Ltd, Grimsby

25.04.1917: Registered at Grimsby (GY1040).   01.1918: Requisitioned for war service as a minesweeper (1-12pdr) (Ad.No.1658). Based Dover.   Post 12.03.1919: Returned.   09.1927: Owners re-styled Consolidated Fisheries Ltd, Grimsby.   04.1937: Sold at Grimsby (£1178) to Metal Industries Ltd, Glasgow.   07.05.1937: Arrived Rosyth for breaking up. 08.05.1937: Grimsby registry closed.   19.05.1937: Breaking commenced.

FAVORITA 139943 Steam trawler GY1039	684 20.06.1916 02.11.1917	314 162	137.0 24.0	Cooper & Greig 87 rhp 3-cyl 11.0 knots	Consolidated Steam Fishing & Ice Co Ltd, Grimsby

25.04.1917: Registered at Grimsby (GY1039).   12.1917: Requisitioned for war service as a minesweeper (1-12pdr) (Ad.No.1655). Based Swansea.   By 12.03.1919: Returned.   09.1927: Owners re-styled Consolidated Fisheries Ltd, Grimsby. 06.03.1937: Stranded on Uskalar Reef (Skagi Reef) off Reykjavik, Iceland; crew member H Robinson struck by davit and died. Fleetwood trawler NORTHERN REWARD (LO168) (655grt/1936) rescued eight men; the rest of the crew were taken ashore in a motor boat.   08.05.1937: Grimsby registry closed - "Total loss".

FLORIO 139946 Steam trawler GY1042	685 03.06.1916 27.11.1917	314 162	137.0 24.0 12.8	Cooper & Greig 87 rhp 3-cyl 11.0 knots	Consolidated Steam Fishing & Ice Co Ltd, Grimsby

26.04.1917: Registered at Grimsby (GY1042).   10.1917: Requisitioned for war service as a minesweeper (1-12pdr) (Ad.No.1653). Based Tyne.   Post 12.03.1919: Returned.   09.1927: Owners re-styled Consolidated Fisheries Ltd.   27.08.1939: Requisitioned for war service as an auxiliary patrol vessel; hire rate £88.19.4d per month.   01.1940: Returned.   29.05.1940: Requisitioned for war service as a minesweeper (P.No.FY.988). Based Lowestoft with M/S & Patrol Group 83.   04.1942: Sold to J Bennett (Wholesale) Ltd, London.   01.1948: Sold to BISCO and allocated to Clayton & Davie Ltd, Dunston, for breaking up. 11.1948: Grimsby registry closed.

RUDYARD KIPLING 144068 Steam trawler H247	686 21.11.1920 21.01.1921	333 140	138.8 23.7 12.9	C D Holmes 94 rhp 3-cyl 11.0 knots	Newington Steam Trawling Co Ltd, Hull

04.02.1921: Registered at Hull. (H247).   16.05.1934: Sold to Sun Steam Trawling Co Ltd, Fleetwood.   05.10.1936: Hull registry closed.   16.10.1936: Registered at Fleetwood (FD33).   09.1939: On a trip to Donegal ground (Sk Charles Robinson); twelve crew. 16.09.1939: Stopped by U-boat (U.27) about 100 miles off Co Donegal coast. Sunk by explosive charges at 3.53pm in position 53.50N 11.10W after crew ordered onto submarine; towed boat towards Irish coast.   17.09.1939: Crew set adrift in early hours, 5 miles off Donegal coast and landed later in Killybegs. Search carried out by destroyers from Scapa Flow based 6th Destroyer Flotilla, HMS MATABELE (P.No.F26) (Cdr G K Whitmy Smith RN) and HMS SOMALI (P.No.F33) (Lt Cdr Nicholson RN) and with aircraft.   29.09.1939: Fleetwood registry closed - "Vessel sunk by enemy submarine".

WILLIAM WESTENBURGH Ad.No.3577 Non-standard Mersey class	687 25.01.1917 17.05.1917	325 130	138.5 23.7 12.8	C D Holmes 87 rhp 3-cyl 11.0 knots	The Admiralty, Whitehall, London

Ordered by Pickering & Haldane's Steam Trawling Co Ltd, Hull. Purchased by the Admiralty on the stocks and completed as a Non-Standard Mersey Class minesweeper (2-12pdrs).   1919: Registered in the Registry of British Ships at London. Official No. 143929. 28.01.1920: Registered by the Admiralty at London as a fishing vessel (LO279).   06.1921: Sold to Pickering & Haldane's Steam Trawling Co Ltd, Hull.   11.06.1921: London registry closed.   Cochrane & Sons Ltd contracted to refurbish as a fishing trawler, allocated yard no.756.   05.07.1921: Registered at Hull (H292).   19.10.1921: Registered at Hull as **LORD TALBOT** (H292) (see yard no.756).

CHARLES ASTIE Ad.No.3578 Non-standard Mersey class	688 25.01.1917 25.05.1917	325 130	138.5 23.7 12.8	C D Holmes 87 rhp 3-cyl 11.0 knots	The Admiralty, Whitehall, London
Ordered by Pickering & Haldane's Steam Trawling Co Ltd, Hull. Purchased by the Admiralty on the stocks and completed as a Non-Standard Mersey class minesweeper (1-12pdr). 26.06.1917: Mined NE of Fanad Head, Lough Swilly, Co Donegal, whilst escorting steamer HARTLAND (4803grt/1906) from Tory Island to Inishowen Head; mine laid 13.06.1917 by U.79. Ty/Sk John Geddes RNR and sixteen crew lost.					
ANTHONY ASLETT Ad.No.3579 Non-standard Mersey class	689 22.02.1917 05.06.1917	305 122	130.3 23.5 12.5	C D Holmes 87 rhp 3-cyl 11.0 knots	The Admiralty, Whitehall, London
Ordered by Roberts & Ruthven Ltd, Grimsby. Purchased by the Admiralty on the stocks and completed as a Non-Standard Mersey class minesweeper (1-12pdr, 1-7.5" Howitzer). 1919: Registered in the Registry of British Ships at London. Official No. 143820. 09.1920: Renamed **ROTHER**. 1922: Sold to J Samuel White & Co Ltd, East Cowes. 1922: Sold to Spanish Navy. Renamed **UAD QUERT**. 1968: Deleted from Spanish Navy lists.					
NORRIX 144043 Steam cargo ship	690 09.12.1919 26.01.1920	576 284	165.0 27.0 11.0	Earle's Co / Drypool Eng 84 rhp 3-cyl 9.5 knots	John Robert Rix Hull
09.04.1920: Registered at Hull to Robert, John, Herbert & Ernest Rix joint owners. 26.03.1921: On a voyage from Par to Antwerp with china clay, capsized and foundered after striking the Zeebrugge Mole. Declared a total loss. 12.10.1921: Registry closed.					
WILLIAM ABRAHAMS Ad.No.3580 Non-standard Mersey class	691 24.02.1917 05.05.1917	248 96	120.3 22.0	Earle's Co 56 rhp 3-cyl 10.0 knots	The Admiralty, Whitehall, London
Ordered by Savoy Steam Fishing Co Ltd, Grimsby. Purchased by the Admiralty on the stocks and completed as a Non-Standard Mersey class minesweeper (1-12pdr). 1919: Registered in the Registry of British Ships at London. Official No. 143890. 25.09.1920: Registered as a fishing trawler (LO469). 01.1922: Sold to H Croft Baker, Grimsby. 30.12.1921: London registry closed. 03.01.1922: Registered at Grimsby (GY1340). 23.02.1922: Registered at Grimsby as **SANTINI** (GY1340). 06.1922: Sold to Savoy Steam Fishing Co Ltd, Grimsby. 26.06.1928: Sold to Ocean Steam Fishing Co Ltd, Hull. 25.06.1928: Grimsby registry closed. 26.06.1928: Registered at Hull (H439). 24.06.1935: Sold to Alexander M Adam, Aberdeen. 06.09.1935: Hull registry closed. 09.09.1935: Registered at Aberdeen (A340). 07.1938: Sold to shipbreakers and broken up. 28.07.1938: Aberdeen registry closed - "Broken up".					
CORNELIUS BUCKLEY Ad.No.3581 Non-standard Mersey class	692 24.02.1917 16.05.1917	248 96	120.3 22.0 12.0	Earle's Co 726 nhp 3-cyl 10.5 knots	The Admiralty, Whitehall, London
Ordered by Savoy Steam Fishing Co Ltd, Grimsby. Purchased by the Admiralty on the stocks and completed as a Non-Standard Mersey class minesweeper (1-12pdr). 11.10.1920: Registered at London as a fishing trawler (LO470). Official No. 145053. 01.1922: Sold to H Croft Baker, Grimsby. 30.12.1921: London registry closed. 05.01.1922: Registered at Grimsby (GY1341). 22.02.1922: Registered at Grimsby as **SAVARIA** (GY1341). 06.1922: Sold to H Croft Baker & John L Green, Grimsby. 09.1927: Sold to H Croft Baker, Grimsby. 1928: Sold to Croft Steam Fishing Co Ltd, Hartlepool. 22.10.1930: Grimsby registry closed. 10.1930: Registered at Hartlepool (HL36). 12.1932: Sold to A Brown, North Shields. 12.1932: Hartlepool registry closed. 29.12.1932: Registered at North Shields as **L H RUTHERFORD** (SN154). 05.1937: Sold to A/S Raagan, Haugesund, Norway. 06.05.1937: North Shields registry closed. Registered at Haugesund as **RAAGAN**. 1940: Taken over by the German Navy, renamed **EBER** (P.No.NS21). Based Stavanger. 17.02.1942: Sunk by Allied aerial torpedo off Skudenes.					
SKALLAGRIMUR Steam trawler RE145	693 26.09.1919 02.03.1920	409 193	150.0 25.0 12.1	Amos & Smith 121 nhp 3-cyl 11.0 knots	H/F Kveldúlfur, Reykavik, Iceland
Completed at a cost of 520,000kr (ca. £23,000). 03.1920: Registered at Reykjavik (RE145). Top trawler in Iceland in 1920-25 and 1931. 1924: Landed a record 2713 barrels of liver, equivalent to 5500-6000 tons of fish. 29.12.1924: When entering Reykjavik outer harbour, rammed and sank the Bergen registered steamer INGER BENEDICTE (1936grt/1883) which was at anchor. 16.06.1940: Rescued the whole crew, 353 men, from Armed Merchant Cruiser HMS ANDANIA (13950grt/1922) (Capt Donald K Bain RN) which was torpedoed by U-boat (UA) some 230 miles W-NW of Faroe Islands. Continued on passage to Hull. 17.06.1940: Survivors transferred to HMS FORESTER (P.No.H74). 1951: Laid up. 16.02.1955: Reykjavik registry closed. 23.05.1955: Sold to Danish shipbreakers. 27.05.1955: Sailed Reykjavik for Esbjerg, Denmark, in tow of Danish motor tug SIGYN (288grt/1916) along with HÖFDABOG (see yard no.649) and THOROLFUR (see yard no.694) for breaking up. Broken up and registry closed.					
THOROLFUR Steam trawler RE134	694 27.09.1919 26.03.1920	409 193	150.0 25.0 12.1	Amos & Smith 121 nhp 3-cyl 11.0 knots	H/F Kveldúlfur, Reykavik, Iceland
Completed at a cost of 520,000 krona (ca. £23,000). 04.1920: Registered at Reykjavik (RE134). Top herring ship in Iceland 1931, 1933 and 1934. 15.09.1940: Rescued 30 men from the Norwegian motor vessel HIRD (4950grt/1924) (Capt Ansgar M Fredhjem) torpedoed by U-boat (U.65) 180 miles from Barra Head. 17.09.1940: Survivors landed at Fleetwood. 1946: Overhauled and new bridge fitted at a cost of 1.5 million krona (£57,500). 16.02.1955: Reykjavik registry closed. 23.05.1955: Sold to Danish shipbreakers. 27.05.1955: Sailed Reykjavik for Esbjerg, Denmark, in tow of Danish motor tug SIGYN (288grt/1916) along with HÖFDABORG (see yard no.649) and SKALLAGRIMUR (see yard no.693) for breaking up. Broken up and registry closed.					
Not built	695				

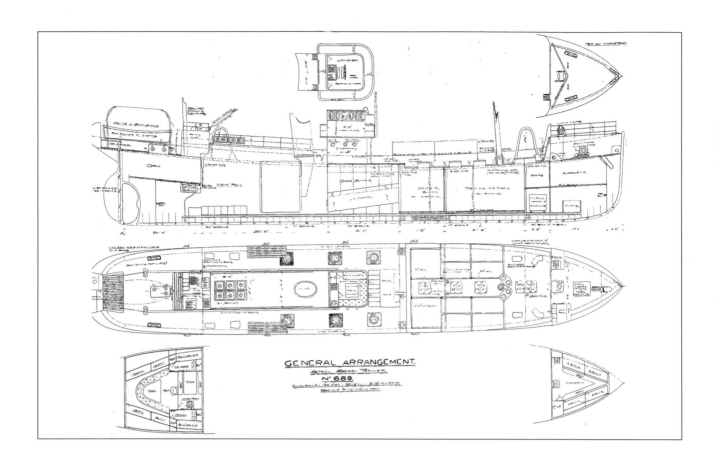

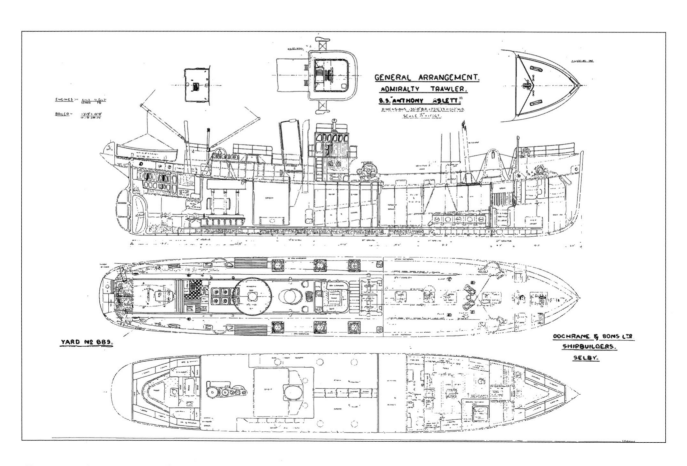

*Two general arrangement drawings of the **Anthony Aslett** (689). The upper view shows her as originally designed, whilst the lower view shows her with modifications as required by the Admiralty.*

BEARDMORE 146871 Motor trawler GY121	696 23.03.1920 03.07.1920	227 120	115.0 22.0 12.0	W Beardmore 100 rhp 4-cyl oil engine 11.0 knots	Grimsby Motor Trawling Co Ltd, Grimsby

14.10.1922: Registered at Grimsby (GY121).   15.07.1927: Sold to John M Scott, Kew, Surrey.   02.08.1927: Registered at Grimsby as **LILIAS** (GY121).   Re-engined with 4-cylinder 91nhp oil engine by J & C G Bolinder, Stockholm. Fishing out of Milford Haven.   08.1931: Sold to J Rio, Lorient, France.   18.08.1931: Grimsby registry closed.   Re-measured to 239grt, 29net.   Registered at Lorient.   1936: Sold to G Gautier and E & A Gautier Fils & Co, Lorient.   1951: Sold to E & A Gautier Frères & Co, Lorient.   1960: Sold to shipbreakers and broken up.   1960: Lorient registry closed.

MAYRIX 144055 Steam cargo ship	697 20.05.1920 02.09.1920	794 375	185.1 31.0 11.7	Earle's Co 111 nhp 3-cyl 9.5 knots	Humber Steam Coasters Ltd, Hull

09.09.1920: Registered at Hull.   15.01.1934: Sold to H Harrison (Shipping) Ltd, London.   24.01.1934: Hull registry closed. Registered at London as **KEMPTON**.   1936: Sold to Polgarth S S Co Ltd, Liverpool.   22.01.1937: Registered at Liverpool as **POLGARTH**.   01.03.1942: On a voyage from Blyth towards Southampton with coal (865 tons), mined 2 miles SSW of Aldeburgh Light Float and although attempts were made to connect and tow, foundered in two hours in position 52.09N 01.42.33E; all sixteen crew saved.   09.04.1942: Registry closed.

Not built	698, 699				

SERFIB 139313 Steam trawler H536	700 09.04.1916 09.03.1917	210 82	112.3 21.5	Cooper & Greig 71 rhp 3-cyl 10.5 knots	East Riding Steam Trawling Co Ltd, Hull

13.03.1917: Registered at Hull (H536).   04.1917: Requisitioned for war service as a minesweeper (1-6pdr) (Ad.No.3034). Based Milford Haven.   By 12.03.1919: Returned.   20.01.1920: Sold to West Riding Steam Fishing Co Ltd, Hull.   08.11.1922: Sold to George C Munro, Devonport, Auckland, New Zealand.   09.09.1924: Hull registry closed.   1924: Registered at Auckland.   1928: Sold to Munro Bros Ltd, Auckland.   06.06.1933: Sailed Auckland for East Coast grounds (Sk A J Flett); nine crew.   08.06.1933: About 3 miles off Waipiro Bay, ingress of water in engine room and by 3.30pm crew decided to abandon. Boat damaged at launch but managed to reach Open Bay and picked up by motor schooner HUIA (257grt/1894) and landed in Tokoman Bay.   Trawler drifted in direction of East Cape and foundered.   Registry closed.

KENRIX 144079 Steam cargo ship	701 27.11.1920 21.07.1921	692 317	175.0 29.1 11.1	J Lewis & Sons 96 rhp 3-cyl 9.0 knots	Humber Steam Coasters Ltd, Hull

20.07.1921: Registered at Hull to Robert, John, Ernest & Herbert Rix, joint owners.   19.10.1926: Robert Rix died.   23.11.1945: Sold to Polpen Shipping Co Ltd, Falmouth.   17.12.1945: Hull registry closed.   1946: Registered at Falmouth as **POLKERRIS**.   1953: Sold to BISCO and allocated to C W Dorkin & Co Ltd, Gateshead & Dunston, for breaking up.   31.12.1953: Arrived River Tyne.   Registry closed.

ERNRIX 144090 Steam cargo ship	702 27.11.1920 28.09.1921	692 317	175.0 29.1 11.3	J Lewis & Sons 96 rhp 3-cyl 9.0 knots	Humber Steam Coasters Ltd, Hull

30.09.1921: Registered at Hull.   23.06.1939: In heavy sea and strong NNW breeze, on passage from Hull towards Thornaby-on-Tees with a cargo of grain, started to take in water when off Staithes. Steam tug KINGS CROSS (282grt/1918) connected and commenced tow but vessel foundered in Tees Bay. All ten crew taken off by Redcar lifeboat LOUISA POLDEN.   18.08.1939: Registry closed.

Not built	703, 704				

GALLEON 145506 Steam cargo ship	705 21.11.1922 06.02.1923	721 349	180.0 29.0 11.5	Amos & Smith 91 rhp 3-cyl 11.0 knots	Galleon Shipping Co Ltd, Newcastle

24.11.1925: On charter to Shipping & Coal Ltd, London, loaded a coal cargo (801 tons) at Blyth. At 6.40pm sailed Blyth for London River (Capt H S Burton); eleven crew.   25/26.11.1925: Bad weather off east coast with very heavy seas, north-easterly gale with snow flurries.   27.11.1925: Trinity House tender ARGUS (661grt/1909) picked up lifeboat between Inner and Outer Dowsing Light vessels but it had not been occupied. Assumed vessel lost with all hands.   12.06.1926: Board of Trade Inquiry (No. 7837) found that the loss was probably due to being overwhelmed by heavy following seas and unable to free herself in consequence of being trimmed by the stern. The exact cause of the casualty could not be determined.

COMMANDER EVANS 147136 Steam trawler H20	706 1924 20.03.1924	344 142	140.2 24.0	C D Holmes 93 rhp 3-cyl 11.0 knots	East Riding Steam Trawling & Fishing Co Ltd, Hull

19.03.1924: Registered at Hull to Hudson Steam Fishing Co Ltd (H20).   08.06.1940: Requisitioned for war service as an auxiliary patrol vessel; hire rate £129.0.0d per month.   05.1941: Fitted out as a minesweeper (P.No.FY.133). Based Ipswich with M/S and Patrol Group 81.   03.1944: Fitted out as a dan layer and assigned to Operation Neptune - Normandy Landings; in readiness at Plymouth.   02.06.1944: Sailed Plymouth for Solent attached to 8th M/S Flotilla.   05.06.1944: Sailed Solent anchorage for Normandy to sweep approach channel Gold Beach - Assault convoy G1.   03.07.1944: Operation Neptune ended.   24.01.1945: Sold to Hudson Brothers Trawlers Ltd, Hull.   28.08.1945: Returned.   28.01.1946: Sold to Loch Fishing Co Ltd, Hull.   07.05.1946: Sold to Sir Thomas Robinson & Son (Grimsby) Ltd, Grimsby.   11.05.1946: Hull registry closed.   06.1946: Registered at Grimsby as **TUNISIAN** (GY278).   22.07.1955: Sold to Onward Steam Fishing Co Ltd, Grimsby.   13.12.1955: Sold to Saint Andrew's Steam Fishing Co Ltd, Hull.   22.03.1956: Sold B J Nijkerk, Antwerp, for breaking up.   05.1956: Grimsby registry closed.

VESPA 146131 Steam tug	707 20.08.1921 23.09.1921	92 -	75.0 21.1 9.5	Earle's Co 92 rhp 3-cyl	Herbert Gaselee & Sons Ltd, London

Completed at a cost of £7,562. 1921: Registered at London. 11.1940: Requisitioned for war service as an auxiliary patrol vessel/harbour tug; hire rate £75.0.0d per month. Based Liverpool. 10.10.1945: Returned. 1946: Sold to Harrisons (London) Ltd, London. Renamed **MARKROCK**. Late 1950s: Sold for breaking up. Registry closed.

EQUITABLE 140808 Steam trawler GY1122	708 05.02.1920 15.06.1920	339 135	140.2 24.0 12.6	C D Holmes 91 rhp 3-cyl 11.0 knots	Equitable Steam Fishing Co Ltd, Grimsby

16.06.1920: Registered at Grimsby (GY1122). 03.1923: Sold to Comissariado Geral Dos Abasjecimentos, Lisbon, Portugal. 20.03.1923: Grimsby registry closed. Re-measured to 358grt, 165net, and registered at Lisbon as **GLAUCO**. 1927: Sold to Companhia Portuguesa de Pesca, Lisbon. Renamed **ALVOR**. 1971: Converted to motor and fitted with 9-cylinder 1110bhp Stork Werkspoor oil engine. 07.1990: Re-engined with 6-cylinder 1100bhp oil engine by Anglo-Belgian Corp NV, Gent. Re-measured to 423grt, 126net. 1992: Sold to Armando & Silva Ltda, Lisbon. 1994: Sold to Ramon Duran Reis, Lisbon. 1997: Lisbon registry closed. Registered in Leixoes. Still registered as a fishing vessel.

CAENEUS 140809 Steam trawler GY1129	709 05.02.1920 16.07.1920	339 135	140.2 24.0 12.6	C D Holmes 91 rhp 3-cyl 11.0 knots	Equitable Steam Fishing Co Ltd, Grimsby

15.07.1920: Registered at Grimsby (GY1129). 1922: Sold to P Delpierre & C Ficheux, Boulogne, France. 22.11.1922: Grimsby registry closed. Registered at Boulogne as **PETIT POILU**. 1940: Captured by Germans at Brest. 1941: Commissioned in Kriegsmarine (P.No.HS04). 05.1942: (P.No.V725). 05.08.1944: Captured by Royal Navy. Not traced further.

KATE LEWIS 139783 Steam trawler A620	710 05.02.1916 07.03.1916	207 79	117.7 22.2 12.3	J Abernethy 80 rhp 3-cyl 11.0 knots	Richard W Lewis, Aberdeen

08.1916: Sold to The Admiralty and fitted out as a minesweeper and later a minelayer (Ad.No.2975). 17.10.1916: Registered at Aberdeen (A620). 28.01.1920: Aberdeen registry closed. 1920: Attached to HMS Vernon and employed as a tender on minelaying trials; later transferred to Mediterranean Station. 01.09.1936: Arrived Portsmouth from Alexandria. 08.09.1936: Paid off to reserve. 02.1939: Sold to Boston Deep Sea Fishing & Ice Co Ltd, Fleetwood. 02.1939: Arrived Fleetwood from Portsmouth. 02. - 04.1929: Converted to a fishing vessel by James Robertson & Sons Ltd, Fleetwood. 24.04.1939: On completion of refit and reclassification registered at Fleetwood as **NOREEN MARY** (FD4). 08.1939: Sold to Carnie & Gibb, Newhaven. 25.08.1939: Fleetwood registry closed. 08.1939: Registered at Granton (GN17). Fishing from Ayr. 01.07.1944: Sailed Ayr via Oban for Butt of Lewis ground (Sk John Flockhart); ten crew. 05.07.1944: At 21.50 shelled by U-boat (U.247) while fishing 20 miles W of Cape Wrath and sunk; eight crew killed. 06.07.1944: At 04.25am two injured survivors (2nd Engineer & deckhand James MacAllister) with shrapnel wounds taken aboard HM Trawler LADY MADELEINE (P.No.FY.283) (H243). 07.1944: Granton registry closed.

ANN LEWIS 139787 Steam trawler A621	711 05.02.1916 13.03.1916	216 83	121.2 22.5 12.3	J Abernethy 80 rhp 3-cyl 11.0 knots	Richard W Lewis, Aberdeen

07.12.1916: Registered at Aberdeen (A621). 12.1916: Requisitioned from the builders and fitted out as a minesweeper (1-6pdr HA) (Ad.No.2985). Based Harwich. Post 12.03.1919: Returned. 01.1920: Sold to J Stookes, Grimsby. 05.01.1920: Aberdeen registry closed. 06.01.1920: Registered at Grimsby. 01.1920: Registered at Grimsby as **FIFTH LANCER** (GY802). 04.1921: Sold to Joseph W Stookes, Grimsby. 04.1920: Registered at Grimsby as **ANN LEWIS** (GY802). 11.1931: Sold to Stephen Fishing Co Ltd, Aberdeen. 26.11.1931: Grimsby registry closed. 30.11.1931: Registered at Aberdeen (A174). 09.01.1932: Registered at Aberdeen as **JEAN EDMONDS** (A174). 07.01.1940: Requisitioned for war service as a boom defence vessel; hire rate £61.4.0d. 16.01.1940: Returned. 26.06.1940: Requisitioned for war service as a minesweeper (P.No.FY.1677). 1944: Sold to R Irvin & Sons Ltd, Aberdeen. 25.09.1945: Returned. 1962: Sold to Scrappingco S.r.l, Antwerp. 16.05.1962: Arrived Boom in tow of tug ERIMUS CROSS (192grt/1960) for breaking up. 05.1962: Aberdeen registry closed.

PREFECT 138941 Steam trawler GY737	712 11.09.1915 18.01.1916	302 159	135.3 23.5 12.4	Gt Central Co-op 84 rhp 3-cyl 10.5 knots	Anchor Steam Fishing Co Ltd, Grimsby

05.11.1915: Registered at Grimsby (GY737). 03.1916: Requisitioned for war service as a minesweeper (1-4", 1-12pdr &1-7.5" Howitzer) (Ad.No.1984). Based Granton. Post 12.03.1919: Returned. 10.1923: Sold to Atlas Steam Fishing Co Ltd, Grimsby. 08.1936: Sold to Earl Steam Fishing Co Ltd, Grimsby. 22.04.1937: Registered at Grimsby as **NORLAND** (GY737). 01.09.1939: Sold to Fishing Vessel Brokers Ltd, Hull. 29.11.1939: Grimsby registry closed. 01.12.1939: Registered at Hull (H266). 12.12.1939: Sold to Boyd Line Ltd, Hull. 17.01.1940: Sold to City Steam Fishing Co Ltd, Hull. 30.05.1940: Requisitioned for war service as an auxiliary patrol vessel (P.No.4.106); hire rate £83.1.0d per month. 09.1941: Employed on miscellaneous naval duties (P.No.FY1561). 1943: Based Grimsby with M/S Group 22. 12.10.1944: Sold to Marine Steam Fishing Co Ltd, Hull. 1945: Sold to Lewis A Walton, Hull. 11.10.1945: Returned. 21.12.1945: Sold to Yorkshire Trawlers Ltd, Hull. 17.11.1949: Sold to George Robb & Sons Ltd, Aberdeen. 11.1949: Hull registry closed. 11.1949: Registered at Aberdeen (A643). 06.1952: Registered at Aberdeen as **VIKING ALLIANCE** (A643). 10.06.1956: Sold to BISCO (£4,900) and allocated to Shipbreaking Industries Ltd, Charlestown, for breaking up. 06.1956: Delivered Charlestown from Aberdeen under own power. Aberdeen registry closed. 08.1956: Breaking commenced.

Kenrix (701)

(World Ship Photo Library)

The **Prefect** *(712) became* **Viking Alliance** *in 1949.*

(Jonathan Grobler collection)

X133	X lighter	713 17.04.1915 18.07.1915	172	105.5 21.0 7.5	Campbell Gas Engine Co, Halifax 60bhp	The Admiralty, Whitehall, London
A batch of the 200 motor landing craft designed by James Pollock of James Pollock & Son for the Admiralty for use in the Gallipoli campaign and ordered February 1915 from various ship builders. Based on Thames barge design with spoon bow so that troops, horses and field guns could be unloaded on to the steeply shelving beaches. Painted black they were nicknamed "Black Beetles". X133, X134, and X135 had wooden supports, halter ropes etc, for tethering horses.						
X134	X lighter	714 17.04.1915 18.07.1915	172	105.5 21.0 7.5	Campbell Gas Engine Co, Halifax 60bhp	The Admiralty, Whitehall, London
X135	X lighter	715 30.04.1915 30.07.1915	172	105.5 21.0 7.5	Campbell Gas Engine Co, Halifax 60bhp	The Admiralty, Whitehall, London

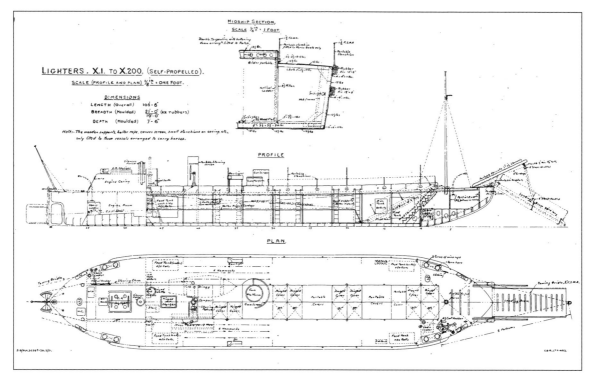

A general arrangement drawing of the X lighters.

*Photographs of X-lighters are comparatively rare. This is the **X48** which was not built at the Selby yard.*

(Derek Grindell)

X130 X lighter	716 30.04.1915 18.08.1915	180	105.5 21.0 7.5	Campbell Gas Engine Co, Halifax 80bhp	The Admiralty, Whitehall, London	

| **X131** X lighter | 717 01.05.1915 03.09.1915 | 180 | 105.5 21.0 7.5 | Campbell Gas Engine Co, Halifax 80bhp | The Admiralty, Whitehall, London | |

21.04.1942: Sunk in Marsamxett Harbour, Malta.   1952: Sold to Greek Government.

| **X132** X lighter | 718 01.05.1915 04.09.1915 | 180 | 105.5 21.0 7.5 | Campbell Gas Engine Co, Halifax 80bhp | The Admiralty, Whitehall, London | |

X131 and **X132**: After completion altered to water carriers at Connells Dry Dock, Hull

| **WYNDHAM** 138975   Steam trawler GY930 | 719 04.04.1916 05.08.1916 | 303 157 | 135.3 23.5 12.4 | Gt Central Co-op 84 rhp 3-cyl 11.0 knots | Welbeck Steam Fishing Co Ltd, Grimsby | |

17.07.1916: Registered at Grimsby (GY930).   08.1916: Requisitioned for war service as a minesweeper (1-12pdr, 1-5" A/S Howitzer) (Ad.No.3303).   Based Portland.   05.1918: Sold to Aldersyde Steam Fishing Co Ltd, Grimsby.   By 12.03.1919: Returned. 07.1923: Sold to Consolidated Steam Fishing & Ice Co (Grimsby) Ltd, Grimsby.   09.1927: Owners restyled Consolidated Fisheries Ltd.   04.1937: Sold at Grimsby to Metal Industries Ltd, Glasgow (£1136) and allocated to Rosyth for breaking up. 08.05.1937: Grimsby registry closed.   05.1937: Arrived Rosyth.   12.05.1937: Breaking up commenced.

| **PRINCESS VICTORIA** 137380   Steam trawler SN321 | 720 22.03.1916 13.04.1916 | 245 93 | 124.8 22.7 12.3 | Cooper & Greig 82 rhp 3-cyl 11.0 knots | Dodds Steam Fishing Co Ltd, Aberdeen | |

11.12.1916: Registered at North Shields (SN321).   01.1917: Requisitioned for war service as a minesweeper (1-6pdr HA) (Ad.No.3320).   Based Newhaven.   Post 12.03.1919: Returned.   12.05.1924: Arrived Aberdeen having lost man overboard. 06.1929: Sold to Boston Deep Sea Fishing & Ice Co Ltd, Fleetwood.   15.06.1929: North Shields registry closed. 19.06.1929: Registered at Fleetwood (FD50).   01.1930: Sold to Northern Steam Fishing Co Ltd, Grimsby.   14.01.1930: Fleetwood registry closed.   16.01.1930: Registered at Grimsby (GY166).   12.1933: Sold to Sir Thomas Robinson & Son (Grimsby) Ltd, Grimsby.   18.01.1934: Registered at Grimsby as **MARANO** (GY166).   11.1939: Requisitioned for war service as a minesweeper (P.No.FY.777); hire rate £69.8.4d per month. Based Great Yarmouth with M/S Group 118.   05.1942: Sold to J Bennett (Wholesale) Ltd, London.   08.01.1945: Returned to owner.   10.1947: Sold to Shire Trawlers Ltd, London.   03.1948: Sold to Benjamin Gelcer & Co, Cape Town. Grimsby registry closed. Registered at Cape Town (CTA306).   1953: Owners re-styled B Gelcer & Co (Pty) Ltd, Cape Town.   1957: Stripped of non-ferrous metals and usable materials. Cape Town registry closed.   04.11.1957: Sunk by SAN gunfire in False Bay.

| **PRINCESS OLGA** 137379   Steam trawler SN326 | 721 22.03.1916 19.04.1916 | 245 93 | 124.8 22.7 12.3 | Cooper & Greig 82 rhp 3-cyl 11.0 knots | Dodds Steam Fishing Co Ltd, Aberdeen | |

05.02.1916: Registered at North Shields (SN326).   04.1916: Requisitioned for war service as a minesweeper (1-6pdr HA) (Ad.No.3031).   14.06.1918: Mined off Le Havre (mine laid on 06.06.1918 by UC.77).   24.01.1920: North Shields registry closed - "Lost on Adm service".

| **GENERAL BOTHA** 139779   Steam trawler A709 | 722 04.07.1916 15.08.1916 | 245 92 | 124.8 22.7 | Cooper & Greig 83 rhp 3-cyl 11.0 knots | Ross Steam Trawl Fishing Co Ltd, Aberdeen | |

01.09.1916: Registered at Aberdeen (A709).   12.1916: Requisitioned for war service as a minesweeper (1-6pdr HA) (Ad.No.3316). Based Tyne.   03.1919: Renamed **ISLAND PRINCE**.   By 12.03.1919: Returned and reverted to **GENERAL BOTHA** (A709). 01.1920: Sold to Canute Steam Trawling Co Ltd, Grimsby.   20.01.1920: Aberdeen registry closed.   02.02.1920: Registered at Grimsby (GY1025).   10.1924: Sold to John Lewis Ltd, Aberdeen.   09.05.1932: Grimsby registry closed.   10.05.1932: Registered at Aberdeen (A194).   22.08.1940: Requisitioned for war service as a minesweeper (P.No.FY.599); hire rate £69.8.4d per month. Based North Shields with M/S Group 68.   1943: Took part in the Ealing Studios film "For Those In Peril" taking the part of the German ship KONIGIN LUISE.   19.11.1945: Returned.   03.1950: Fitted for burning oil fuel. Re-measured to 236grt, 87net. 1953: Sold to North Eastern Fisheries Ltd, Aberdeen.   11.1959: Sold to BISCO (£2150) and allocated to Shipbreaking Industries Ltd, Charlestown, Fife, for breaking up.   15.11.1959: Arrived Charlestown from Aberdeen under own power.   21.11.1959: Delivered. 11.1959: Aberdeen registry closed.   16.02.1960: Breaking up commenced.

| **MAGRIX** 139306   Steam cargo ship | 723 14.09.1916 22.11.1916 | 314 124 | 135.3 23.1 9.5 | Hall Russell/Drypool Eng Co 57 rhp 3-cyl 8.0 knots | Robert Rix & Sons, Hull | |

17.11.1916: Registered at Hull to Robert, John, Ernest & Herbert Rix, joint owners.   19.10.1926: Robert Rix deceased. 14.05.1937: Sold to Alexander M Massie, Aberdeen.   25.05.1937: Hull registry closed.   05.1937: Registered at Aberdeen as **DEEDON**.   1946: Sold to Deeside Shipping Co Ltd, Sunderland.   1955: Sold to Bremner & Co, Stromness, Orkney. Registered at Kirkwall as **ORKNEY DAWN**.   1957: Sold to Haulbowline Industries Ltd, Passage West, Co Cork, for breaking up. 25.01.1957: Arrived Passage West.   01.1957: Registry closed.

ROBRIX	724	314	135.3	Drypool Eng Co	Humber Steam Coasters
139307 Steam cargo ship	28.09.1916	124	23.1	50 rhp 3-cyl	Ltd,
	28.12.1916		9.5	7.5 knots	Hull

22.12.1916: Registered at Hull.   14.04.1929: On a voyage from Hull towards Teignmouth, with a cargo of oil cake extract. In thick fog off Haisborough, foundered after being in collision with Sunderland-registered steamer ANDELLE (1832grt/1922) approximately 2 miles SSE of Newarp Light vessel in position 52.45.30N 01.54.30E. One crew member lost.   30.05.1929: Registry closed.

FEUGH	725	227	121.2	R W Lewis & Sons	Richard W Lewis & Sons,
138782 Steam trawler	18.07.1916	87	22.2	80 rhp 3-cyl	Aberdeen
A706	11.08.1916		12.3	11.0 knots	

17.10.1916: Registered at Aberdeen (A706).   06.1917: Requisitioned for war service as a minesweeper (1-6pdr HA) (Ad.No.1278). Based Peterhead.   Post 12.03.1919: Returned.   1919: Sold to British Trawling Co Ltd, Bootle.   1920: Sold to Derby Steam Trawling Co Ltd, Fleetwood.   02.1922: Sold to Godby Steam Fishing Co Ltd, Fleetwood.   20.02.1922: Aberdeen registry closed. 24.02.1922: Registered at Fleetwood (FD403).   08.06.1923: Driven ashore at Bispham, Blackpool; catch and crew saved. 1923: Refloated and returned to service.   09.1924: Sold to Thomas D Lees, Bonnington, Edinburgh.   11.10.1924: Fleetwood registry closed.   13.10.1924: Registered at Granton (GN24).   11.1924: Sold to Crampin Steam Fishing Co Ltd, Grimsby. 23.11.1925: Granton registry closed.   25.11.1925: Registered at Grimsby (GY366).   11.1927: Sold to Trawlers (White Sea & Grimsby) Ltd, Grimsby.   12.1927: Registered at Grimsby as BERENGA (GY366).   25.11.1939: Requisitioned for war service as a minesweeper (P.No.FY.774); hire rate £64.6.4d.   17.02.1940: Returned.   19.04.1940: Requisitioned for war service for barrage balloon towing duties.   01.1942: Sold to Trawlers Grimsby Ltd, Grimsby.   3.09.1945: Returned.   19.12.1945: Sold to United Trawlers Ltd, Milford Haven.   30.01.1951: Sailed Milford for the fishing grounds SW of Ireland (Sk.Arthur Howie).   31.01.1951: Responded to call for assistance from trawler BRAES O' MAR (M100) (Sk John H. Ryan) taking in water some 15 miles WNW of the Skelligs.   Transferred crew and stood by.   01.02.1951: At 9.00am, BRAES O' MAR foundered. Crew landed at Berehaven, Co. Cork.   10.1951: Sold to Atlantic Trawlers Ltd, Edinburgh.   17.10.1951: Registered at Milford as SPRINGLEIGH (M192). Fishing from Milford Haven.   1952: Sold to J C Llewellin (Trawlers) Ltd, Milford Haven.   1953: Sold to S W Trawlers Ltd, Milford Haven. 01.1953: Registered at Milford as LYDSTEP (M192).   1955: Sold to BISCO and allocated to Thos W Ward Ltd, Sheffield, for breaking up at Castle Pill, Milford Haven.   23.05.1955: Delivered Castle Pill.   13.06.1955: Milford registry closed.

JARRIX	726	429	150.2	Shields Eng & DD	Humber Steam Coasters
139308 Steam cargo ship	28.10.1916	203	24.6	69 rhp 3-cyl	Ltd,
	16.02.1917		11.0	9.0 knots	Hull

30.12.1916: Registered at Hull.   26.05.1939: Sold to Ribble Shipping Co Ltd, Liverpool.   26.07.1939: Hull registry closed. 07.1939: Registered at Liverpool as GORSETHORN.   08.12.1940: On a voyage from Preston towards Cork with a cargo of coal, foundered in Liverpool Bay, 11 miles NW of Hoylake in approximate position 53.32N 03. 22.1W. No survivors.   Registry closed.

EBBRIX	727	429	150.2	Shields Eng & DD	Robert Rix & Sons,
139311 Steam cargo ship	11.11.1916	203	24.6	69 rhp 3-cyl	Hull
	10.03.1917		11.0	8.0 knots	

23.01.1917: Registered at Hull to Robert, John, Ernest & Herbert Rix, joint owners.   19.10.1926: Robert Rix died. 30.06.1939: Sold to Ribble Shipping Co Ltd, Liverpool.   26.07.1939: Hull registry closed.   07.1939: Registered at Liverpool as BANNTHORN.   1943: Sold to Springfal Shipping Co Ltd, London.   1946: Registered at Liverpool as SPRINGOUSE.   1947: Sold to Ribble Shipping Co Ltd, Liverpool. Registered at Liverpool as BANNTHORN.   1948: Sold to Thomas Stone (Shipping) Ltd, Swansea.   1949: Registered at Liverpool as BROOKSTONE.   1950: Sold to Thorn Line Ltd, Liverpool. Registered at Liverpool as BANNTHORN.   1954: Sold to BISCO and allocated to West of Scotland Shipbreaking Co Ltd, Troon, for breaking up. 08.10.1954: Arrived Troon.   Registry closed.

CARBILL	728	242	120.2	Great Central Co-op	John W Smethurst,
139960 Steam trawler	12.03.1917	94	22.2	74 rhp 3-cyl	Grimsby
GY1100	01.09.1917		12.0	10.5 knots	

01.09.1917: Requisitioned from the builders for war service and fitted out as a minesweeper (1-12pdr, 1-6pdr HA) (Ad.No.1648). 16.11.1917: Registered at Grimsby (GY1100). Based Granton.   Post 12.03.1919: Returned.   05.1924: Sold to Sir Alec Black, Bart, Grimsby.   06.1924: Sold to John W Smethurst, Grimsby.   05.1935: Sold to Andrew Christie, Aberdeen, & others. 09.05.1935: Grimsby registry closed.   13.05.1935: Registered at Aberdeen (A309).   30.05.1935: Registered at Aberdeen as EURYALUS (A309).   09.1939: Requisitioned for war service as a minesweeper; hire rate £70.11.0d. Renamed HOVERFLY (P.No.FY.557). Based Granton with M/S Group 105.   09.11.1943: Reverted to trawling.   24.07.1944: Sold to Boston Deep Sea Fishing & Ice Co Ltd, Fleetwood.   15.01.1945: Returned and reverted to EURYALUS (A309).   04.1946: Sold to Humber Trawlers Ltd, Grimsby.   04.1946: Aberdeen registry closed.   12.04.1946: Registered at Grimsby (GY245).   04.1951: Sold to Seafield Fishing Co Ltd, Aberdeen.   04.1951: Grimsby registry closed.   27.04.1951: Registered at Aberdeen (A682).   1956: Sold to BISCO and allocated to Malcolm Brechin, Granton, for breaking up.   29.02.1956: Arrived Granton from Aberdeen under own power. 15.10.1956: Aberdeen registry closed.

LITHIUM	729	301	135.2	Shields Eng Co	United Alkali Co Ltd,
137540 Steam cargo ship	12.12.1916	113	23.1	69 rhp 3-cyl	Liverpool
	30.03.1917		9.4	8.0 knots	

15.03.1917: Registered at Liverpool.   23.08.1932: Owners re-styled I.C.I. (General Chemicals) Ltd, Liverpool. 28.03.1935: Owners re-styled I.C.I. (Alkali) Ltd, Liverpool.   11.06.1945: Owners re-styled Imperial Chemical Industries Ltd, Liverpool.   31.03.1950: Sold to T G Irving Ltd, Sunderland.   04.1950: Liverpool registry closed.   27.04.1950: Registered at Sunderland as MAYDENE.   01.1955: Sold to BISCO and allocated to Clayton & Davie Ltd, Dunston, for breaking up. 14.01.1955: Arrived Dunston-on-Tyne.   23.07.1955: Registry closed.

Jarrix *(726)*

(Eric Hammal collection)

Ebbrix *(727)*

(Eric Hammal collection)

Lithium *(729)*

(World Ship Photo Library)

HELIUM	730	301	135.2	Shields Eng co	United Alkali Co Ltd,
137540 Steam cargo ship	27.12.1916	113	23.1	69 rhp 3-cyl	Liverpool
	10.05.1917		9.4	8.0 knots	

05.04.1917: Registered at Liverpool.   23.08.1932: Owners re-styled I.C.I. (General Chemicals) Ltd, Liverpool.   28.03.1935: Owners re-styled I.C.I. (Alkali) Ltd, Liverpool.   11.06.1945: Owners re-styled Imperial Chemical Industries Ltd, Liverpool.   1949: Sold to J Johnson & Sons (Shipping) Ltd, Liverpool. Registered at Liverpool as **HOLLYLEAF**.   1953: Sold to Johnson Bretland Ltd, Liverpool.   1954: Sold to Kendall Bros (Portsmouth) Ltd, Southsea.   1955: Registered at Liverpool as **HOLLYBRANCH**. 1956: Sold to Henry G Pounds, Portsmouth. Resold to Stolk's Handelsonderneming, Hendrik ido Ambacht, Holland, for breaking up. 07.11.1956: Arrived Maasluis under tow by tug RIFLEMAN (333grt/1945).   01.1957: Registry closed.

SUN VIII	731	196	100.3	Earle's Co	W H J Alexander,
143951 Steam tug	26.07.1919	-	25.6	678 ihp 3-cyl	London
	09.12.1919		11.8	10.0 knots	

12.1919: Registered at London.   1929: Transferred to W P & G F Alexander, London.   1929: Transferred to W H J Alexander Ltd, London.   10.1939: Requisitioned for war service under naval control; hire rate £111.19.6d per month.   26.05.1940: 'Operation Dynamo' (Dunkirk evacuation) put into effect.   31.05.1940: Crossed to Dunkirk towing 12 ship's lifeboats (Sk S Smith). 01.06.1940: Returned with 120 troops.   1940-45: Assisting ships damaged or grounded in Thames estuary.   18.04.1946: Returned. 02.1960: Converted to burn oil fuel.   27.01.1969: Transferred to London Tugs, Ltd, London.   02.1969: Sold to Scrappingco S.r.l., Brussels, for breaking up at Antwerp.   Registry closed.

SUN IX	732	196	100.3	Earle's Co	W H J Alexander,
144405 Steam tug	29.07.1919	-	25.6	750 ihp 3-cyl	London
	25.02.1920			10.0 knots	

01.1920: Registered at London.   1929: Transferred to W P & G F Alexander, London.   1929: Transferred to W H J Alexander Ltd, London.   11.1939: Requisitioned for war service; hire rate £120.9.0d per month. Based Southend - Naval Control of Shipping. 21.12.1940: Mined and foundered between buoys 1 & 2, Yantlet Channel, Thames estuary; three crew lost. Transferred to Ministry of War Transport. London registry closed.   06.1942: Salvaged, taken to Southend but beyond repair and laid up. Sold to Thos W Ward Ltd, Sheffield, for breaking up at Grays, Essex.

SUN X	733	196	100.3	Earle's Co	W H J Alexander,
144657 Steam tug	29.07.1919	-	25.6	99 rhp 3-cyl	London
	23.01.1920			10.0 knots	

01.1920: Registered at London.   31.08.1923: Attended Japanese steamer on fire off Gravesend, injecting steam in hold. 1929: Transferred to W P & G F Alexander, London.   1929: Transferred to W H J Alexander Ltd, London.   18.12.1936: Foundered off Tilbury following collision with steamer TURQUOISE (570grt/1924).   Salved and repaired.   03.05.1940: Towed damaged steamer PACIFIC COAST (1210grt/1935) from Brest to Bristol Channel.   26.05.1940: 'Operation Dynamo' (Dunkirk evacuation) put into effect.   31.05.1940: Bound Dunkirk with sailing barge SPURGEON (46net/1883/rebuilt 1924) in tow; bombed and damaged and turned back.   02.06.1940: In Dunkirk harbour (Sk W A Fothergill) unsuccessfully attempted to move grounded French steamer ROUEN (1882grt/1912); embarked some of her troops.   03.06.1940: At Dover landed 211 troops.   25.08.1942: Requisitioned for war service; hire rate £120.9.0d per month. Based River Clyde - Naval Control of Shipping.   08.05.1945: Returned. 05.1957: Converted to burn oil fuel.   27.01.1969: Transferred to London Tugs, Ltd, London.   02.1969: Sold to Scrappingco S.r.l., Brussels, for breaking up at Antwerp.   Registry closed.

LEIFUR HEPPNI	734	346	140.2	Amos & Smith	Geir Thorsteinsson,
Steam trawler	14.08.1919	170	24.0	90 nhp 3-cyl	Reykjavik,
RE146	31.03.1920		10.9	11.0 knots	Iceland

Completed for Geir Thorsteinsson (1/3) & Th Thorsteinsson (2/3), Reykjavik.   06.1920: Registered at Reykjavik (RE146). 11.09.1920: Sk Gisli M Oddsson became a partner.   04.10.1924: After death of Th Thorsteinsson, Sk Giali M Oddsson increased his shareholding to 1/3.   07-08.02.1925: Foundered off Vestfirdir, Iceland, in a severe storm known in Iceland as 'Halavedrid'; Sk Oddsson and thirty two crew lost.   Reykjavik registry closed.

ARI	735	342	140.1	Amos & Smith	F Langley,
Steam trawler	15.08.1919	172	24.0	90 nhp 3-cyl	Reykjavik,
RE147	29.04.1920		10.9	11.0 knots	Iceland

Completed for H/F Ari Frodi, Reykjavik, Iceland.   08.05.1920: Arrived Reykjavik.   09.06.1920: Registered at Reykjavik (RE147). 14.01.1928: Sold to H/F Kári, Videy, Iceland. Reykjavik registry closed. Registered at Videy (GK328).   1928 & 1930: Herring season, top landing Icelandic ship.   09.01.1932: Repossessed by mortgagee, Utvegsbanki Islands, Reykjavik. Videy registry closed. Registered at Reykjavik (RE147).   03.09.1932: Sold to Olafur Johannesson & Co, Patreksfördur. Reykjavik registry closed. Registered at Patreksfördur as **LEIKNIR** (BA167).   01.10.1936: Sprang a leak when fishing off Vestfirdir, Iceland. Crew taken off and ship taken in tow by trawler GYLFI (BA77) (336 grt/1915), but foundered off Saudanes on 02.10.1936.

Helium *(730)*

Sun X *(733)*

SUMMERTIME Swim barge	752 1921 05.01.1921	132 129	88 21	N/A	Tester Bros, London
WINTERTIME Swim barge	753 1921 05.01.1921	132 129	88 21	N/A	Tester Bros, London
LORD BYNG 143857 Steam trawler H288	754 15.01.1918 05.07.1921	327 130	138.5 23.7	C D Holmes 69 rhp 3-cyl 11.0 knots	Pickering & Haldane's Steam Trawling Co Ltd, Hull

Built as Mersey Class trawler **WILLIAM JACKSON** (Ad.No.3831) for the Admiralty (see yard no.838).
06.1921: Sold to Pickering & Haldane's Steam Trawling Co Ltd, Hull. 11.06.1921: London registry closed. Cochrane & Sons Ltd contracted to refurbish as a fishing trawler, allocated yard no.754. 05.07.1921: Registered at Hull (H288). 18.08.1921: Registered at Hull as **LORD BYNG** (H288). 24.01.1929: Sold to Bunch Steam Fishing Co Ltd, Grimsby. 28.01.1929: Hull registry closed. 29.01.1929: Registered at Grimsby (GY9). Fitted for lining to pursue the Greenland halibut fishery. 05.1936: Sold to Boston Deep Sea Fishing & Ice Co Ltd, Fleetwood. 07.1936: Registered at Grimsby as **EVELYN ROSE** (GY9). Operating out of east coast ports. 1939: Transferred to Fleetwood. 04.1940: Employed on Fishery Protection (WAS/Fort William/Fleetwood). 27.05.1940: Requisitioned for war service; hire rate £98.2.0d per month. 01.06.1940: To Dunkirk, embarked 150 troops. Returning struck wreck and lost one propeller blade. Badly damaged by air attack, beached at Ramsgate. Repaired and fitted out for auxiliary patrol duties (P.No.4.136). 05.1941: Fitted out as a minesweeper. 1945: Returned. 08.1945: Sold to Cevic Steam Fishing Co Ltd, Fleetwood. 22.11.1949: Homeward from an Icelandic trip (Sk Pegler); twenty-two crew. Stranded in darkness while on passage through the Sound of Islay. 23.11.1949: Twelve crew members taken off by Port Askaig lifeboat and returned to standby. Concrete poured into vessel in early forenoon but could not seal the hull. 24.11.1949: Part catch discharged to CEVIC (FD7) (248grt/1908) for shipment to Fleetwood. About 02.12.1949: Refloated and berthed at Port Askaig pier. 02.1950: Repairs completed and returned to fishing. 30.12.1954: Sailed Fleetwood for Faroe fishing grounds (Sk William Dawson); thirteen crew. 31.12.1954: At 12.30am stranded about 15 yards from Ardtornish Light, Morvern, while in transit through the Sound of Mull in southerly wind, fresh breeze, good visibility. While attempting to launch boat, slipped off rocks and foundered quickly; two survivors walked five miles to nearest habitation. (Position of wreck is uncertain, possibly located in 130m, 400m from shore; original loss in approximate position 56°31N/5°45W in 60-80m). 23.07.1955: At MoT formal inquiry (S.433) the court found Sk Dawson had made an error in navigation by misinterpreting image on radar screen, resulting in vessel stranding. 07.1955: Fleetwood registry closed.

LORD BIRKENHEAD 143884 Steam trawler H291	755 (22.08.1918) * 05.07.1921	326 132	138.3 23.7	C D Holmes 89 rhp 3-cyl 11.0 knots	Pickering & Haldane's Steam Trawling Co Ltd, Hull

Built as Mersey Class trawler **WILLIAM JOHNSON** (Ad.No.3843) for the Admiralty (see yard no.850).
06.1921: Sold to Pickering & Haldane's Steam Trawling Co Ltd, Hull. 11.06.1921: London registry closed. Cochrane & Sons Ltd contracted to refurbish as a fishing trawler, allocated yard no.755. 05.07.1921: Registered at Hull (H291). 06.10.1921: Registered at Hull as **LORD BIRKENHEAD** (H291). 10.05.1928: Sold to Crampin Steam Fishing Co Ltd, Grimsby. 15.05.1928: Hull registry closed. 16.05.1928: Registered at Grimsby (GY462). 09.06.1934: Foundered 10 miles ES-E of North Rona, Inner Hebrides, in approximate position 59.06N 05.30W. 26.07.1934: Grimsby registry closed - "Total loss".

LORD TALBOT 143929 Steam trawler H292	756 (25.01.1917) 05.07.1921	325 130	138.5 23.7 12.8	Richardsons, Westgarth 87 rhp 3-cyl 11.0 knots	Pickering & Haldane's Steam Trawling Co Ltd, Hull

Built as Non-Standard Mersey Class trawler **WILLIAM WESTENBURGH** (Ad.No.3577) for the Admiralty (see yard no.687).
1919: Registered in the Registry of British Ships at London. Official No.143929. 28.01.1920: Registered by the Admiralty at London as a fishing vessel (LO279). 06.1921: Sold to Pickering & Haldane's Steam Trawling Co Ltd, Hull. 11.06.1921: London registry closed. Cochrane & Sons Ltd contracted to refurbish as a fishing trawler, allocated yard no.756. 05.07.1921: Registered at Hull (H292). 19.10.1921: Registered at Hull as **LORD TALBOT** (H292). 17.05.1928: Sold to Perihelion Steam Fishing Co Ltd, Grimsby. 21.05.1928: Hull registry closed. 22.05.1928: Registered at Grimsby (GY463). 01.1931: Sold to Walker Steam Trawl Fishing Co Ltd, Aberdeen. 08.01.1931: Grimsby registry closed. 09.01.1931: Registered at Aberdeen (A147). 13.12.1932: Registered at Aberdeen as **STAR OF THE REALM** (A147). 02.1933: Sold to Crampin Steam Fishing Co Ltd, Grimsby. 02.02.1933: Aberdeen registry closed. 06.02.1933: Registered at Grimsby (GY475). 06.1934: Sold to Malmata Fishing Co Ltd, Grimsby. 02.1938: Sold to P/F Uvak A/S, Tórshavn, Faroe Islands. 10.02.1938: Grimsby registry closed. Registered at Tórshavn as **NORDSTJÖRNAN**. Re-measured to 293grt, 120net. 16.02.1940: Sold to A Wright, Hull. Renamed **STAR OF THE REALM**. 17.02.1940: Sold to the Admiralty and converted to a boom defence vessel (P.No.Z.105). Based Granton. 06.1946: Sold to William R Metcalfe, Dover, 'as is' a boom defence conversion. 05.1948: Converted to a mooring vessel. Re-measured to 325grt, 149net and registered at Falmouth. Renamed **S 48**. 1952: Sold to George A Ferguson, Borstal, Rochester. 1952: Sold to Italian shipbreakers and broken up. Falmouth registry closed.

* Where a date is given in brackets, this is the date of the original launch. The date below that is the date of completion as a trawler.

LORD CARSON 144409 Steam trawler H302	757 (07.06.1917) 30.09.1921	324 130	138.5 23.7 12.8	Cooper & Greig 87 rhp 3-cyl 11.0 knots	Pickering & Haldane's Steam Trawling Co Ltd, Hull

Built as Mersey Class trawler **WILLIAM RAM** (Ad.No.3550) for the Admiralty (see yard no.810).
30.09.1921: Sold to Pickering & Haldane's Steam Trawling Co Ltd, Hull. 05.10.1921: Registered at Hull (H302). 10.1921: London registry closed. Cochrane & Sons Ltd contracted to refurbish as a fishing trawler, allocated yard no.757. 28.10.1921: Registered at Hull as **LORD CARSON** (H302). 12.1929: Sold to J Rushworth, Grimsby. 10.12.1929: Hull registry closed. 12.12.1929: Registered at Grimsby (GY165). 09.01.1930: Registered at Grimsby as **WELBECK** (GY165). 10.1935: Sold to Harry Franklin Ltd, Grimsby. 01.06.1940: Requisitioned for war service as an auxiliary patrol vessel; hire rate £94.10.0d per month. 05.1941: Fitted out as a minesweeper (P.No.FY.1609). Based Lowestoft / Yarmouth. 1944: Towed converted London barges to south coast in preparation for D-Day. 16.05.1946: Returned. 09.1944: Sold to Shire Trawlers Ltd, London. 04.1950: Sold to Northern Trawlers Ltd, London. 1951: Sold to Belgian shipbreakers. 30.10.1951: Sailed Grimsby for Antwerp. 10.1951: Grimsby registry closed.

SPACE Wooden steam H293 drifter	758 (08.10.1920) 08.1921	96 34	86.6 20.0 9.9	S Richards & Co 43 rhp 3-cyl 9.25 knots	The Admiralty, Whitehall, London

Built by Richard Dunston Ltd, Thorne (yard no.93) (wooden Admiralty drifter) for the Admiralty as **SPLASH** (Ad.No.4101) and completed as a fishing vessel. 11.1920: Transferred to the Ministry of Agriculture & Fisheries, London, for disposal. Registered in the Registry of British Ships at London as **SPACE**. Official No.145186. 06.1921: Sold to Niels Kristian Nielsen, Cottingham. 06.1921: Cochrane & Sons Ltd contracted to refurbish as a fishing vessel (seine net), allocated yard no.758. 08.1921: London registry closed. 18.08.1921: Registered at Hull (H293). 19.01.1922: Sold to Nielsen Fishing Co, Hull. 03.02.1925: Sold to John Robinson (Grimsby) Ltd, Grimsby. 20.12.1926: Hull registry closed. 22.12.1926: Registered at Grimsby as **BELOVAR** (GY410). 12.11.1928: Reported in collision with Grimsby trawler **DELILA** (GY1237) (202grt/1919) off the Humber. Taken in tow but after 20 minutes started to settle and with deck awash crew of five taken off. 20.02.1929: Grimsby registry closed - "Total loss".

DORBIE 144120 Steam trawler/ H361 fish carrier	759 10.1917 22.07.1921	304 122	135.5 23.5 12.3	Amos & Smith 87 rhp 3-cyl 10.5 knots	Kelsall Bros & Beeching, Hull

Completed as **T19**, a replacement for the Russian Navy trawler T19 that was lost on 03.10.1916 whilst on trials in the North Sea before acceptance (see yard no.673). 07.1921: Sold to Kelsall Bros & Beeching, Hull. 22.07.1921: Cochrane & Sons Ltd contracted to recondition and convert into a steam trawler/fish carrier, allocated yard no.759. 29.12.1921: Registered at Hull as **DORBIE** (H361). Official No. 144120. 09.01.1932: Homeward from Faroe grounds (Sk J H Mason); eleven crew. In thick fog stranded on Tor Ness, Hoy, Orkney Islands. Longhope lifeboat K.T.J.S. (Cox John Swanson) launched and in dangerous and trying circumstances took off eight of the crew; three crew jumped into the sea and rescued by shore party. 08.02.1932: Hull registry closed - "Total loss". Insurance paid - £8,000.

NIGHTFALL Wooden steam H317 drifter	760 (04.07.1918) 30.11.1921	95 41	88.0 19.9 9.5	W Beardmore 43 rhp 3-cyl 10.0 knots	John McCann, Hull

Built by S Richards & Co Ltd, Lowestoft (yard no. 209) (Non-Standard wooden Admiralty Drifter) for the Admiralty as a minesweeper (1-6pdr) (Ad.No.3932).
1921: Sold to John McCann, Hull. 1921: Cochrane & Sons Ltd contracted to refurbish as a fishing vessel (seine net), allocated yard no.760. 30.11.1921: Registered at Hull (H317). Official No.144113. 19.07.1922: Sold to Pickering & Haldane's Steam Trawling Co Ltd, Hull. 11.02.1924: Sold to S & D Franklin and E & R Pearson, Grimsby. 1927: Sold to A.V.P. Fishing Co Ltd, Grimsby. 1932: Sold to H Franklin Ltd, Grimsby. 07.1940: Requisitioned for war service as a boom drifter. 09.1941: Compulsorily acquired by Ministry of War Transport. 28.10.1944: Advertised for sale 'in poor condition and no boiler'. 27.01.1947: Sold to shipbreakers and broken up.

ABELIA 146438 Steam drifter H404	761 31.12.1921 13.01.1922	97 35	85.2 19.1 9.0	Goldie/McCulloch Design 33 nhp 2-cyl 8.0 knots	Pickering & Haldane's Steam Trawling Co Ltd, Hull

All machinery new 1917 by International Engine Works, Amherst, NS and ex Canadian wooden Admiralty drifter CD.18.
21.02.1922: Registered at Hull (H404). 17.03.1925: Sold to Thomas Baskcomb Ltd, Grimsby. 20.03.1925: Hull registry closed. 23.03.1925: Registered at Grimsby(GY294). 02.1929: Sold to George H Catchpole & Sydney E Catchpole, Lowestoft. 01.03.1929: Grimsby registry closed. 02.03.1929: Registered at Lowestoft (LT8). 27.03.1929: Registered at Lowestoft as **SCATTAN** (LT8). 12.06.1929: Lowestoft registry closed in consequence of material alterations. Machinery replaced; engine T.3-cylinder 270ihp by S Richards & Co Ltd, Lowestoft; boiler by Riley Bros (Boilermakers) Ltd, Stockton. 12.06.1929: Re-registered at Lowestoft as **SCATTAN** (LT8). 30.12.1929: Sold to Sydney E Catchpole, Lowestoft. 20.05.1937: In fog off Cromer Light vessel, at about 4.00pm in collision with Greenock steamer LYLEPARK (5186grt/1929), Tyne for Key West. Returned to Lowestoft with heavy damage. 12.08.1938: Sold to Torbay Trawlers Ltd, Brixham. 02.01.1941: Sold to Arthur C Mitchell, Milford Haven. 29.01.1941: Sold to Scattan Ltd, Milford Haven. 11.01.1952: Registered at Lowestoft as **DICKETA** (LT8). 1959: Sold to Dutch shipbreakers and broken up. 11.11.1959: Lowestoft registry closed.

BIOTA	762	97	85.2	Goldie/McCulloch Design	John McCann,
146439 Steam drifter	31.12.1921	35	19.1	33 nhp 2-cyl	Hull
H425	23.01.1922		9.0	8.0 knots	

All machinery new 1917 by International Engine Works, Amherst, NS and ex Canadian wooden Admiralty drifter CD.24.
21.02.1922: Transferred to Pickering & Haldane's Steam Trawling Co Ltd, Hull. 21.02.1922: Registered at Hull (H425).
26.03.1925: Sold to Soc Anon Armement Ostendais, Ostend, Belgium. 26.03.1925: Hull registry closed. Registered at Ostend as
PAUL PASTEUR (O234). 03.04.1925: Arrived Ostend in company with FERNAND HARDYNS (O235) (see yard no.764)
14.06.1930: Laid up. 06.02.1936: Sold to Jubilee Fishing Co Ltd, Lowestoft. 13.07.1936: Registered at Lowestoft as **CICERO**
(LT141). 12.11.1941: Sold to Berrys (Stranraer) Ltd, Stranraer. 03.12.1941: Lowestoft registry closed - "No longer used for
fishing". 15.08.1943: Requisitioned for war service with Ministry of Aircraft Production; hire rate £25.0.0d per month.
Post 1945: Returned to owner. 1948: Sold for breaking up.

COLUTEA	763	97	85.2	Goldie/McCulloch Design	Pickering & Haldane's
146440 Steam drifter	16.01.1922	35	19.1	33 nhp 2-cyl	Steam Trawling Co Ltd,
H421	02.02.1922		9.0	8.0 knots	Hull

All machinery new 1917 by International Engine Works, Amherst, NS and ex Canadian wooden Admiralty drifter CD.38.
21.01.1922: Registered at Hull (H421). 03.1925: Sold to Sigurdur Thorvardsson and Thorvardur Sigurdsson, Hnífsdalur, Iceland.
23.03.1925: Hull registry closed. Registered at Hnífsdalur as **THURIDUR SUNDAFYLLIR**. 28.05.1927: Sold to Ingvar
Benediktsson & Ludvig C Magnússon, Reykjavik. Hnífsdalur registry closed. Registered at Reykjavik as **FJÖLNIR** (RE271).
31.12.1930: Sold to H/F Fjölnir, Reykjavik. 17.03.1933: Sold to H/F Fjölnir, Thingeyri, Dyrafjordur. Registered at Thingeyri
(IS7). 1941: Lengthened to 98.9 ft; tonnages amended to 123grt, 55net. 10.04.1945: On a return voyage as fish carrier to
England in collision with Glasgow steamer LAIRDSGROVE (1227grt/1898). Five crew lost and five taken aboard the
LAIRDSGROVE.

DEUTZIA	764	97	85.2	Goldie/McCulloch Design	Pickering & Haldane's
146446 Steam drifter	16.01.1922	35	19.1	33 nhp 2-cyl	Steam Trawling Co Ltd,
H435	13.02.1922		9.0	8.0 knots	Hull

All machinery new 1917 by International Engine Works, Amherst, NS and ex Canadian wooden Admiralty drifter CD.39.
08.03.1922: Registered at Hull (H435). 26.03.1925: Sold to Soc Anon Armement Ostendais, Ostend, Belgium. 03.04.1925: Hull
registry closed. Registered at Ostend as **FERNAND HARDYNS** (O235). Arrived Ostend in company with PAUL PASTEUR (O235)
(see yard no.762). 14.05.1930: Laid up. 17.01.1936: Sold to Emiel Danneel & Engel Verhaeghe, Ostend. Registered at Ostend as
DE ROZA (O235). 1936: Converted to motor and fitted with 240bhp Deutz oil engine. Remeasured to 98.94grt, 29.43net.
05.1940: Escaped to England. 1940: Transferred to Belgian Economic Mission, London. 09.10.1940: Requisitioned for war
service as an auxiliary patrol vessel. 08.1942: Employed on miscellaneous naval duties. 28.08.1945: Returned. 1960: Engine
uprated to 280bhp. 06.06.1966: Broken up. Ostend registry closed.

FORSYTHIA	765	97	85.2	Goldie/McCulloch Design	Pickering & Haldane's
146451 Steam drifter	30.01.1922	35	19.1	33 nhp 2-cyl	Steam Trawling Co Ltd,
H469	24.02.1922		9.0	8.0 knots	Hull

All machinery new 1917 by International Engine Works, Amherst, NS and ex Canadian wooden Admiralty drifter CD.21.
05.04.1922: Registered at Hull (H469). 05.05.1925: Sold to Soc Anon Armement Ostendais, Ostend, Belgium. 05.05.1925: Hull
registry closed. Registered at Ostend as **BURGEMEESTER DEBUNNE** (O236). 04.1930: Laid up. 21.10.1935: Sold to Henri
Laplasse, Ostend. Registered at Ostend as **HENRIETTE** (O236). 1935: Converted to auxiliary motor/sail and fitted with a 240bhp
Deutz oil engine. Remeasured to 98.82grt, 30.63net. 19.04.1940: Seized by Germans at La Rochelle. Converted to vorpostenboot
(auxiliary patrol trawler) (1-88mm). 1940-1942: Hafenschutzgruppe (Harbour protection group) La Rochelle.
1942-1944: At Lorient. 1944: Scuttled at La Rochelle. 1948: Salved and broken up.

MYRICA	766	97	85.2	Goldie/McCulloch Design	Pickering & Haldane's
146452 Steam drifter	30.01.1922	35	19.1	33 nhp 2-cyl	Steam Trawling Co Ltd,
H471	01.03.1922			8.0 knots	Hull

All machinery new 1917 by International Engine Works, Amherst, NS and ex Canadian wooden Admiralty drifter CD.34.
05.04.1922: Registered at Hull (H471). 27.11.1924: Sold to Johann J Eyfirdingur & Co h/f, Isafjord, Iceland. 23.03.1925: Hull
registry closed. Registered at Ísafjödur as **FRODI** (IS454). 23.12.1934: Sold to Thorsteinn J Eyfirdingur, Karvel Jonsson & Jon
Jonsson, Isafjordur, Iceland. 1941: Thorsteinn J Eyfirdingur became sole owner. 1941: Lengthened to 97.8 ft; tonnage amended
to 123grt. 11.03.1941: On a voyage with fish cargo from Reykjavik to Fleetwood (Sk Gunnar J Árnason); eleven crew total. At
8.00am when about 200 miles SE of Vestmannaeyjar, U-boat (U.37) closed and opened fire causing extensive damage.
12.03.1941: Arrived Vestmannaeyjar with five crew dead and six survivors. 15.03.1941: Returned to Reykjavik. 09.02.1942: On a
voyage from Stykkisholmur to Grundarfjordur, stranded on Vesturbodi, Snaefellsnes; came afloat and foundered. All nine crew safe.

TELIA	767	97	85.2	Goldie/McCulloch Design	John McCann,
146456 Steam drifter	14.02.1922	35	19.1	33 nhp 2-cyl	Hull
H477	24.03.1922		9.0	8.0 knots	

All machinery new 1917 by International Engine Works, Amherst, NS and ex Canadian wooden Admiralty drifter CD.19.
24.04.1922: Transferred to Pickering & Haldane's Steam Trawling Co Ltd, Hull. 25.04.1922: Registered at Hull (H477).
17.03.1925: Sold to T Baskcomb Ltd, Grimsby. 20.03.1925: Hull registry closed. 23.03.1925: Registered at Grimsby (GY299).
12.03.1929: Grimsby registry closed. 13.03.1929: Sold to William J Westgate, Lowestoft. 28.06.1929: Registered at Lowestoft as
PEACE WAVE (LT47). 06.06.1937: Sold to Ernest Edward Butcher & Ernest Herbert Holland, Lowestoft. 21.09.1937: Sold to
P W Watson & Sons Ltd, Lowestoft. 28.10.1937: Prunier Trophy winner. 01.10.1943: Sold to Jubilee Fishing Co Ltd, London.
06.1955: Sold to Jas. de Smedt, Antwerp, for breaking up at Boom. 13.07.1955: Sailed Lowestoft for Antwerp in tow of steam
drifter LANDBREEZE (LT1296) (94grt/1919) also sold for breaking up. 14.07.1955: Arrived Boom.
03.08.1955: Lowestoft registry closed.

OLEARIA 146459 Steam drifter H478	768 14.02.1922 29.03.1922	97 35	85.2 19.1 9.0	Goldie/McCulloch Design 33 nhp 2-cyl 8.0 knots	John McCann, Hull

All machinery new 1917 by International Engine Works, Amherst, NS and ex Canadian wooden Admiralty drifter CD.48 (see yard no.775).
25.04.1922: Registered at Hull (H478).   08.05.1922: Transferred to Pickering & Haldane's Steam Trawling Co Ltd, Hull.
02.1925: Sold to Lauritz Espersen, Esbjerg, Denmark.   17.02.1925: Hull registry closed. Registered at Esbjerg (E444).
16.11.1925: Sold to Soc Anon Armement Ostendais, Ostend, Belgium.   11.1925: Esbjerg registry closed.   25.11.1925: Registered at Ostend as **HECTOR DENIS** (O237).   16.09.1930: Laid up.   06.02.1936: Sold to Jubilee Fishing Co Ltd, Lowestoft. Ostend registry closed.   16.04.1936: Registered at Lowestoft as **ALCOR** (LT140).   24.11.1939: Requisitioned for war service as a minesweeping drifter (P.No.FY960); hire rate £35.3.3d per month.   03.1942: Employed on miscellaneous naval duties.
12.08.1943: Sold to Northern Trawlers Ltd, London.   12.1943: Employed on port duties.   08.04.1945: Arrived Lowestoft for restoration and survey.   17.09.1945: Returned.   08.1948: Sold to Jozef Arts, Ostend.   14.08.1948: Lowestoft registry closed.
12.05.1948: Taken in hand for conversion to motor; fitted with 270bhp Ruston & Hornsby oil engine.   20.09.1948: Renamed **MARJOLENE** on completion. Remeasured to 99.72grt, 42.98net.   31.09.1948: Registered as a motor trawler at Ostend as **MARJOLENE** (O337).   05.1950: Sold to P.V.B.A. Jozef Arts & Co, Ostend.   04.03.1955: Crewman Emiel Makelberghe washed overboard and drowned.   22.12.1956: Whilst on passage home from Newlyn for Christmas when off Start Point started to take in water in engine room. Taken in tow by Brixham motor trawler ROGER BUSHELL (BM76) (117grt/1946) but started to settle and foundered in position 50.14.12 N 03.08.45 W. All crew picked up by ROGER BUSHELL and landed at Brixham.
01.1957: Ostend registry closed.

COLEUS 146472 Steam drifter H498	769 13.03.1922 25.04.1922	97 35	85.2 19.1 9.10	Goldie/McCulloch Design 33 nhp 2-cyl 8.0 knots	Pickering & Haldane's Steam Trawling Co Ltd, Hull

All machinery new 1917 by International Engine Works, Amherst, NS and ex Canadian wooden Admiralty drifter CD.10.
18.05.1922: Registered at Hull (H498).   26.03.1925: Sold to Armement Ostendais, Ostend, Belgium.   26.03.1925: Hull registry closed.   27.03.1925: Arrived Ostend. Registered at Ostend as **KAMIEL HUYSMANS** (O233).   30.10.1930: Laid up until sold.
02.10.1935: Sold to Van Loocke Amand, Ostend.   22.10.1935: Registered at Ostend as **MARGUERITE** (O233).
04.12.1936: Converted to motor; fitted with a 250bhp MAN oil engine.   10.12.1938: Sold to Gauthier Frères, Lorient, France, for 240,000 francs.   No further information.

SILENE 146480 Steam drifter H551	770 13.03.1922 16.05.1922	97 35	85.2 19.1	Goldie/McCulloch Design 33 nhp 2-cyl 8.0 knots	Pickering & Haldane's Steam Trawling Co Ltd, Hull

All machinery new 1917 by International Engine Works, Amherst, NS and ex Canadian wooden Admiralty drifter CD.76.
03.1925: Sold to Magnus Thorberg, Reykjavik, Iceland.   28.03.1925: Hull registry closed. Registered at Reykjavik as **HAFTHÓR** (IS453).   01.12.1927: Sold to Arni Thorarinsson, Sigurjon Högnason, Eyvindur Thorarinsson, Gudmundur Helgason, Thorarin Bernodusson & Julius Jonsson, Vestmann Islands. Reykjavik registry closed. Registered at Vestmannaeyjar as **VENUS** (VE20).
1933: Sold to Julius Gudmundsson & others, Thingeyri. Vestmannaeyjar registry closed. Registered at Thingeyri (IS160).
1935: Sold to Gudmundur J Asgeirsson, Thingeyri.   1940: Sold to Petur O Johnson & others, Reykjavik. Thingeyri registry closed. Registered at Reykjavik as **REYKJANES** (RE94).   24.07.1942: Foundered off Tjörnes, all eighteen crew taken on board Icelandic trawler/longliner OLAFUR BJARNASON (MB57) (197grt/1914) from Akranes.   Reykjavik registry closed.

EXTENSION 146474 Steam drifter H504	771 28.02.1922 25.05.1922	103 36	85.2 19.8 9.1	Goldie/McCulloch Design 20 rhp 2-cyl 8.0 knots	Nielson Fishing Co Ltd, Hull

All machinery new 1917 by International Engine Works, Amherst, NS and ex Canadian wooden Admiralty drifter CD.42.
29.05.1922: Registered at Hull (H504).   14.01.1926: Sold to Soc Anon Pêcheries du Nord, Ostend, Belgium.   14.01.1926: Hull registry closed. Registered at Ostend as **ELIANE** (O115).   1931: Sold to P Tartanson, Marseilles, France. Ostend registry closed. Registered at Marseilles as **CALENDAL**.   1933: Sold to Criée du Chalutage, Marseilles.   1941: Sold to Louis Le Boulch, Lorient. Marseilles registry closed. Registered at Lorient.   1947: Re-registered in Concarneau.   1958: Vessel removed from Lloyd's Register of Shipping.

AREA 146487 Steam drifter H594	772 28.02.1922 29.06.1922	103 36	85.2 19.8 9.1	Goldie/McCulloch Design 20 rhp 2-cyl 8.0 knots	Nielson Fishing Co Ltd, Hull

All machinery new 1917 by International Engine Works, Amherst, NS and ex Canadian wooden Admiralty drifter CD.85.
30.06.1922: Registered at Hull (H594).   14.01.1926: Sold to Soc Anon Pêcheries du Nord, Ostend, Belgium.   14.01.1926: Hull registry closed. Registered at Ostend as **JULIA** (O106).   1931: Sold to Marquis de Bourdeilles, Dieppe, France.   1932: Sold to Criée du Chalutage, Marseilles. Registered at Marseilles as **NERTO**.   1941: Sold to Louis Le Boulch, Lorient.   1948: Marseilles registry closed. Registered at Concarneau as **NOTRE DAME DE TROGWALL**   1949: Converted to motor; fitted with 6-cylinder Fiat oil engine by Soc Anon. Fiat S.G.M. Turin.   1962: Sold to Corneillet, Doula, Cameroons. Re-engined with 6-cylinder oil engine by Soc Gen de Constr Méc, La Corneuve.   1971: Vessel removed from Lloyd's Register of Shipping.

Not built	773, 774 Orders cancelled.				

CD.48 Canadian built wooden drifter	775 1922 02.02.1922			N/A	John McCann, Hull

Converted to a coal hulk - see yard no. 768.

*The **William Jackson** (754/838) seen under her later name of **Evelyn Rose**.*

(Authors' collection)

Abelia *(761)*

(Authors' collection)

*The Icelandic **Hafthór** (770) was originally named **Silene**.*

(Authors' collection)

E WILSON'S No. 67 Built as a cargo lighter	776 1922 11.02.1922			N/A	Ellerman Wilson Line, Hull

Converted to an oil lighter.

LORD LASCELLES	777 (01.12.1917) 01.06.1922	326 131	138.5 23.7	C D Holmes 87 rhp 3-cyl 11.0 knots	Pickering & Haldane's Steam Trawling Co Ltd, Hull

Built as Mersey Class trawler **THOMAS WHIPPLE** (Ad.No.3574) for the Admiralty (see yard no.834).
05.1922: Sold to Pickering & Haldane's Steam Trawling Co Ltd, Hull. 26.05.1922: London registry closed. Cochrane & Sons Ltd contracted to refurbish as a fishing trawler; allocated yard no.777. 01.06.1922: Registered at Hull (H514). 18.07.1922: Registered at Hull as **LORD LASCELLES** (H514). 12.02.1926: Sold to Storr's Steam Trawling Co Ltd, Hull. 11.03.1926: Registered at Hull as **SABIK** (H514). 04.1929: Sold to Dale Steam Fishing Co (Grimsby) Ltd, Grimsby. 11.04.1929: Hull registry closed. 12.04.1929: Registered at Grimsby (GY58). 10.1933: Sold to Rushworth Steam Fishing Co Ltd, Grimsby. 26.01.1934: Sheltering in Dyrafjord, west coast of Iceland (Sk Frank Walker). After discussion with Fleetwood trawler LORINDA (FD182) (348grt/1928) decided to resume fishing. Sailed at 10.30am for fishing grounds but at 1.25pm in collision with Grimsby trawler EUTHAMIA (GY716) (342grt/1912) which struck her amidships in the starboard bunker and shell plates fractured. Vessel foundered in three to four minutes in approximate position 66.7N 24.4W; twelve crew lost and two survivors picked up by EUTHAMIA and landed at Dyrafjord. 11.04.1934: Grimsby registry closed - "Total loss".

MUDD Coal lighter	778 27.07.1922 20.09.1922	149 101	82.0 20.5	Kromhout Perman & Co 90 bhp 2-cyl 9.0 knots	Great Grimsby Coal Salt & Tanning Co Ltd, Grimsby
MEADOWS Coal lighter	779 28.08.1922 19.10.1922	149 101	82.0 20.5	Plenty & Son 100 bhp 2-cyl 9.0 knots	Great Grimsby Coal Salt & Tanning Co Ltd, Grimsby
CARTER Coal lighter	780 23.08.1922 09.11.1922	148 91	82.0 20.5	Plenty & Son 110 bhp 2-cyl 9.0 knots	Great Grimsby Coal Salt & Tanning Co Ltd, Grimsby
MUSCA 146648 Steam tug	781 24.08.1922 03.10.1922	75 -	72.5 18.6 9.1	Earles 380 bhp 2-cyl 9.0 knots	Gaselee & Son Ltd, London

Completed at a cost of £7663. 10.1922: Registered at London. Operated as "London Bridge tug'. 07.1940: Requisitioned for war service as an auxiliary patrol vessel; hire rate £71.5.0d per month. 10.10.1945: Returned. 12.1960: Sold to Thos W Ward Ltd, Sheffield, for breaking up. 22.12.1960: Arrived Grays, Essex. 12.1960: London registry closed.

BERBERIS 147968 Steam drifter H798	782 06.01.1923 15.02.1923	97 34	85.2 19.1 9.0	Goldie/McCulloch Design 33 nhp 2-cyl 9.0 knots	Pickering & Haldane's Steam Trawling Co Ltd, Hull

All machinery new 1917 by International Engine Works, Amherst, NS and ex Canadian wooden Admiralty drifter.
13.03.1923: Registered at Hull (H798). 02.1925: Sold to Lauritz Espersen, Esbjerg, Denmark. 17.02.1925: Hull registry closed. Registered at Esbjerg. 16.11.1925: Sold to Soc Anon Armement Ostendais, Ostend, Belgium. Registered at Ostend as **JAN DE RIDDER** (O238). 1930s: Laid up. 18.02.1935: Returned to service. 22.03.1937: Sold to Chantiers & Armement A Seghers, Ostend. Registered at Ostend as **INDEPENDENCE** (O309). 1937: Converted to motor; fitted with 300bhp Deutz oil engine. 21.05.1940: Bombed and sunk in Dieppe by German aircraft with loss of 21 refugees and one crewman. (May have been subsequently salved by German authorities).

RIBES 147073 Steam drifter H804	783 06.01.1923 15.02.1923	97 34	85.2 19.1 9.0	Goldie/McCulloch Design 33 nhp 2-cyl 9.0 knots	Pickering & Haldane's Steam Trawling Co Ltd, Hull

Built with materials from cancelled orders for Mersey Class Trawlers.
All machinery new 1917 by International Engine Works, Amherst, NS and ex Canadian wooden Admiralty drifter.
20.03.1923: Registered at Hull (H804). 02.1925: Sold to Lauritz Espersen, Esbjerg, Denmark. 17.02.1925: Hull registry closed. Registered at Esbjerg. 16.11.1925: Sold to Soc Anon Armement Ostendais, Ostend, Belgium. Registered at Ostend as **CELESTIN DEMBLON** (O239). 10.12.1925: Arrived Ostend. 26.05.1931: Laid up. 19.05.1934: Sold to Samvinnufelagid Tindastoll, Saudarkrokur, Iceland. 22.05.1934: Ostend registry closed. Registered at Saudarkrokur as **SKAGFIRDINGUR** (SK1). 31.10.1940: Sold to Jon Gislason & Sigurjon Einarsson, Hafnarfjördur. Registered at Hafnarfjördur as **BUDAKLETTUR** (GK250). 1941: Converted to motor; fitted with 200bhp Newbury oil engine. Re-measured to 101grt. 23.12.1944: Stranded and wrecked near Reykjanes lighthouse; eight crew got ashore but two passengers drowned. Hafnarfjördur registry closed.

SUPERMAN	784	200	96.6	Earles Co	United Towing Co Ltd,
147148 Steam tug	17.02.1923	1	24.5	750 ihp 3-cyl	Hull
	09.04.1923		11.8	11.0 knots	

06.04.1923: Registered at Hull.   First new vessel built for United Towing Co Ltd.   28.07.1928: Sold to Compañia Argentina de Navegación Angel Gardella Ltda, Buenos Aires, Argentina.   28.07.1928: Hull registry closed. Registered at Buenos Aires as **JUAN JOSÉ**.   1939: Registered at Buenos Aires as **CELSO R**.   1949: Sold to Flota Argentina de Navegación de Ultramar, Buenos Aires.   1958: Transferred to Flota Argentina de Navegación Fluvial, Buenos Aires.   1985: Vessel removed from Lloyd's Register of Shipping - continued existence in doubt.

MASTERMAN	785	200	96.6	Earles Co	United Towing Co Ltd,
147079 Steam tug	17.02.1923	1	24.5	750 ihp 3-cyl	Hull
	25.04.1923			11.0 knots	

23.04.1923: Registered at Hull.   10.02.1925: Sold to George Edgley, Gravesend & others (T/A Gamecock Steam Towing Co, London) for £12,900.   19.02.1925: Hull registry closed.   02.1925: Registered at London as **WATER COCK**.   1928: Transferred to Gamecock Steam Towing Co Ltd, London.   26.05.1940: 'Operation Dynamo' (Dunkirk evacuation) put into effect. At Dover on harbour duty.   06.1940: Requisitioned for war service with War Department; hire rate £128.5.0d per month.   30.08.1942: Employed as a salvage tug/coastal convoy work.   23.06.1944: Assigned to 'Operation Neptune' - Normandy landings.   25.06.1944: At Dungeness pumping out 'Phoenix' sections.   08.02.1946: Returned.   1948: Sold to Ocean Salvage & Towage Co Ltd, London.   01.02.1950: Sold to Gamecock Tugs Ltd, London.   1964: Sold to William Watkins Ltd, London.   1966: Sold to Jas de Smedt, Antwerp, Belgium, for breaking up.   05.07.1966: Arrived at Willebroek for breaking up.   Registry closed.

TORRIS	786	131	90.1	C D Holmes	Thompson Towage Co Ltd,
147083 Steam tug	07.03.1923		22.1	73 rhp 3-cyl	Hull
	10.05.1923			11.0 knots	

18.05.1923: Registered at Hull.   23.10.1926: Sold to United Towing Co Ltd, Hull.   17.01.1927: Registered at Hull as **PRESSMAN**.   26.10.1938: Sold to Soc Anon les Goelands, Oran, Algeria.   26.10.1938: Hull registry closed. Registered at Oran as **GOELAND II**.   1956: Lengthened to 104.11ft, tonnage amended to 135grt.   1961: Sold to Nicolas E Vernicos, Piraeus, Greece.   1962: Oran registry closed. Registered at Piraeus as **VERNICOS FANNY**.   30.01.1964: Stranded at Kali Limenes, southern Crete, during a gale and became a total loss.   Registry closed.

MARK LANE	787	81	74.6	C D Holmes	Tilbury Contracting &
147487 Steam tug	07.03.1923	36	19.1	68 nhp 2-cyl	Dredging Co Ltd,
	18.05.1923		9.3	8.5 knots	London

Employed in the company's dredging fleet towing mud hoppers.   1963: Sold to Thos W Ward Ltd, Sheffield, for breaking up.   06.03.1963: Arrived Grays, Essex.   Registry closed.

MALRIX	788	703	175.1	C D Holmes	Rix Steamships Ltd,
147086 Steam cargo ship	19.04.1923	354	29.0	96 rhp 3-cyl	Hull
	21.06.1923		11.4	9.0 knots	

20.06.1923: Registered at Hull.   17.12.1940: On a voyage from Hull towards London River with a cargo of 781 tons of coal. Mined 1.8 miles S by W of the Nore Light Vessel; eight of twelve crew lost.   22.09.1942: After part lifted.   17.10.1942: Fore part lifted.   23.10.1942: Remainder of wreckage beached at Southend and area cleared.   22.01.1941: Registry closed.

LESRIX	789	703	175.1	C D Holmes	Rix Steamships Ltd,
147126 Steam cargo ship	16.05.1923	354	29.0	96 rhp 3-cyl	Hull
	15.01.1924		11.4	9.0 knots	

11.01.1924: Registered at Hull.   08.09.1941: Sold to Williamstown Shipping Co Ltd, London.   26.01.1942: On a voyage from Sunderland towards Belfast (Capt Grant) with a cargo of coal, in storm conditions stranded on rocks off Hackley Head, near Cruden, Aberdeenshire; four crew rescued from forecastle by shore party with breeches buoy but ten crew lost when stern section of vessel broke away.   07.05.1942: Registry closed.

WELTONDALE	790	883	195.6	Amos & Smith	Yorkshire Dale Steamship
147119 Steam cargo ship	08.01.1924	442	31.1	98 rhp 3-cyl	Co Ltd,
	27.02.1924		12.6	9.0 knots	Hull

25.02.1924: Registered at Hull.   21.01.1936: Sold to "Toft" Steamship Co Ltd, Middlesbrough.   03.04.1936: Renamed **WHITETOFT**.   12.09.1936: Hull registry closed. Registered at Middlesbrough.   29.04.1940: On a voyage from Ghent towards the Tees with a cargo of iron ore, stranded at North Cheek, Robin Hood's Bay, North Yorkshire, in approximate position 54.26N 0.31W.   Registry closed.

RYE	791	70	61.3		Furley & Co Ltd,
147129 Sheffield keel	23.01.1924	67	15.3	N/A	Hull
lighter	15.02.1924		7.6		

13.02.1924: Registered at Hull.   12.08.1956: Registered anew after conversion to motor, fitted with 30bhp oil engine by R A Lister Ltd, Dursley. 6 knots.   17.06.1965: Sold to Ernest V Waddington, Mexborough.   16.11.1999: Registry closed - "Not renewed, broken up".

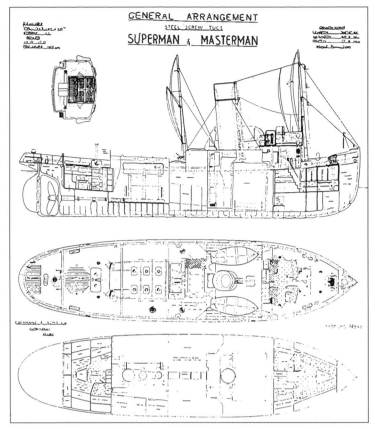

A general arrangement drawing of the **Superman** (784) and **Masterman** (785)

Superman (784)

(World Ship Photo Library)

Masterman (785)

(Stuart Emery collection)

Lesrix (789)

(World Ship Photo Library)

NAR 147128 Sheffield keel lighter	792 23.01.1924 15.02.1924	70 67	61.3 15.3 7.6	N/A	Furley & Co Ltd, Hull

13.02.1924: Registered at Hull. 1962: Rebuilt, lengthened to 85ft and converted to motor, fitted with 65bhp oil engine by F Perkins Ltd, Peterborough. 6 knots. 20.03.1963: Registered anew as motor lighter. 31.03.1968: Foundered in River Humber; two crewmen rescued by Dutch coaster named by a newspaper as BEUJALAND but which cannot be otherwise traced. 07.11.1968: Registry closed - "Total Loss in River Humber".

SALVAGE PRINCE 147612 Steam tug	793 1924 28.03.1924	184 61	92.5 26.1 10.8	Plenty & Son 69 rhp 2-cyl 11.0 knots	Grant Pyke, Kingston, Ontario

03.1924: Registered at London. 05.1924: Delivered Montreal, Province of Quebec, Canada (Capt J C Leslie). 1931: Sold to Pyke Towing & Salvage Co, Kingston, ON. By 1944: Sold to Pyke Salvage Co, Kingston, ON. 1946: Sold to Léon R Beaupre, Kingston, ON. 1949: Sold to Pyke Salvage & Navigation Co Ltd, Kingston, Ontario. London registry closed. Registered at Kingston, ON. 1963: Sold to McAllister-Pyke Salvage Ltd, Kingston, ON. 1970: Sold to McAllister Towing Ltd, Kingston, ON. 1976: Sold to McAllister Towing & Salvage Ltd, Kingston, ON. 08.1976: Sold to Joost Brender, Kingston, ON, for breaking up. Re-sold to Jock & Susanne Brandis and converted to houseboat. Removed from Lloyd's Register of Shipping.

BLUE GALLEON 148074 Steam cargo ship	794 1924 21.06.1924	712 337	180.2 29.0 11.4	Amos & Smith 82 rhp 3-cyl 9.0 knots	Galleon Shipping Co Ltd, Newcastle

06.1924: Registered at Newcastle. 15.11.1940: On a voyage from London River towards Sunderland with a cargo of cement, attacked and bombed by German aircraft 5 miles E of Hammond Knoll and foundered in approximate position 52.57N 01.56E; three of the fourteen crew lost. Register closed.

LORY 147133 Lighter	795 21.02.1924 21.03.1924	107 104	71.0 19.0	N/A	John A Scott Ltd, Hull

14.03.1924: Registered at Hull. 27.03.1980: Registry closed on advice of owner, vessel broken up.

COLY 147135 Lighter	796 21.02.1924 21.03.1924	107 104	71.0 19.0	N/A	John A Scott Ltd, Hull

14.03.1924: Registered at Hull. 27.03.1980: Registry closed on advice of owner, vessel broken up

BAZA 147132 Lighter	797 23.02.1924 28.03.1924	107 104	71.0 19.0	N/A	John A Scott Ltd, Hull

14.03.1924: Registered at Hull. 29.06.1979: Registry closed on advice of owner, vessel broken up.

RHEA 147134 Lighter	798 23.02.1924 28.03.1924	107 104	71.0 19.0	N/A	John A Scott Ltd, Hull

14.03.1924: Registered at Hull. 11.04.1983: Registry closed on advice of owner, vessel broken up

TRADESMAN 147148 Steam tug	799 24.03.1924 29.05.1924	177 1	96.6 24.6 11.8	Earle's Co 84 rhp 3-cyl 12.0 knots	United Towing Co Ltd, Hull

05.06.1924: Registered at Hull. 11.1928: Sold to Argentine Nav. Co (Nicolas Mihanovich) Ltd, Buenos Aires, Argentina. 16.11.1928: Hull registry closed. Registered at Buenos Aires as **MEDIADOR**. 1932: Sold to Cia Argentina de Nav Mihanovich Ltda, Buenos Aires. 1943: Sold to Cia Argentina de Nav Dodero SA, Buenos Aires. 1958: Sold to Flota Argentina de Navegación de Ultramar, Buenos Aires. 1961: Sold to Empresa Lineas Maritimas Argentinas, Buenos Aires. 1962: Removed from Lloyd's Register of Shipping - noted as no longer in existence.

HEADMAN 147150 Steam tug	800 24.03.1924 11.06.1924	177 1	96.5 24.6	Earle's Co 84 rhp 3-cyl 12.0 knots	United Towing Co Ltd, Hull

10.06.1924: Registered at Hull. 1939-1945: Local towage and salvage work. 23.01.1962: Sold to Blyth Tug Co Ltd, Blyth. 06.02.1962: Hull registry closed. Registered at Newcastle as **HILLSIDER**. 1972: Sold to Hughes Bolckow Ltd, Blyth. 09.1972: Broken up at Blyth. Registry closed.

JOHN QUILLIAM Ad.No.3541 Mersey class	801 12.03.1917 26.06.1917	324 132	138.2 23.7 12.8	Richardsons 600 rhp 3-cyl 11.0 knots	The Admiralty, Whitehall, London

Completed as an armed trawler (1-12pdr HA & W/T). First of the Mersey class trawlers.
07.02.1920: Registered by the Admiralty at London as a fishing vessel (LO322). Official No.144374. 1921: Sold to Danish Government (Landbrugsministeriet), Copenhagen. 03.03.1921: Hull registry closed. Registered at Copenhagen as **DANA**. Employed on research. 1931: Sold to Den Dansk Stat (Fiskeridirektoratet), Korsør. 22.06.1935: Foundered off the west coast of Denmark having been in collision with German trawler PICKHUBEN (238grt/1920). Copenhagen registry closed.

GEORGE BLIGH Ad.No.3542 Mersey class	802 24.03.1917 03.07.1917	324 132	138.5 23.7 12.8	Campbell Gas 600 ihp 3-cyl 11.0 knots	The Admiralty, Whitehall, London

Completed as an armed trawler (1-12pdr, 1-7.5" A/S Howitzer & W/T).
03.02.1920: Registered by the Admiralty at London as a fishing vessel (LO309). Official No.144324. 10.06.1921: Transferred to Minister of Agriculture and Fisheries, London. Employed on fishery research. 1930: Laid up. 1935: Engaged with Danish Government in fishery research in Icelandic waters. 09.1939: Redeployed for war service as an escort vessel.
06.1940: Converted for boom defence duties (P.No.Z.178). Based Lyness. 12.1945: Released. 1947: Sold to Inch Fishing Co Ltd, Granton. London registry closed. Registered at Granton as **INCHKENNETH** (GN26). 11.1954: Sold to BISCO (£2,400) and allocated to Shipbreaking Industries Ltd for breaking up at Charlestown, Fife. 13.11.1954: Arrived Charlestown and breaking up commenced. 11.1954: Granton registry closed.

JOHN YULE Ad.No.3543 Mersey class	803 24.03.1917 11.07.1917	324 133	138.5 23.7 12.8	Richardsons 600 ihp 3-cyl 11.0 knots	The Admiralty, Whitehall, London

Completed as an armed trawler (1-12pdr, Hydrophone & W/T). 14.07.1917: Delivered. 1919: Registered in the Registry of British Ships at London. Official No.144299. 03.02.1920: Registered by the Admiralty at London as a fishing vessel (LO305). 1922: Sold to Gournay-Delpierre & Co, Boulogne, France. 02.05.1922: London registry closed. Registered at Boulogne as **NOTRE DAME DE LORETTE**. 1933: Sold to Gournay Frères, Boulogne. 1939: Requisitioned for war service by the French Navy (P.No.AD.85). 25.01.1940: Attacked and bombed by German aircraft and foundered off Dunkirk. 26.01.1940: Salved and repaired. 1947: Sold to shipbreakers and broken up.

JOHN PASCO Ad.No.3544 Mersey class	804 19.04.1917 24.07.1917	325 131	138.5 23.7 12.8	Campbell Gas 600 ihp 3-cyl 11.0 knots	The Admiralty, Whitehall, London

Completed as an escort vessel (1-12pdr, W/T). 27.07.1917: Delivered. 06.11.1920: Registered by the Admiralty at London as a fishing vessel (LO485). Official No.145084. 22.12.1922: Sold to Pearl Steam Trawling Co Ltd, Scarborough. 14.02.1923: Registered at Hull (H791). 16.02.1923: London registry closed. 11.1924: Sold to H/F Kveldulfur, Reykjavik, Iceland. 01.12.1924: Hull registry closed. Registered at Reykjavik as **ARINBJORN HERSIR** (RE1). 16.09.1940: Returning to Iceland in company with SNORRI GODI (373grt/1921) having landed at Fleetwood. At 2.30am witnessed the attack by a German aircraft on the troopship ASKA (8323grt/1939), Bathurst for Liverpool, which was between Rathlin Island and the Maiden's Rock and was set on fire and abandoned. With SNORRI GODI picked up from the sea and from boats and liferafts between 250-300 men, all of whom were transferred to HMS JASON (P.No.N99) and landed at Greenock. 26.06.1944: Sold to Oskar Halldorsson, Gudridur Erna Oskarsdottir and Gudrun Oskarsdottir, Reykjavik. Registered at Reykjavik as **FAXI** (RE17). 29.11.1944: Sold to H/F Faxaklettur, Hafnarfjordur Iceland. 1949: Laid up in Hafnarfjordur harbour. 05.01.1952: In storm conditions parted mooring and driven across Faxa-bay fetching up aground inside Borgarfjordur, near Borgarnes. 30.01.1952: Refloated undamaged, towed to Borganess, re activated and returned to Reykjavik under own power. Surveyed but considered beyond economical repair. 27.11.1952: Register closed. 28.06.1955: Sailed Reykjavik for Esbjerg, Denmark, in tow of Danish motor tug SIGYN (288grt/1916) with TRYGGVI GAMLI (see yard no.737) and one other trawler for breaking up. Broken up, registry closed.

ANDREW KING Ad.No.3545 Mersey class	805 19.04.1917 01.08.1917	324 131	138.5 23.7 12.8	Richardsons, Westgarth 600 ihp 3-cyl 11.0 knots	The Admiralty, Whitehall, London

Completed as a minesweeper (1-12pdr, Hydrophone & W/T). 04.08.1917: Delivered. 09.1920: Re-commissioned as HMS **OUSE** ("Colne" class, unarmed). Fleet Target Service. 1939: Mediterranean Station. Armed (2x1-3") (P.No.T.80). 20.02.1941: Mined off Tobruk, Libya. Twelve crew killed and the CO, Sub Lt Wilfred V Fitzmaurice RNVR and nine crew, all wounded, survived.

THOMAS ATKINSON Ad.No.3546 Mersey class	806 08.05.1917 03.08.1917	325 130	138.5 23.7 12.8	Cooper & Greig 600 ihp 3-cyl 11.0 knots	The Admiralty, Whitehall, London

Completed as a minesweeper (1-12pdr and W/T). 1919: Registered in the Registry of British Ships at London. Official No.143797. 11.05.1921: Registered by the Admiralty at London as a fishing vessel (LO509). 12.1923: Sold to Hudson Steam Fishing Co Ltd, Hull. 08.12.1923: London registry closed. 10.12.1923: Registered at Hull (H909). 18.12.1923: Registered at Hull as **CAVENDISH** (H909). 07.1938: Sold to Towarzystwo Dalekomorskich Polowoe "Pomorze" Sp.z.o.o., Gdynia. 28.07.1938: Hull registry closed. 1938: Registered at Gdynia as **EUGENIUSZ** (GDY118). 1939: Sold to Adam Steam Fishing Co. Ltd, London. 08.1939: Gdynia registry closed. 08.08.1939: Registered at Fleetwood as **ERITH** (FD93). 04.02.1940: Requisitioned for war service as a minesweeper (P.No.FY.578); hire rate £94.15.10d per month. 01.1941: Based Grimsby with M/S Group 21. 31.05.1943: Sold to Winzenty Bartosiak, Gdynia, Poland (Baltycka Spolka Okretowa sp.z.o.o., Gdynia (Baltic Shipping Co Ltd)). 04.06.1943: Fleetwood registry closed. 06.1945: Returned. Registered at Gdynia as **POLESIE** (GDY89). 06.1946: Fishing from IJmuiden with Dutch crews until end of year. 12.1946: Returned to Poland. 16.12.1949: By Order of the Ministry of Navigation, the holding company and assets to be placed under control of the Polish People's Republic. 1950: Company and assets transferred to "Dalmor" Przedsiobiorstwo Polowow Dalekomorskich Sp.z.ogr.odp, Gdynia (Polish Government). 1957: Registered at Gdynia as **FENIKS** (GDY89). 1957: New boiler fitted. 12.1959: Sold to Polish shipbreakers and broken up. 1960: Gdynia registry closed.

THOMAS BAILEY Ad.No.3558 Mersey class	818 04.08.1917 07.11.1917	324 133	138.5 23.7 12.8	Cooper & Greig 600 ihp 3-cyl 11.0 knots	The Admiralty, Whitehall, London

Completed as a minesweeper (1-12pdr, W/T). 13.11.1917: Delivered. 1919: Registered in the Registry of British Ships at London. Official No.143848. 24.08.1920: Registered by the Admiralty at London as a fishing vessel (LO443). 1922: Sold to E Dominguez Macaya, Vigo. 04.08.1922: London registry closed. Registered at Vigo as **PANXON**. 01.03.1948: Lost off Cape Bojador, West Africa.

ROBERT BARTON Ad.No.3559 Mersey class	819 28.08.1917 10.11.1917	321 134	138.5 23.7 12.8	C D Holmes 600 ihp 3-cyl 11.0 knots	The Admiralty, Whitehall, London

Completed as a minesweeper (1-12pdr, W/T). 14.11.1917: Delivered. 1919: Registered in the Registry of British Ships at London. Official No.144289. 23.12.1920: Registered by the Admiralty at London as a fishing vessel (LO494). Laid up. 10.1922: Sold to Ernest Wilfred & William John Robins, Hull. 25.05.1923: Sold to West Dock Steam Fishing Co Ltd, Hull. 05.10.1922: London registry closed. 18.10.1922: Registered at Hull as **HAYBURN WYKE** (H717). 25.04.1930: Sold to Dinas Steam Trawler Co Ltd, Fleetwood, for £8250. 25.04.1930: Hull registry closed. 26.04.1930: Registered at Fleetwood (FD99). 10.1939: Sold to Oddsson & Co Ltd, Hull. 23.05.1940: Fleetwood registry closed. 27.05.1940: Registered at Hull (H334). 28.05.1940: Requisitioned for war service as an auxiliary patrol vessel; hire rate £94.10.0d per month. 08.1941: Fitted out as a minesweeper (P.No.FY.139). Based Swansea. 02.01.1945: At anchor off Ostend (Sk Lieut Francis Wilson RNR). Torpedoed by German 'Seehund' midget submarine and foundered rapidly. Crew of twenty-two missing presumed killed. 17.09.1947: Hull registry closed - "Lost on Admiralty service 1945". Wreck lies in position 51.15.27N 02.48.44E.

RICHARD BULKELEY Ad.No.3560 Mersey class	820 21.08.1917 16.11.1917	324 133	138.5 23.7 12.8	Campbell Gas 600 ihp 3-cyl 11.0 knots	The Admiralty, Whitehall, London

Completed as an armed trawler (1-12pdr, W/T). 21.11.1917: Delivered. 31.05.1919: Loaned to the United States Navy for clearance work on the Northern Mine Barrage. 12.07.1919: Mined whilst 'sweeping in the North Sea off the Orkney Islands. Seven crew lost; eighteen survivors.

MICHAEL CLEMENTS Ad.No.3561 Mersey class	821 21.08.1917 22.11.1917	324 133	138.5 23.7 12.8	C D Holmes 600 ihp 3-cyl 11.0 knots	The Admiralty, Whitehall, London

Completed as a minesweeper (1-12pdr HA, W/T later fitted with Hydrophone). 27.11.1917: Delivered. 08.08.1918: Off St. Catherine's Point, Isle of Wight, struck by HM Trawler JOHN CATTLING (Ad.No.3676) and foundered in position 50.21N 01.25W. No casualties.

JOHN CORMACK Ad.No.3562 Mersey class	822 04.09.1917 30.11.1917	324 133	138.5 23.7 12.8	C D Holmes 600 ihp 3-cyl 11.0 knots	The Admiralty, Whitehall, London

Completed as an armed trawler (1-12pdr HA ,W/T). 05.12.1917: Delivered. 1919: Registered in the Registry of British Ships at London (O.N.143867). 28.01.1920: Registered by the Admiralty at London as a fishing vessel (LO263). 1922: Sold to Pickering & Haldane's Steam Trawling Co Ltd, Hull. 28.07.1922: London registry closed. 04.08.1922: Registered at Hull (H660). 21.08.1922: Registered at Hull as **LORD PIRRIE** (H660). 06.04.1929: Sold to W B Willey & Sons Ltd, Hull. 28.06.1929: Registered at Hull as **CHILTERN** (H660). 15.05.1936: Sold to H Elliott & Sons Trawlers Ltd, Fleetwood. 03.1937: Fishing from Fleetwood. 16.08.1939: Sold to Boston Deep Sea Fishing & Ice Co Ltd, Fleetwood. 04.1940: Employed on Fishery Protection (WA/Fort William/Fleetwood). 04.06.1940: Requisitioned for war service as an auxiliary patrol vessel (1-12pdr) (P.No.4.125); hire rate £94.10.0d per month. 15 - 25.06.1940: Operation Ariel. 18.06.1940: At St. Nazaire, rescued women and children from advancing German forces. The last British ship to leave the port. 30.05.1941: Shot down twin-engined German bomber off West Country (Ty/Sk A J Drake RNR). 09.1941: Fitted out as a minesweeper. Based Plymouth. 01.1942: At Falmouth for arcticisation. 03.1942 - 05.1942: At Reykjavik as escort (part) of Russian convoys PQ.12, PQ.14 and PQ.15. 26.08.1944: Sold to Eton Fishing Co Ltd, Hull. 1945: Returned. 01.06.1946: Sold to Ross & Fullerton Ltd, Glasgow. 12.09.1946: Sold to David G Watson, Edinburgh. 25.10.1946: Hull Registry closed. 25.10.1946: Sold to Planet Fishing Co Ltd, Edinburgh. 10.1946: Registered at Granton (GN25). 28.10.1945: Laid up at Granton. Flooded engine room due to leak. 26.01.1950: Fishing about 110 miles NE of Buchan Ness (Sk John Paterson) in company with trawler KUVERA (GN39) (203grt/1919) which started to take in water. Before vessel settled and foundered, all thirteen crew taken onboard and later landed at Granton. 1952: Sold to Medway Yacht Basin Ltd, Borstal, Rochester. 1954: Sold to BISCO and allocated to James A White & Co Ltd, St David's, for breaking up. Granton registry closed.

CHRISTOPHER DIXON Ad.No.3563 Mersey class	823 04.09.1917 11.01.1918	323 131	138.5 23.7 12.8	Crossley Bros 600 ihp 3-cyl 11.0 knots	The Admiralty, Whitehall, London

Completed as an armed trawler (1-12pdr, W/T). 14.01.1918: Delivered. 07.03.1922: Registered by the Admiralty at London as a fishing vessel (LO544). Laid up. 02.1923: Sold to Irish Free State Government, Dublin. 28.02.1923: London registry closed. 02.1923: Registered at Dublin. 04.05.1923: Commissioned in the Irish Free State Coastal & Marine Service, Dublin. 31.03.1924: Decommissioned. Transferred to Commissioners of Public Works in the Saorstat Eireann, Dublin. For sale. 1924: Sold to Pickering & Haldane's Steam Trawling Co Ltd, Hull. 10.1924: Dublin registry closed. 15.10.1924: Registered at Hull as **LORD GAINFORD** (H73) (see yard no. 941).

SAMUEL DOWDEN	824	324	138.5	C D Holmes	The Admiralty,
Ad.No.3564	18.09.1917	133	23.7	600 ihp 3-cyl	Whitehall, London
Mersey class	07.12.1917		12.8	11.0 knots	

Completed as an armed trawler (1-12pdr, 1-3.5" A/S Howitzer, hydrophone & W/T). 11.12.1917: Delivered.
29.01.1921: Registered by the Admiralty as a fishing vessel at London (LO499). 09.1922: Sold to Jutland Amalgamated Trawlers Ltd, Hull. 18.09.1922: London registry closed. 26.09.1922: Registered at Hull as **ROYAL REGIMENT** (H683). 05.11.1934: Sold to Hudson Brothers Trawlers Ltd, Hull. 05.01.1935: Registered at Hull as **CAPE GRENVILLE** (H683). 28.07.1938: Sold to Towarzystwo Dalekomorskich Polowoe "Pomorze" Sp.z.o.o., Gdynia. 21.08.1938: Hull registry closed. 1938: Registered at Gdynia as **DOROTA** (GDY117). 09.1939: Sold to Adam Steam Fishing Co Ltd, London. 09.1939: Gdynia registry closed.
03.11.1939: Registered at Fleetwood as **DUNCAN** (FD92). 02.1940: Requisitioned for war service as a minesweeper and renamed **SEA MIST** (P.No.FY1640); hire rate £94.10.0d per month. Based Grimsby with M/S Group 21. 31.05.1943: Sold to Winzenty Bartosiak, Gdynia, Poland (Baltycka Spolka Okretowa sp.z.o.o., Gdynia (Baltic Shipping Co Ltd). 01.06.1943: Fleetwood registry closed. 06.1943: Registered at Gdynia as **POKUCIE** (GDY98). 10.12.1945: Returned. 08.1946: Fishing from IJmuiden with Dutch crews until end of year. 16.12.1949: By Order of the Ministry of Navigation, the holding company and assets to be placed under control of the Polish People's Republic. 1950: Company and assets transferred to "Dalmor" Przedsiobiorstwo Polowow Dalekomorskich Sp.z.ogr.odp, Gdynia (Polish Government). 06.06.1955: Bunkering at Silesia wharf, Gdynia, at 5.56am, sank alongside due to leaking valve. Salved but due to "the general wear and tear", declared beyond economical repair and sold for breaking up. 1956: Gdynia registry closed.

JAMES BUCHANAN	825	324	138.5	C D Holmes	The Admiralty,
Ad.No.3565	18.09.1917	132	23.7	600 ihp 3-cyl	Whitehall, London
Mersey class	13.12.1917		12.8	11.0 knots	

Completed as a minesweeper (1-12pdr HA & W/T, later fitted with hydrophone). 15.12.1917: Delivered. 23.08.1920: Registered by the Admiralty at London as a fishing vessel (LO396). 02.1922: Sold to City Steam Fishing Co Ltd, Hull. 24.08.1922: London registry closed. 14.09.1922: Registered at Hull as **STONEFERRY** (H676). 19.01.1934: Sold to Hudson Brothers Trawlers Ltd, Hull. 11.06.1934: Sold to Hudson Steam Fishing Co Ltd, Hull. 11.06.1934: Registered at Hull as **CAPE TARIFA** (H676). 07.1938: Sold to Towarzystwo Dalekomorskich Polowoe "Pomorze" Sp.z.o.o., Gdynia. 28.07.1938: Hull registry closed. 1938: Registered at Gdynia as **FRANCISZKA** (GDY119). 1939: Sold to Adam Steam Fishing Co Ltd, London. 11.1939: Gdynia registry closed. 07.11.1939: Registered at Fleetwood as **FORCE** (FD100). 12.02.1940: Requisitioned for war service as a minesweeper (P.No.FY.NI); hire rate £94.10.0d per month. 28.06.1941: At anchor six miles off Winterton Ness, Norfolk (Act/Ty Sk C E Smalley RNR), attacked by German aircraft, damaged and set on fire and in twenty minutes foundered in position 52.48.55N 01.47.48E. Eleven crew lost. Fleetwood registry closed.

JOHN EBBS	826	324	138.5	C D Holmes	The Admiralty,
Ad.No.3566	02.10.1917	132	23.7	600 ihp 3-cyl	Whitehall, London
Mersey class	19.12.1917		12.8	11.0 knots	

Completed as an armed trawler (1-12pdr, 1-3.5" A/S Howitzer & W/T later fitted with Hydrophone). 20.12.1917: Delivered.
1922: Sold to the Belgian pilotage service, converted to a pilot cutter. Renamed **PILOTE No. 4**. 26.10.1939: Requisitioned by the Marinekorps (Belgian Navy) for war service. Renamed **A.4**. Based Ostend with 1ste Escadrille patrolling Belgian waters; 33 mines destroyed with gunfire. 06.1940: Interned in Portugalete, near Bilbao, Spain. 10.1946: Returned to the Belgian pilotage service. Reverted to **PILOTE NO. 4**. 15.10.1948: Sold to shipbreakers and broken up.

FRASER EAVES	827	324	138.5	C D Holmes	The Admiralty,
Ad.No.3567	02.10.1917	131	23.7	600 ihp 3-cyl	Whitehall, London
Mersey class	22.12.1918		12.8	11.0 knots	

Completed as an armed trawler (1-4", 1-12pdr HA, 1-7.5" A/S Howitzer & W/T). 22.12.1917: Delivered.
09.1920: Re-commissioned as HMS **DOON** (1-12pdr). Fishery Protection duties. Based west coast of Ireland. 1937: Based Portland (P.No.T.35). 09.1939: At Portsmouth fitting out as a minesweeper (P.No.T.35). 1940: Western Approaches Command. 05.1944: Fitted out for dan laying and assigned to Operation Neptune - Normandy landings. 23.05.1944: Attached to the 18th Minesweeping Flotilla as a dan layer. 05.06.1944: Sailed Solent anchorage for Gold Beach as part of Assault Convoy G2. 03.07.1944: Operation Neptune ended. 1946: Sold to Easton Trawling Co Ltd, Swansea. Registered at Swansea as **DONESSE** (SA21). Official No.168571. 1948: Sold to East Fisheries Ltd, Cape Town, South Africa. Swansea registry closed. Registered at Cape Town. 10.06.1957: Having been stripped of all usable materials, used as a target and sunk by SAN off Robben Island. Cape Town registry closed.

GEORGE FENWICK	828	324	138.5	C D Holmes	The Admiralty,
Ad.No.3568	18.10.1917	132	23.7	600 ihp 3-cyl	Whitehall, London
Mersey class	05.01.1918		12.8	11.0 knots	

Completed as an armed trawler (1-12pdr, W/T). 10.01.1918: Delivered. 03.02.1920: Registered by the Admiralty at London as a fishing vessel (LO542). Official No. 146527. 12.1923: Sold to Hudson Steam Fishing Co Ltd, Hull. 08.12.1923: London registry closed. 10.12.1923: Registered at Hull (H912). 18.12.1923: Registered at Hull as **CAPE OTWAY** (H912). 09.1938: Sold to the Royal Hellenic Navy. 03.10.1938: Hull registry closed. Converted to an "Aixos" class minelayer (50 mines) and on completion renamed RHS **STRYMON**. 04.1941: Battle of Greece. 23.04.1940: In Gulf of Athens, attacked by German aircraft and sunk. Later salved by Germans, repaired and commissioned in Kriegsmarine as a submarine chaser. Renamed **UJ 2101**.
01.06.1944: North of Crete, attacked by Allied aircraft and sunk.

HENRY FORD Ad.No.3569 Mersey class	829 18.10.1917 15.01.1918	324 134	138.5 23.7 12.8	C D Holmes 600 ihp 3-cyl 11.0 knots	The Admiralty, Whitehall, London

Completed as a minesweeper (1-12pdr HA, W/T). 18.01.1918: Delivered. 02.1919: Renamed **BOADICEA II**. 02.1920: Reverted to **HENRY FORD**. 03.02.1920: Registered by the Admiralty at London as a fishing vessel (LO493). Official No. 145115. 09.1921: Sold to Bourgain-Vincent, Boulogne, France. 09.09.1921: London registry closed. Registered at Boulogne as **DUPERRÉ**. 1933: Sold to Fourmentin - Avisse & Cie, Boulogne. 1939: Requisitioned for war service in French Navy as a patrol vessel (P.No.P.64). 26.05.1940: 'Operation Dynamo' (Dunkirk evacuation) put into effect. 03.06.1940: At Ramsgate landed 307 troops. 05.06.1940: Lost at Dunkirk.

JOHN FELTON Ad.No.3570 Mersey class	830 01.11.1917 24.01.1918	324 132	138.5 23.7 12.8	C D Holmes 600 ihp 3-cyl 11.0 knots	The Admiralty, Whitehall, London

Completed as an armed trawler (1-12pdr HA, 1-6" A/S Howitzer & W/T). 31.01.1918: Delivered. 1919: Registered in the Registry of British Ships at London. Official No.143895. 28.01.1920: Registered by the Admiralty at London as a fishing vessel (LO264). 1921: Sold to Fisheries Board for Scotland, Edinburgh. Converted to a research vessel. Re-measured to 351grt, 146net. 02.1922: Renamed **EXPLORER**. 05.07.1922: London registry closed - "No longer required". 08.1940: Requisitioned for war service as an examination vessel in the Firth of Forth. 12.04.1946: Returned. 1955: Withdrawn from service and laid up. 08.1956: Sold by Scottish Home Department, Edinburgh, to BISCO (£5,600) and allocated to Shipbreaking Industries Ltd, Charlestown, Fife. 24.08.1956: Arrived Charlestown and breaking up commenced.

DANIEL FEARALL Ad.No.3571 Mersey class	831 02.11.1917 29.01.1918	324 132	138.5 23.7 12.8	C D Holmes 600 ihp 3-cyl 11.0 knots	The Admiralty, Whitehall, London

Completed as a minesweeper (1-12pdr, 1-7.5" A/S Howitzer & W/T). 03.02.1918: Delivered and used as a training ship. 09.1920: Renamed **STOUR**. 01.09.1922: Re-commissioned as HMS **PEMBROKE** ("Colne" class (2-3pdrs). Employed on various duties. 1939: Fitted out as a minesweeper and renamed **STOUR** (2-3pdrs) (P.No.FY1592). Based Harwich with M/S Group 56. 1946: Sold to Easton Trawling Co Ltd, Swansea. Registered at Swansea as **STORESSE** (SA22). Official No.168575. 1948: Sold to East Fisheries Ltd, Cape Town, South Africa. Swansea registry closed. Registered at Cape Town (CTA37). 1967: Stripped of non-ferrous metals and usable materials. Cape Town registry closed. 02.1967: Scuttled at 'Irvin Johnson' artificial reef in False Bay by South African Navy.

THOMAS THRESHER Ad.No.3572 Mersey class	832 17.11.1917 05.02.1918	324 134	138.5 23.7 12.8	C D Holmes 600 ihp 3-cyl 11.0 knots	The Admiralty, Whitehall, London

Completed as a minesweeper (1-12pdr, W/T). 08.02.1918: Delivered. 07.02.1920: Registered by the Admiralty at London as a fishing vessel (LO321). Official No.144373. 1923: Laid up. 02.1923: Sold to Irish Free State Government, Dublin. 28.02.1923: London registry closed. 02.1923: Registered at Dublin. 04.05.1923: Commissioned in the Irish Free State Coastal & Marine Service, Dublin. 31.03.1924: Decommissioned. Transferred to Commissioners of Public Works in the Saorstat Eireann, Dublin. For sale. 1924: Sold to George E J Moody, Grimsby. Dublin registry closed. 03.03.1925: Registered at Grimsby (GY228). 06.1928: Sold to Grimsby Steam Fishing Co Ltd, Grimsby. 01.1939: Sold to Earl Steam Fishing Co Ltd, Grimsby. 04.01.1939: Sold to Hellyer Bros Ltd, Hull. 03.01.1939: Grimsby registry closed. 04.01.1939: Registered at Hull (H47). 19.11.1939: Registered at Hull as **SYRIAN** (H47). 07.06.1940: Requisitioned for war service as an auxiliary patrol vessel. Renamed **TYPHOON** (P.No.FY.1703); hire rate £97.14.0d per month. Based Harwich. 10.1941: Fitted out as a minesweeper. 15.08.1942: Sold to H Markham Cook, Grimsby. 03.10.1945: Returned and reverted to **SYRIAN** (H47). 27.11.1946: Hull registry closed. 11.1946: Registered at Grimsby (GY419). 10.1947: Sold to Shire Trawlers Ltd, London. 04.1950: Sold to Northern Trawlers Ltd, London & Grimsby. 1953: Sold to A R Hope-Vere, Spain. 03.1955: Sold to Spanish shipbreakers and broken up. 11.1955: Grimsby registry closed.

JOHN WELSTEAD Ad.No.3573 Mersey class	833 17.11.1917 12.02.1918	324 134	138.5 23.7 12.8	C D Holmes 600 ihp 3-cyl 11.0 knots	The Admiralty, Whitehall, London

Completed as an armed trawler (1-12pdr, W/T). 15.02.1918: Delivered. 1919: Registered in the Registry of British Ships at London. Official No.143926. 28.01.1920: Registered by the Admiralty at London as a fishing vessel (LO270). 07.1922: Sold to Pickering & Haldane's Steam Trawling Co Ltd, Hull. 28.07.1922: London registry closed. 04.08.1922: Registered at Hull (H657). 21.08.1922: Registered at Hull as **LORD HAREWOOD** (H567). 31.01.1929: Sold to Bunch Steam Fishing Co Ltd, Grimsby. 01.02.1929: Hull registry closed. 02.02.1929: Registered at Grimsby (GY12). 05.1937: Sold to A/S Havfiskedamper Sydøen, Bergen, Norway. 19.05.1937: Grimsby registry closed. Registered at Bergen as **SYDØEN**. 1939: Sold to A/S M/S Myrland, Haugesund. Bergen registry closed. Registered at Haugesund as **MYRLAND**. 1939: Converted to motor fitted with 99nhp 6-cylinder oil engine by A/B Atlas-Diesel, Stockholm. 1940: Requisitioned by the Royal Norwegian Navy for war service but demobilised upon occupation of Norway by German forces. 06.03.1941: Captured by the Royal Navy at Lofoten, ownership transferred to Royal Norwegian Ministry of Commerce, London. 01.04.1940: Requisitioned for war service as a minesweeper (P.No.FY1784); hire rate £81.0.0d per month. 09.1944: Employed as a fire-float. 1946: Returned. 1947: Re-engined with 680bhp 6-cylinder oil engine by Mirrlees, Bickerton & Day Ltd, Stockport. 1955: Sold to P/R Brödr Davik, Ålesund. Haugesund registry closed. Registered at Ålesund as **HELLEFISK**. 1966: Re-engined with 850bhp 6-cylinder oil engine by Masch-Kiel GmbH, Kiel. 1977: Sold to I/S Jade, Ålesund. 01.1977: Sold to shipbreakers and broken up by Hansen Edmund, Tonsberg, Norway. Ålesund registry closed.

THOMAS WHIPPLE	834	324	138.5	C D Holmes	The Admiralty,
Ad.No.3574	01.12.1917	149	23.7	600 ihp 3-cyl	Whitehall, London
Mersey class	23.02.1918		12.8	11.0 knots	

Completed as an armed trawler (1-12pdr, hydrophone & W/T).   1919: Registered in the Registry of British Ships at London. Official No.143884.   03.02.1920: Registered by the Admiralty at London as a fishing vessel (LO278).   06.1921: Sold to Pickering & Haldane's Steam Trawling Co Ltd, Hull.   26.05.1922: London registry closed.   01.06.1922: Registered at Hull (H514).   18.07.1922: Registered at Hull as **LORD LASCELLES** (see yard no.777).

GEORGE WESTPHALL	835	324	138.5	C D Holmes	The Admiralty,
Ad.No.3575	15.12.1917	150	23.7	600 ihp 3-cyl	Whitehall, London
Mersey class	04.03.1918		12.8	11.0 knots	

Completed as an armed trawler (1-12pdr, hydrophone & W/T).   07.03.1918: Delivered.   1919: Registered in the Registry of British Ships at London. Official No.143785.   1921: Sold to Victor Fourny, Boulogne, France.   1921: London registry closed. Registered at Boulogne as **ESTELLE-YVONNE**.   1922: Sold to Lecae, Leroy & Cie, Boulogne.   15.01.1923: Stranded at Oualidia, north of Cape Safi, Morocco. Total loss. Boulogne registry closed.

JAMES WRIGHT	836	326	138.5	C D Holmes	The Admiralty,
Ad.No.3576	17.12.1917	130	23.7	600 ihp 3-cyl	Whitehall, London
Mersey class	12.03.1918		12.8	11.0 knots	

Completed as a minesweeper (1-12pdr, hydrophone & W/T).   15.03.1918: Delivered.   03.02.1920: Registered by the Admiralty at London as a fishing vessel (LO311).   07.1922: Sold to Pickering & Haldane's Steam Trawling Co Ltd, Hull.   02.08.1922: London registry closed.   07.08.1922: Registered at Hull (H662).   21.08.1922: Registered at Hull as **LORD ANCASTER** (H662).   12.07.1935: Sold to J Marr & Son Ltd, Fleetwood (£4500). Fishing from Hull.   04.11.1935: Registered at Hull as **WESTCOATES** (H662).   25.08.1938: Sold to Fishing Vessel Brokers Ltd, Hull.   20.03.1939: Sold to Loch Fishing Co (Hull) Ltd, Hull (£3000).   01.04.1939: Registered at Hull as **LOCH MOIDART** (H662).   08.06.1940: Requisitioned for war service as an auxiliary patrol vessel (P.No.4.229); hire rate £97.16.0d per month.   10.1941: Fitted out as minesweeper. Based Grimsby with A/S Group 34, later A/S Group 179.   14.01.1946: Sold to A & M Smith Ltd, Hull.   18.01.1946: Laid up.   01.1946: Returned.   03.03.1948: Sold to Henry J Richards, Johnston, Haverfordwest.   14.05.1948: Hull registry closed.   15.05.1948: Registered at Milford as **GOODLEIGH** (M294).   07.06.1948: Sold to Goodleigh Fisheries Ltd, Milford Haven.   03.1949: Laid up.   08.1950: Sold to Associated Fisheries Trawling Co Ltd, Hull, for £16,000.   08.08.1950: Milford registry closed.   10.8.1950: Registered at Hull (H134).   15.11.1950: Registered at Hull as **LORD LYNWOOD** (H134).   1952: Laid up pending survey.   02.10.1952: Sold to BISCO (£2,650) and allocated to Clayton & Davie Ltd, Dunston-on-Tyne, for breaking up.   14.10.1952: Arrived River Tyne.   06.03.1953: Hull registry closed.

CHARLES HAMMOND	837	324	138.5	C D Holmes	The Admiralty,
Ad.No.3830	29.12.1917	150	23.7	600 ihp 3-cyl	Whitehall, London
Mersey class	19.03.1918		12.8	11.0 knots	

Completed as an armed trawler (1-12pdr, hydrophone & W/T).   26.03.1918: Delivered.   02.11.1918: In Firth of Forth off Kirkcaldy, Fife, in collision with HM Destroyer MARKSMAN (P.No.F66) and foundered in approximate position 56.15N 02.96W. No casualties.

WILLIAM JACKSON	838	327	138.5	C D Holmes	The Admiralty,
Ad.No.3831	15.01.1918	130	23.7	600 ihp 3-cyl	Whitehall, London
Mersey class	27.04.1918		12.8	11.0 knots	

Completed as an A/S trawler (1-12pdr, W/T & hydrophone).   03.02.1920: Registered by the Admiralty at London as a fishing vessel (LO293). Official No.143857.   06.1921: Sold to Pickering & Haldane's Steam Trawling Co Ltd, Hull.   05.07.1921: Registered at Hull (H288).   18.08.1921: Registered at Hull as **LORD BYNG** (H288) (see yard no.754).

JOHN JOHNSON	839	324	138.5	C D Holmes	The Admiralty,
Ad.No.3832	17.01.1918	134	23.7	600 ihp 3-cyl	Whitehall, London
Mersey class	04.04.1918		12.8	11.0 knots	

Completed as an armed trawler (1-12pdr, hydrophone and W/T).   19.04.1918: Delivered.   03.02.1920: Registered by the Admiralty at London as a fishing vessel (LO291). Official No.143856.   1922: Sold to Ernest Wilfred & William John Robins, Hull.   05.10.1922: London registry closed.   18.10.1922: Registered at Hull as **CLOUGHTON WYKE** (H705).   25.05.1923: Sold to West Dock Steam Fishing Co Ltd, Hull.   31.05.1929: Sold to Dinas Steam Trawling Co Ltd, Fleetwood.   03.06.1929: Hull registry closed.   04.06.1929: Registered at Fleetwood (FD46).   01.1931: Stranded on Grey Island, Sound of Mull. Refloated and returned to service.   04.1940: Employed on Fishery Protection (WA/Fort William/Fleetwood).   04.06.1940: Requisitioned for war service as an auxiliary patrol vessel; hire rate £97.4.0d per month.   15-25.06.1940: 'Operation Ariel' evacuation from France and Channel Islands.   18.06.1940: Sailed St Nazaire for Plymouth.   09.1941: Fitted out as a minesweeper.   02.02.1942: Attacked by German aircraft in Humber estuary and sunk in position 52.59N 01.18.30E (Ty/Sk C S Larter OBE DSC RNR) (four crew MPK, Sk Larter wounded). CAPE SPARTEL (H23) (Lieut J R Grundy RNR) (see yard no.1037) also sunk in the same attack.   22.10.1942: Fleetwood registry closed.

JOHN JACOBS Ad.No.3833 Mersey class	840 13.02.1918 11.04.1918	325 150	138.5 23.7 12.8	C D Holmes 600 ihp 3-cyl 11.0 knots	The Admiralty, Whitehall, London

Completed as an armed trawler (1-12pdr, hydrophone & W/T). 15.04.1918: Delivered. 03.02.1920: Registered by the Admiralty at London as a fishing vessel **JOHN JACOB** (LO312). Official No.144330. 1921: Sold to Fourmentin-Avisse & Cie, Boulogne, France. 23.06.1922: London registry closed. Registered at Boulogne as **CASTELNAU**. 1939: Requisitioned for war service with the French Navy (P.No.AD.46). 03.07.1940: Seized by the Admiralty at Southampton. 08.1940: Commissioned as an auxiliary patrol vessel (P.No.FY.355). Based Granton. 08.02.1946: Returned to original owner. 1951: Sold to André Fourmentin & Cie, Boulogne. 1956: Sold to Jas de Smedt, Antwerp, for breaking up. 06.1956: Arrived at Antwerp. Boulogne registry closed.

JOHN JEFFERSON Ad.No.3834 Mersey class	841 13.02.1918 18.04.1918	324 131	138.5 23.7 12.8	C D Holmes 600 ihp 3-cyl 11.0 knots	The Admiralty, Whitehall, London

Completed as an armed trawler (1-12pdr, 1-3.5" A/S Howitzer, hydrophone & W/T). 23.04.1918: Delivered. 03.02.1920: Registered by the Admiralty as a fishing vessel at London (LO302). Official No.144277. 09.1922: Sold to Thomas Hamling & Co Ltd, Hull. 04.10.1922: London registry closed. 18.10.1922: Registered at Hull as **ST AMANT** (H702). 03.1926: Arrested at Iceland for illegal fishing. 05.11.1935: Sold to Trident Steam Fishing Co Ltd, Hull. 12.12.1935: Registered at Hull as **LYNESS** (H702). 30.12.1938: Sold to Jutland Amalgamated Trawlers Ltd, Hull. 24.04.1939: Registered at Hull as **LADY ENID** (H702). 28.08.1939: Requisitioned for war service on examination service and as a minesweeper (P.No.FY.547); hire rate £96.18.0d per month. 06.1941: Based Portland with M/S Group 49. 13.08.1942: Sold to City Steam Fishing Co Ltd, Hull. 11.12.1945: Reclassed at Manchester and returned. 21.12.1945: Sold to Henderson's Trawling Co Ltd, Hull. 07.02.1949: Sold to Dinas Steam Trawling Co Ltd, Fleetwood. 21.02.1949: Hull registry closed. Registered at Fleetwood (FD4). 04.05.1954: Sold to J Marr & Son Ltd, Fleetwood, for £7000. 01.06.1954: Sold to BISCO for breaking up and allocated to Rees Shipbreaking Co Ltd, Llanelli. 06.06.1954: Sailed Fleetwood for Llanelli. 1954: Fleetwood registry closed.

THOMAS JAGO Ad.No.3835 Mersey class	842 29.05.1918 25.07.1918	324 128	138.5 23.7 12.8	C D Holmes 600 ihp 3-cyl 11.0 knots	The Admiralty, Whitehall, London

Completed as an escort (1 - 4" and W/T). 31.07.1918: Delivered. 24.08.1920: Registered by the Admiralty at London as a fishing vessel (LO450). Official No.144587. 10.1922: Sold to Thomas Hamling & Co Ltd, Hull. 04.10.1922: London registry closed. 18.10.1922: Registered at Hull as **ST VALERY** (H691). 01.11.1935: Sold to Trident Steam Fishing Co Ltd, Hull. 09.12.1935: Registered at Hull as **CLEE NESS** (H691). 30.12.1938: Sold to Jutland Amalgamated Trawlers Ltd, Hull. 25.04.1939: Registered at Hull as **LADY ELEANOR** (H691). 08.1939: Requisitioned for war service as a minesweeper; hire rate £97.4.0d. 10.1939: Returned. 29.05.1940: Requisitioned for war service as an A/S trawler. 11.1940: Fitted out for boom defence duties (P.No.Z.226). Cost of conversion £26,193. Based Greenock. 13.08.1942: Sold to J Marr & Son Ltd, Fleetwood. 23.11.1943: Compulsorily acquired by Ministry of War Transport. 10.02.1944: Hull registry closed. 1946: Estimated cost of re-conditioning £8,750. 31.01.1947: Sold to James N Connell, Coatbridge, for breaking up at Glasgow. 09.1947: Breaking up completed.

RICHARD JEWELL Ad.No.3836 Mersey class	843 06.08.1918 31.07.1918	312 130	138.5 23.7 12.8	C D Holmes 600 ihp 3-cyl 11.0 knots	The Admiralty, Whitehall, London

Completed as an armed trawler (1-6pdr HA and W/T). 05.08.1918: Accepted. 18.10.1920: Registered by the Admiralty as a fishing vessel at London (LO476). Official No.145062. 1922: Sold to Pickering & Haldane's Steam Trawling Co Ltd, Hull. 28.07.1922: London registry closed. 04.08.1922: Registered at Hull (H646). 21.08.1922: Registered at Hull as **LORD KNARESBOROUGH** (H646). 21.12.1924: Off Dunnet Head, homeward from Icelandic grounds, picked up crew of Norwegian steamer VARG (1436grt) which presume foundered. 22.12.1924: Landed survivors at Hull. 31.10.1928: Sold to Joseph G Little, Grimsby. 09.11.1928: Hull registry closed. 10.11.1928: Registered at Grimsby (GY488). 03.12.1928: Registered at Grimsby as **FAIRWAY** (GY488). 08.05.1929: Sold to Rinovia Fishing Co Ltd, Grimsby. 04.1940: Employed on Fishery Protection (Nore/Humber/Grimsby). 29.05.1940: Requisitioned for war service as an A/S trawler (P.No.4.23); hire rate £93.12.0d. 05.1941: Fitted out as a minesweeper (P.No.FY.1551). 22.01.1942: Sold to J Marr & Son Ltd, Fleetwood for £9250. 1944: Fitted out for dan laying and assigned to Operation Neptune - Normandy landings. 23.05.1944: Attached to the 6th Minesweeping Flotilla as a dan layer. 05.06.1940: Sailed Solent for Gold Beach ahead of Assault Convoy G1. 22.06.1944: Damaged by mine. 03.07.1944: Operation Neptune ended. 25.06.1945: Sold to K Percival (Trawlers) Ltd, Hull. 28.06.1945: Grimsby registry closed. 06.1945: Registered at Hull (H130). 11.1945: Restored and surveyed at Londonderry. 18.03.1946: Returned. 19.05.1947: Sold to Henderson's Trawling Co Ltd, Hull. 07.02.1951: Sold to Fern Leaf Co Ltd, Fleetwood. 18.04.1953: Hull registry closed. 19.04.1953: Registered at Fleetwood (FD140). 1955: Sold to Van Heyghen Frères, Ghent, for breaking up. 04.10.1955: Fleetwood registry closed. 08.10.1955: Arrived Ghent from Fleetwood.

THOMAS JOHNS Ad.No.3837 Mersey class	844 10.06.1918 30.08.1918	324 150	138.5 23.7 12.8	C D Holmes 600 ihp 3-cyl 11.0 knots	The Admiralty, Whitehall, London

Completed as an armed trawler (1-12pdr, W/T). 03.09.1918: Delivered. 09.1920: Renamed **EDEN**. 11.01.1922: Loaned to the Royal South African Navy. 1926: Renamed HMSAS **IMMORTELLE**. 1934: Due to the Great Depression, returned and reverted to **EDEN** (P.No.T.49). 1939: Laid up and placed on disposal list. 1941: Brought forward for harbour service. 1942: Reduced to a hulk. 1945: Sold to shipbreakers and broken up.

*The **Chiltern** (822) was originally named **John Cormack**.*

(Authors' collection)

*The **Lady Enid** (841), originally **John Jefferson**, in Fleetwood registry after 1941.*

(Authors' collection)

WILLIAM JONES Ad.No.3838 Mersey class	845 10.06.1918 05.09.1918	324 150	138.5 23.7 12.8	C D Holmes 600 ihp 3-cyl 11.0 knots	The Admiralty, Whitehall, London

Completed as a minesweeper (1-12pdr, W/T). 08.09.1918: Delivered. 09.1920: Re-commissioned as HMS **BOYNE** (1-12pdr). Fishery Protection duties. North Sea and Iceland. 1937: Based Portland. 01.1938: At Gt Yarmouth landed bodies of crew of Yarmouth steam drifter GIRL NORAH (YH) (Sk Harris) lost off French coast. 09.1939: At Portsmouth fitting out as a minesweeper (P.No.T.29). 1940: Based Port Edgar with M/S Group 60 (Training Flotilla). 04.1946: Sold to Faroe-British Trawler Co, Tórshavn, Faroe Islands. Registered at Tórshavn (TN35). 1949: Sold to P/F Vagaklettur A/S, Midvaag, Faroe Islands. Registered at Midvaag as **NYPUBERG** (VA178). 1957: Sold to Eckhardt & Co, Germany, for breaking up. 04.1957: Arrived Hamburg. Registry closed.

SAMUEL JAMESON Ad.No.3839 Mersey class	846 27.06.1918 20.09.1918	324 149	138.5 23.7 12.8	C D Holmes 600 ihp 3-cyl 11.0 knots	The Admiralty, Whitehall, London

Completed as an armed trawler (1 - 12pdr and W/T). 10.10.1918: Delivered. 09.1920: Re-commissioned as HMS **ETTRICK** (1-12pdr). Fishery Protection duties. Based Falmouth. 1926: Sold to Sam Robford & Co Ltd, London. 12.03.1927: Registered at Fleetwood as **LOUGHRIGG** (FD148). 27.02.1928: Sailed Fleetwood for St Kilda with mails (11 bags). Could not locate island due to dense fog, eventually anchored in Village Bay and islanders came out. Very short of flour and other provisions. 08.03.1928: Returned Fleetwood, coaled and took on provisions. 09.03.1928: Sailed Fleetwood for St. Kilda. 1929: Sold to Clifton Steam Trawlers Ltd, Fleetwood. 21.08.1929: Registered at Fleetwood as **PHYLLISIA** (FD148). 27.03.1930: Sold to New Docks Steam Trawling Co (Fleetwood) Ltd, Fleetwood. 17.07.1939: Sold to Clifton Steam Trawlers Ltd, Fleetwood. 12.11.1939: When homeward off St Kilda, at 4.42pm closed by U-boat (U.41) that had onboard survivors from steam trawler CRESSWELL (M129) (275grt/1917) which she had shelled and sunk earlier in the day 18 miles NW by N of the Flannan Islands (approx 58.39N 07.36W). Took onboard survivors, seven in number. 14.11.1939: Landed at Fleetwood. 04.12.1939: Requisitioned for war service as a boom defence vessel (P.No.Z.144); hire rate £97.4.0d. Cost of conversion £17,984. Deployed South Atlantic Command. 16.11.1942: Transferred to West Africa Command. Based at Freetown, Sierra Leone. 08.10.1943: On loan to Portuguese Government (P.No.B1). 23.11.1943: Compulsorily acquired by Ministry of War Transport, remaining on loan to Portuguese Government. 17.01.1944: Fleetwood registry closed. 19.08.1945: Returned to Ministry of War Transport. Based at Plymouth. 06.1946: Surveyed and restored at Plymouth at estimated cost of £8,730. 07.1946: Sold to East Fisheries Ltd, Cape Town. Registered at Cape Town (CTA126). 07.09.1952: Sold to South African Navy. Stripped of all useable parts and non-ferrous metals and used as a target. Subsequently scuttled off Robben Island.

THOMAS JARVIS Ad.No.3840 Mersey class	847 27.06.1918 23.10.1918	324 149	138.5 23.7 12.8	C D Holmes 600 ihp 3-cyl 11.0 knots	The Admiralty, Whitehall, London

Completed for special service (1-12pdr, W/T). 24.10.1918: Delivered. 09.1920: Re-commissioned as HMS **EXE** (1-12pdr). Fishery Protection duties. Based Moray Firth under Scottish Fisheries Board operational control. 1928: Sold to Soc Anon Armement Ostendais, Ostend, Belgium. Registered at Ostend as **JAN VOLDERS** (O150). 24.12.1933: In darkness and gathering storm stranded near Reykjanes, SW coast of Iceland. All fifteen crew including skipper Oscar Verkouille rescued at the last minute by boat from the Icelandic gunboat ODIN (512grt/1926). Ostend registry closed. 1934: Eight crew from ODIN received a medal from the King of Belgium for the daring rescue.

WILLIAM INNWOOD Ad.No.3841 Mersey class	848 11.07.1918 25.10.1918	324 149	138.5 23.7 12.8	C D Holmes 600 ihp 3-cyl 11.0 knots	The Admiralty, Whitehall, London

Completed as an armed trawler (1-12pdr, W/T). 30.10.1918: Delivered. 09.1920: Re-commissioned as HMS **BLACKWATER** "Colne" class (2-3pdrs). Employed on various duties. 01-02.1932: Involved in search for missing submarine 'M2' lost in Lyme Bay, Dorset. 09.1939: At Swansea fitting out as a minesweeper (P.No.T.04). 1940: Based Port Edgar with M/S Group 60 (Training Flotilla). 1941: At Port Edgar with M/S Group 164 (Training). 04.1946: Sold to D/S A/S Borgundøy, Haugesund, Norway. Converted for coastal trading. Registered at Haugesund as **SPLEIS**. 12.1946: Sold to Peder Jacobsen & Heitmann Jansen, Tromsø. Haugesund registry closed. Registered at Tromsø. 1947: Sold to Magnus & Anders Stokka, Mosterhamn/Haugesund. Tromsø registry closed. Registered at Stavanger as **SAGVAAG**. 1947: Rebuilt as a motor vessel by Aasheim & Valvatnes Mek Verksted, Sågvåg; fitted with 5-cylinder oil engine by Newbury Diesel Co Ltd, Newbury, (engine built in 1942). Re-measured to 372grt, 160net. 02.1949: Sold to Anders Stokka, Hetland. Stavanger registry closed. Registered at Haugesund. 03.1952: Sold to Skips-AS Sagvaag (H T Haver), Stavanger. 02.1953: Managers now Haver & Stokka. 1954: Sold to Einar S Haver, Stavanger. 12.02.1956: Disappeared off Lindesnes when on a voyage from Odda to Oslo with a cargo of carbide in drums. Several days later, a Swedish fishing vessel found a boat containing six dead crewmen. The body of a further crewman was washed ashore near Skagen. The bodies of two others were never found. Register closed.

JAMES JONES Ad.No.3842 Mersey class	849 11.07.1918 05.11.1918	324 149	138.5 23.7 12.8	C D Holmes 600 ihp 3-cyl 11.0 knots	The Admiralty, Whitehall, London

Completed as an armed trawler (1-12pdr, W/T). 09.11.1918: Delivered. 09.1920: Re-commissioned as HMS **CHERWELL** (1-12pdr). Fishery Protection duties. Employed Irish Channel. 1939: Allocated P.No.T.03, laid up. 01.1941: At Portsmouth for disposal. Used as boom gear store. 1942: At Lymington, sea traffic control. 05.1946: Sold to P Baurer, London, for onward sale for breaking up.

The **William Jones** (845) was completed as a minesweeper and was renamed **Boyne** in 1920.

(Authors' collection)

The **William Innwood** (848) was completed as an armed trawler and became **Blackwater** in 1920.

(Authors' collection)

Also completed as an armed trawler, the **James Jones** (849) became **Cherwell**, again, in 1920.

(Authors' collection)

WILLIAM JOHNSON Ad.No.3843 Mersey class	850 22.08.1918 18.11.1918	324 149	138.5 23.7 12.8	C D Holmes 600 ihp 3-cyl 11.0 knots	The Admiralty, Whitehall, London

Completed as a minesweeper (1-12pdr, W/T). 22.11.1918: Delivered. 31.05.1919 to 31.08.1919: Loaned to the United States Navy for clearance work on the Northern Mine Barrage. 1919: Registered in the Registry of British Ships at London. Official No.143884. 28.01.1920: Registered by the Admiralty at London as a fishing vessel (LO278). 06.1921: Sold to Pickering & Haldane's Steam Trawling Co Ltd, Hull. 11.06.1921: London registry closed. 05.07.1921: Registered at Hull (H219). 05.10.1921: Registered at Hull as **LORD BIRKENHEAD** (see yard no.755).

ANDREW JEWER Ad.No.3844 Mersey class	851 22.08.1918 28.11.1918	324 152	138.5 23.7 12.8	C D Holmes 600 ihp 3-cyl 11.0 knots	The Admiralty, Whitehall, London

Completed as an armed trawler (1-12pdr, W/T). 04.12.1918: Delivered. 09.1920: Re-commissioned as HMS **NITH** (1-12pdr). Employed on various duties. 06.1922: Renamed **EXCELLENT**. At Portsmouth as gunnery tender (later disarmed). Base ship for HMS **EXCELLENT**, Whale Island, Portsmouth. 1939: Allocated P.No.T.47. 1942: New boiler. 06.1946: Sold to Malvern Fishing Co Ltd, Aberdeen. 16.10.1946: Registered at Aberdeen as **MALVERN** (A234). Official No.181009. 09.1948: Sold to Yolland Bros Ltd, Milford Haven. 04.09.1948: Aberdeen registry closed. 09.09.1948: Registered at Milford as **LADY JILL** (M295). 1954: Sold to Haulbowline Industries Ltd, Passage West, Co Cork, for breaking up. 05.11.1954: Arrived Passage West (Sk Grenville Williams). 18.11.1954: Milford registry closed.

KILDALKEY Ad.No.4047 Kil class patrol gunboat	852 13.03.1918 23.07.1918	895 disp	175.3 30.0 15.8	C D Holmes 1400 ihp 3-cyl 13.0 knots	The Admiralty, Whitehall, London

Completed (1-4", depth charges). 14.02.1920: Sold to Robinson, Brown & Joplin Ltd, Newcastle upon Tyne. Converted by Shields Engineering and Dry Dock Co Ltd, North Shields, on behalf of Irvin & Johnson Ltd, Cape Town, South Africa, to a factory ship/tanker to prosecute the elephant seals around the Kerguelen Islands for their meat, skins and oil. On completion, registered to Irvin & Johnson Ltd, Cape Town. Measured 624grt, 271net. 12.08.1920: Registered at North Shields. Official No.139886. 1923: Sold to Kerguelen Sealing & Whaling Co Ltd, Cape Town. 1923: North Shields registry closed. Registered in Cape Town, South Africa. 18.11.1936: Stranded near Donkergat, Saldanha Bay, Western Cape, and abandoned. Registry closed.

KILDANGAN Ad.No.4048 Kil class patrol gunboat	853 15.03.1918 28.08.1918	895 disp	172.4 30.0 15.8	MacColl & Pollock 1400 ihp 3-cyl 13.0 knots	The Admiralty, Whitehall, London

Completed (1-4", depth charges). 14.02.1920: Sold to Robinson Brown & Joplin, Newcastle upon Tyne. 1920: Sold to Bryan Burletson, Newcastle. Measured 620grt, 266net. Registered at Newcastle as **BEBSIDE**. Official No.144897. 1922: Sold to Johann M K Blumenthal, Hamburg, Germany. 1923: Newcastle registry closed. 1923: Registered at Hamburg as **JOHANN**. 1925: Sold to Pietro Schenone, Leghorn, Italy. Hamburg registry closed. Registered at Leghorn as **LABRONE**. 1928: Sold to Soc An di Nav L'argonauta, Genoa. Converted to motor; fitted with 4-cylinder oil engine by J & C G Bollinder, Stockholm. Re-measured to 636grt, 364net. Leghorn registry closed. Registered at Genoa as **ANITA**. 1930: Sold to Banca Casareto, Genoa, Italy. 1939: Sold to Capt Adolfo Calzi, Trieste. Genoa registry closed. Registered at Trieste. 1940: Sold to Soc Italiana Ernesto Breda, Venice. Trieste registry closed. Registered at Venice as **GIOVANNI MARIA**. 10.01.1941: On a voyage from Derna towards Tobruk, mined 12 miles off Tobruk. Register closed.

KILDARE Ad.No.4049 Kil class patrol gunboat	854 10.04.1918 10.09.1918	895 disp	172.4 30.0 15.8	C D Holmes 1400 ihp 3-cyl 13.0 knots	The Admiralty, Whitehall, London

Completed (1-4", depth charges). 14.02.1920: Sold to Robinson, Brown & Joplin Ltd, Newcastle on Tyne. 1920: Sold to Bryan Burletson, Newcastle. Measured 616grt, 265net. Registered at Newcastle as **MITFORD**. Official No.144898. 1923: Sold to Reederei Johannes Ick, GmbH, Hamburg. Newcastle registry closed. Registered at Hamburg as **MUNDUS**. 1925: Sold to Eriksen & Andersen, Bergen, Norway. Hamburg registry closed. Registered at Bergen as **EINA**. 14.12.1925: On a voyage from River Tyne to Isafjordur, Iceland, with 480 tons of coal, stranded on a reef at Medallandsfjara, south coast of Iceland. Crew of fourteen got into boats and after waiting half a day were guided by locals through the surf to shore. Total loss. Register closed.

KILDONAN Ad.No.4030 Kil class patrol gunboat	855 11.04.1918 29.09.1918	895 disp	213.5 30.1 15.8	C D Holmes 1400 ihp 3-cyl 13.0 knots	The Admiralty, Whitehall, London

Completed (1-4", depth charges). 21.11.1919: Sold to John I Thornycroft & Co Ltd, London. Rebuilt at Southampton; lengthened 213.5ft; tonnages amended to 803grt, 447net. 1920: Sold to Marlborough Steamship Co Ltd, Cardiff. Registered at Southampton as **WATKIN**. Official No.143563. 1921: Sold to Mary Steam-Ship Co Ltd, Cardiff. 1922: Sold to Det Söndenfjeldske Norske D/S, Oslo, Norway. Southampton registry closed. Registered at Oslo as **KONG RAGNAR**. 24.10.1930: On a voyage from Kragerø towards West Hartlepool with a cargo of timber, stranded off Rando near Kristiansand. Total loss. Register closed.

KILDRESS Ad.No.4031 Kil class patrol gunboat	856 13.04.1918 21.10.1918	895 disp	213.5 30.0 15.8	MacColl & Pollock 1400 ihp 3-cyl 13.0 knots	The Admiralty, Whitehall, London

Completed (1-4", depth charges).   21.11.1919: Sold to John I Thornycroft & Co Ltd, London. Rebuilt at Southampton, lengthened to 213.5ft; remeasured to 825grt, 415net.   1920: Sold to Evan Jones, Carmarthen. Registered at Southampton as **GLYNARTHEN**. Official No.145328.   1925: Sold to Hannevig Brothers Ltd, Cardiff.   1925: Sold to D/S Martha A/S, Horten, Norway. Southampton registry closed.   Registered at Horten as **ELFI**.   1930: Sold to K Salvesen, Kragerø. Horten registry closed. Registered at Kragerø. 1936: Sold to Birgir Ekerholt, Oslo. Kragerø registry closed. Registered at Oslo as **REIÁS**.   1937: Sold to Rederi A/B Niord, Gothenburg. Oslo registry closed. Registered at Gothenburg as **RUNA**.   1938: Sold to A F Bjørnstads Rederi A/S, Oslo. Gothenburg registry closed. Registered at Oslo as **BJORNVIK**.   29.01.1942: On a voyage from Newport towards Fowey with a cargo of patent fuel, when approximately 2.8 miles E of Lizard Head, attacked and sunk by German aircraft; three survivors from crew of nineteen. Register closed.

KILDWICK Ad.No.4032 Kil class patrol gunboat	857 27.04.1918 20.11.1918	895 disp	213.5 30.0 15.8	C D Holmes 1400 ihp 3-cyl 13.0 knots	The Admiralty, Whitehall, London

Completed (1-4", depth charges).   21.11.1919: Sold to John I Thornycroft & Co Ltd, London. Rebuilt at Southampton, lengthened to 213.5ft; remeasured to 825grt, 415net.   1920: Sold to Ashburnham Steamship Co Ltd, Cardiff. Registered at Cardiff as **PENGAM**. Official No. 143524.   1924: Owners re-styled Ashburnham Steamship & Coal Co Ltd, Cardiff.   1931: Sold to J Salcmans & K Jansons, Riga, Latvia. Cardiff registry closed. Registered at Riga as **CURONIA**.   1932: Sold to Navigazione Italia Soc Anon, Genoa, Italy. Riga registry closed. Registered at Genoa.   1932: Sold to Ligure-Sicula Soc di Nav, Genoa. Registered at Genoa as **SANDRINA**.   03.1932: Fitted for burning oil fuel.   1938: Sold to A Lauro, Naples. Genoa registration closed. Registered at Naples. 1952: Sold to Nicola late Alfredo Cacciapolli, Naples. Converted to motor and fitted with an 8-cylinder Fiat oil engine by Soc An "Fiat" S G M, Turin. Registered at Naples as **SAN SILVERIO**.   23.05.1954: On a voyage from Elba towards Savona with a cargo of pyrites, capsized off Camigli.   Register closed.

KILFINNY Ad.No.4033 Kil class patrol gunboat	858 10.05.1918 10.12.1918	895 disp	213.5 30.0 15.8	MacColl & Pollock 1400 ihp 3-cyl 13.0 knots	The Admiralty, Whitehall, London

Completed (1-4", depth charges).   21.11.1919: Sold to John I Thornycroft & Co Ltd, London. Rebuilt at Southampton, lengthened to 213.5ft; remeasured to 825grt, 411net.   1920: Sold to Ashburnham Steamship Co Ltd, Cardiff. Registered at Cardiff as **KENRHOS**. 1924: Owners re-styled Ashburnham Steamship & Coal Co Ltd, Cardiff.   1930: Sold to F Jürgenson & Co, Pärnu, Estonia. Cardiff registry closed. Registered at Pärnu as **HELJO**.   1934: Sold to D/S Viking A/S, Copenhagen, Denmark. Pärnu registry closed. Registered at Copenhagen as **HORSIA**.   1937: Sold to A/S Risøy, Mandal, Norway. Copenhagen registry closed. Registered at Mandal as **RISØY**.   20.03.1942: On a voyage from Southampton to Swansea with a 450 ton cargo of steel scrap, attacked by German aircraft off Trevose Head and foundered in approximate position 50.40N 05.01'W. One crewman lost.   Registry closed.

KILFREE Ad.No.4034 Kil class patrol gunboat	859 11.05.1918 21.05.1918	823 411	213.5 30.0 15.8	MacColl & Pollock 1400 ihp 3-cyl 13.0 knots	The Admiralty, Whitehall, London

Completed (1-4", depth charges).   21.11.1919: Sold to John I Thornycroft & Co Ltd, London. Rebuilt at Southampton, lengthened to 213.5ft; remeasured to 825grt, 411net.   1920: Sold to Richard P Care, Cardiff.   1920: Registered at Southampton as **PORTHMINSTER**. Official No.143583.   1924: Sold to Clodoald Shipping Co Ltd, Cardiff. Registered at Southampton as **CLODOALD**.   1928: Southampton registry closed. Registered at Gibraltar.   1931: Sold to S Dumartin & V Lourties, Bordeaux, France. Gibraltar registry closed.   Registered at Bordeaux.   17.03.1934: On a voyage from Antwerp towards Bayonne with general cargo, stranded at St Jean de Luz. Total loss.   Register closed.

Not built Kil class gunboats	860 to 873 inclusive. Order cancelled on 02.03.1918.				

HENRY LANCASTER Ad.No.4231 Mersey class	874 26.05.1918 31.03.1918	326 153	138.3 23.7 12.7	C D Holmes 600 ihp 3-cyl 11.0 knots	The Admiralty, Whitehall, London

Completed as a minesweeper 'Mark buoy' vessel (unarmed, W/T).   08.04.1919: Delivered.   08.1921: Sold to Aberdeen Mutual & General Marine Insurance Co Ltd, Aberdeen. Converted to a salvage tug. Re-measured to 337grt, 143net. Registered at Aberdeen. Official No.145251.   1937: Sold to James Dredging, Towage & Transport Co Ltd, London. Aberdeen registry closed. Registered at London as **LONGTOW**.   09.1939: Requisitioned for war service as a salvage tug (P.No.W.93); hire rate £105.5.0d per month. 13.09.1940: Returned.   23.10.1940: Requisitioned for war service as a salvage tug (P.No.W.93).   1943: Sold to Risdon Beazley Ltd, Southampton.   29.11.1945: Returned.   1947: Sold to Overseas Towage & Salvage Co Ltd, London.   1950: Sold to BISCO and allocated to Thos W Ward Ltd, Sheffield, for breaking up.   08.01.1951: Arrived Grays, Essex.   Register closed.

JAMES LUDFORD Ad.No.4232 Mersey class	875 26.08.1918 30.04.1919	326 153	138.3 23.7 12.8	C D Holmes 600 ihp 3-cyl 11.0 knots	The Admiralty, Whitehall, London

Completed as a minesweeper 'Mark buoy' vessel (unarmed, W/T).   01.05.1919: Delivered.   1921: Laid up.   1930: Commissioned as an A/S trawler, for instruction and training.   09.1939: Commissioned as a minesweeper (1-12pdr, depth charges) (P.No.T.16). 14.12.1939: Mined off the River Tyne in position 55.02.30N 01.16.15W. Minefield laid by German destroyers on 12/13.11.1939. Seventeen crew lost including CO, Lt Cdr H R J Lewis RN (Rtd); ship's boat washed ashore on Cambois beach, Northumberland.

WILLIAM LEECH Ad.No.4233 Mersey class	876 21.09.1918 11.03.1919	324 148	138.3 23.7 12.8	C D Holmes 600 ihp 3-cyl 11.0 knots	The Admiralty, Whitehall, London

Completed as a minesweeper (unarmed, W/T). 02.1919: Renamed **EXCELLENT**. 12.03.1919: Delivered. At Portsmouth as base ship for HMS EXCELLENT, Whale Island, Portsmouth. 1922: Sold to P Lépine, Boulogne, France. Registered at Boulogne as **WILLIAM LEECH**. 1929: Registered at Boulogne as **EXCELLENT**. 1939: Taken over by the French Navy as a patrol vessel (P.No.P.69). 1942: Captured by the German Navy and used as a patrol vessel (P.No.U.1804). 1945: Returned to original owners. 11.1962: Sold to H P Heuvelmen NV, Krimpen aan den IJssel for breaking up. 10.12.1962: Breaking commenced at Krimpen aan den IJssel. Boulogne registry closed.

JEREMIAH LEWIS Ad.No.4234 Mersey class	877 21.09.1918 25.03.1919	324 148	138.3 23.7 12.8	C D Holmes 600 ihp 3-cyl 11.0 knots	The Admiralty, Whitehall, London

Completed as a minesweeper (unarmed, W/T). 25.03.1919: Delivered. Laid up. 27.10.1919: Sold to Hellyer Bros Ltd, Hull, for £16,000 and completed as a fishing vessel (£17,277 fitted out). 04.11.1919: Registered at Hull as **FIELD MARSHAL ROBERTSON** (H104). Official No.139358. 02.1925: Sailed Hull for the Icelandic fishing grounds (Sk Charles Beard). At Reykjavik picked up Icelandic skipper (Sk Einar Magnusson) and additional crew for a 6 month salting trip. Total complement thirty-five men. 07 - 09.02.1925: Believed foundered in the storm known in Iceland as 'Halavedrid'. 19.02.1925: Vessel posted missing. 10.03.1925: A memorial service was held in Reykjavik. 27.10.1925: Hull registry closed - "Lost". 1926: A plaque donated by Hellyer was placed in the church in Hafnarfjordur.

JAMES LONG Ad.No.4235 Mersey class	878 25.09.1918 08.05.1919	326 150	138.3 23.7 12.8	C D Holmes 600 ihp 3-cyl 11.0 knots	The Admiralty, Whitehall, London

1919: Sold to Harry Smethurst, Grimsby, and completed as a fishing vessel. 19.05.1919: Registered at Grimsby (GY316). Official No.140786. 02.01.1920: Sold to Hellyer Bros Ltd, Hull, for £21,150 (£25,635 fitted out). 06.01.1920: Grimsby registry closed. 09.01.1920: Registered at Hull (H141). 29.01.1933: Sailed Hull for Icelandic grounds (Sk Horace Cuthbert); thirteen crew. 04.02.1933: Last sighting off Patreksfjördur, Iceland. HMS GODETIA (P.No.K226) of the Fishery Protection Squadron and a Danish patrol vessel searched but nothing was found. 18.02.1933: Posted missing. Believed lost when homeward bound; no survivors. 27.04.1933: Hull registry closed - "Missing".

NICHOLAS COUTEUR Ad.No.4236 Mersey class	879 25.09.1918 20.05.1919	325 149	138.3 23.7 12.8	C D Holmes 600 ihp 3-cyl 11.0 knots	The Admiralty, Whitehall, London

1919: Sold to James Johnson, Scarborough, and completed as a fishing vessel. 05.1919: Registered at Scarborough as **MARY A JOHNSON** (SH91). Official No.143258. 23.01.1920: Off Eyrarbakki, Iceland, (Sk Nielson) took off crew of steamer EOS (293grt/1886) of Helsingfors as she was driven ashore at Stokkseyri. 02.1920: Connected to Icelandic motorboat JÓN ARASON which was ashore at Patreksfjördur and refloated her. 04.1920: Arrested for alleged illegal fishing, fined £85 with gear and catch confiscated. 30.10.1920: On an Icelandic trip. In an easterly gale and heavy seas, grounded on reef close to 'Geirfuglasker' rock, SE of Reykanes. With considerable damage it was considered that she might slip off the reef and founder. In deteriorating weather boat was launched and all sixteen crew left the ship; there was no time to take on any provisions. Attempts to pull towards the shore were thwarted and the skipper decided to let the boat drift. With the need for constant baling they drifted for two days at the end of which the water had run out and some of the crew were in poor shape. On the third day the wind changed and they again attempted to pull towards the land but with no compass the direction was determined by the stars. On the fourth day at about 3.00pm they spotted a trawler and as they pulled towards her the gear was hauled and the Fleetwood trawler DONNA NOOK (FD237) (see yard no.646) steamed towards them and all were taken onboard. 03.11.1920: Survivors landed at Reykjavik where all were taken to hospital. Despite their ordeal all recovered. 11.1920: Scarborough registry closed.

DEGARA LEROSA Ad.No.4237 Mersey class	880 24.10.1918 06.06.1919	325 149	138.3 23.7	C D Holmes 87 nhp 3-cyl 11.0 knots	The Admiralty, Whitehall, London

1919: Sold to James Johnson, Scarborough, and completed as a fishing vessel. 06.1919: Registered at Scarborough as **JAMES JOHNSON** (SH109). Official No.143262. 10.1924: Sold to Hudson Steam Fishing Co Ltd, Hull. 10.1924: Scarborough registry closed. 23.10.1924: Registered at Hull (H84). 22.11.1924: Registered at Hull as **CAPE GRISNEZ** (H84). 16.12.1927: Sold to West Riding Steam Trawling Co Ltd, Hull. 26.03.1929: Sold to Hudson Steam Fishing Co Ltd, Hull. 09.01.1932: On Icelandic grounds, went to the assistance of Grimsby trawler MORAVIA (GY1018) (307grt/1917) struck by heavy seas and severely damaged. After thirty-six hours found the MORAVIA with ten surviving crew members. Wheelhouse wrecked, funnel and mizzen mast swept away. Skipper and one crewman washed overboard and lost. Connected and after approximately 900 mile tow, delivered Grimsby. 10.1938: Sold to Hellenic Royal Navy. 03.10.1938: Hull registry closed. Converted to an Aixos Class minelayer (40 mines). Renamed **AXIOS**. 28.04.1941: At Syros, attacked by German aircraft and sunk. Later salved. 1948: Sold to Domestinis Bros, Piraeus. Registered at Piraeus as **CORALIA**. 1955: Sold to Ziya Kalavan KS, Istanbul. Piraeus registry closed. Registered at Istanbul as **SEFER KALKAVAN**. 1987: Sold to Cavasoglu Deniszcilik ve Turizm, Istanbul. Registered at Istanbul as **SELIM CAVASOGLU**. 21.08.1987: On a voyage Canakkale towards Istanbul with a cargo of cement, foundered following collision 8 nautical miles N of Marmara Island, Sea of Marmara. Declared a total loss. Registry closed.

JAMES MANSELL Ad.No.4238 Mersey class	881 24.10.1918 25.06.1919	326 150	138.3 23.7 12.8	C D Holmes 600 ihp 3-cyl 11.0 knots	The Admiralty, Whitehall, London

1919: Sold to Harry Smethurst, Grimsby, and completed as a fishing vessel. 10.07.1919: Registered at Grimsby (GY409). Official No. 140794. 11.1920: Sold to Kveldulfur Ltd, Reykjavik, Iceland. 19.11.1920: Grimsby registry closed. 11.1920: Registered at Reykjavik as **SNORRI STURLUSSON** (RE242). 01.1923: Sold to J Hollingsworth, Hull. Reykjavik registry closed. 30.01.1923: Registered at Hull as **JAMES MANSELL** (H782). 19.02.1923: Registered at Hull as **TRIER** (H782). 29.12.1924: Sold to Hudson Steam Fishing Co Ltd, Hull. 23.01.1925: Registered at Hull as **CAPE HATTERAS** (H782). 04.01.1926: Sold to Trident Steam Fishing Co Ltd, Hull. 20.04.1926: Registered at Hull as **GIRDLENESS** (H782). 07.12.1931: Sailed Hull for Faroes grounds (Sk A Edward George): eleven crew. 18.12.1931: In severe weather, stranded at Famien, Sydero Island, Faroes; no survivors. 14.01.1932: Hull registry closed - "Total loss'.

DANIEL MUNRO Ad.No.4239 Mersey class	882 06.11.1918 20.06.1919	324 148	138.3 23.7 12.8	C D Holmes 600 ihp 3-cyl 11.0 knots	The Admiralty, Whitehall, London

1919: Sold to Henry Samman Jnr, Cottingham, and completed as a fishing vessel. 20.08.1919: Registered at Hull (H74). Official No.139346. 01.02.1922: Sold to Storr's Steam Trawling Co Ltd, Hull. 06.06.1924: Sold to Munro Steam Trawling Co Ltd, Hull. 10.1926: Sold to Estrella d'Alva Ltda Empreza de Pesca a Vapor, Lisbon, Portugal. 19.10.1926: Hull registry closed. Registered at Lisbon as **ESTRELLA DO NORTE**. 1940: Sold to The Admiralty. Lisbon registry closed. Fitted out as a minesweeper (P.No.FY.1807). 04.1942: Renamed **STORMCENTRE**. 08.1946: Sold to Ch Pandelis & D Samaridis, Alexandria, Egypt. Converted to dry cargo, re-measured to 357grt, 177net. Registered at Panama as **TOLIS**. 1959: Sold to Aden Coal Co Ltd, Aden. Panama registry closed. Registered at Aden as **ROMILLY**. 1960: Sold to A O Fuad, Aden. 1962: Sold to G I Abdurheman, Aden. 1965: Vessel beached at Slave Island, Back Bay, Aden; all usable material removed and abandoned. Aden registry closed.

LEWIS McKENZIE Ad.No.4240 Mersey class	883 06.11.1918 26.06.1919	324 148	138.3 23.7	C D Holmes 87 nhp 3-cyl 11.0 knots	The Admiralty, Whitehall, London

1919: Sold to James Johnson, Scarborough, and completed as a fishing vessel. 22.07.1919: Registered at Scarborough as **FLORENCE JOHNSON** (SH118). Official No.143263. 24.09.1919: On an Icelandic trip, struck a reef off Ondverdames, north-west tip of Snæfellsnes, Faxa Bay, at low tide; came clear on the flood but leaking. Headed for Reykjavik in company with Hull trawler MARCONI (H488) (322/1916). Off Myrar started to settle, crew of thirteen abandoned in boat, stood off as ship foundered; picked up by MARCONI and landed at Reykjavik. 1919: Scarborough registry closed.

ALEXANDER McBETH Ad.No.4241 Mersey class	884 05.12.1918 14.07.1919	324 148	138.3 23.7 12.8	C D Holmes 600 ihp 3-cyl 11.0 knots	The Admiralty, Whitehall, London

1919: Sold to James Johnson, Scarborough, and completed as a fishing vessel. 25.09.1919: Registered at Scarborough as **JOHN W JOHNSON** (SH137). Official No.143266. 05.11.1924: Sold to Hudson Steam Fishing Co Ltd, Hull. 06.05.1919: Registered at Hull (H95). 22.11.1924: Registered at Hull as **CAPE AGULHAS** (H95). 05.1925: Sold to Belleoram Trawling Co Ltd, St John's, Newfoundland. 06.05.1925: Hull registry closed. 1925: Registered at St John's, NFL. 1929: Sold to Cape Agulhas Co Ltd, Halifax, NS. St John's registry closed. Registered at Halifax, NS. 1930: Sold to Harvey & Co Ltd, St John's, NFL. Halifax registry closed. Registered at St John's, NFL. 1931: Sold to The Government of Newfoundland, St John's (Minister of Marine & Fisheries). 1937: Sold to Newfoundland Trawling Co Ltd, St John's. NFL. 1941: Sold to Cape Agulhas Co Ltd, Halifax, NS. 1947: Sold to National Sea Products Ltd, Halifax, NS. St John's registry closed. Registered at Halifax, NS. 06.01.1956: Inbound in storm conditions following a trip to Grand Banks, stranded off Portugese Cove, Halifax, NS. Deckhand Ernest Thornhill swam ashore and although injured secured a line enabling all eighteen crew to reach the shore. Vessel slipped off rocks and foundered. Halifax registry closed. Ernest Thornhill was awarded the George Medal, The Royal Canadian Humane Association Silver Medal and a gold watch from the City of Halifax for his bravery.

DANIEL McPHERSON Ad.No.4242 Mersey class	885 05.12.1918 15.08.1919	326 148	138.3 23.7 12.8	C D Holmes 600 ihp 3-cyl 11.0 knots	The Admiralty, Whitehall, London

1919: Sold to Pickering & Haldane's Steam Trawling Co Ltd, Hull, and completed as a fishing vessel. 01.09.1919: Registered at Hull as **LORD HALIFAX** (H79). Official No.139349. 02.02.1925: Sold to H/F Togarafelag, Isfirdinga, Isafjordur, Iceland. 02.02.1925: Hull registry closed. Registered at Isafjordur as **HAVARDUR ISFIRDINGUR** (IS451). 18.02.1936: Sold to H/F Havardur, Isafjordur. 29.12.1938: Sold to H/F Valur, Isafjordur. 01.1939: Registered at Isafjordur as **SKUTULL** (IS451). 1939: Top herring ship in Iceland. 02.03.1940: Bombed and machine-gunned by German aircraft in the North Sea. No casualties and negligible damage. 03.08.1940: About 8 nautical miles S-E of Skerryvore lighthouse picked up twenty-one crew and six passengers, survivors from the Swedish steamer ATOS (2161grt/1902) torpedoed that morning by U-boat (U.57), 35 miles north of Malin Head. Vessel foundered quickly after boiler explosion. 20.03.1942: Sold to H/F Askur, Reykjavik. Isafjordur registry closed. Registered at Reykjavik (RE142). 10.03.1948: Sold to Oddsson & Co Ltd, Hull. Laid up in Hull. 1952: Sold to Belgian shipbreakers. 25.07.1952: Arrived Antwerp and broken up. Reykjavik registry closed.

LANGDON McKENNON Ad.No.4243 Mersey class	886 19.12.1918 20.10.1919	324 148	138.3 23.7 12.8	C D Holmes 600 ihp 3-cyl 11.0 knots	The Admiralty, Whitehall, London

1919: Sold to Andrew Hardie, Aberdeen, and completed as a fishing vessel. 21.10.1919: Delivered. 28.10.1919: Registered at Hull as **DOUGLAS H SMITH** (H94). Official No.139357. 03.01.1920: Sold to Horace E Stroud, Aberdeen. 09.08.1921: Stranded off Storkenaes, south coast of Iceland. Total loss. 31.01.1922: Hull registry closed - "Total wreck".

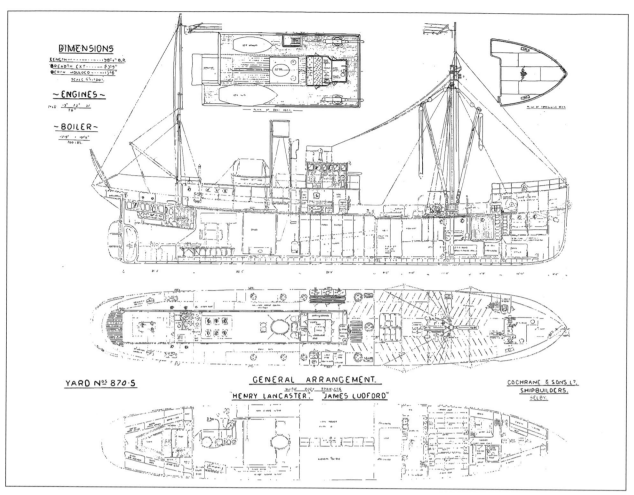

*A general arrangement drawing of **Henry Lancaster** (874) and **James Ludford** (875).*

*The **Cape Grisnez** (880) was originally named **Degara Lerosa** and the **Cape Hatteras** (881) was **James Mansell**. This photograph can be dated to 1925, the only year that **Cape Hatteras** was thus named.*

(Authors' collection)

JAMES McDONALD Ad.No.4244 Mersey class	887 20.12.1918 08.09.1919	324 148	138.3 23.7 12.8	C D Holmes 600 ihp 3-cyl 11.0 knots	The Admiralty, Whitehall, London

1919: Sold to Jutland Steam Trawling Co Ltd, Hull, and completed as a fishing vessel. 16.09.1919: Registered at Hull (H80). Official No.139350. 20.10.1920: Registered at Hull as **GRAND FLEET** (H80). 29.05.1920: Sold to Jutland Amalgamated Trawlers Ltd, Hull. 30.03.1929: Sold to Crampin Steam Fishing Co Ltd, Grimsby. 05.04.1929: Hull registry closed. 06.04.1929: Registered at Grimsby (GY44). Fitted for lining to pursue the Greenland halibut fishery. 03.1938: Sold to C. R. Mauritzen, Newbridge, Midlothian. 28.04.1938: Grimsby registry closed. Transferred to Danish flag. 05.10.1938: Arrived Leith from Spitsbergen having fished the summer season in Arctic waters. Landed salt fish. 21.10.1938: Registered at Leith (LH216). 29.03.1939: Registered at Leith as **BARBARA ROBERTSON** (LH216). 26.08.1939: Leith registry closed. 08.09.1939: Registered at Fleetwood (FD50). 17.09.1939: Sold to Boston Deep Sea Fishing & Ice Co Ltd, Fleetwood. 08.1939: Armed trawler under T124 Articles (1-12pdr). 09.12.1939: Sailed Hull for Icelandic grounds (Sk A E Hall); eighteen crew. Outward in convoy with ADAM (FD65) (see yard no.890), CHILTERN (H660) (see yard no.822) and FORCE (FD100) (see yard no.825). 28.12.1939: Homeward to Hull. At about 2.10am when 35 miles NW of the Butt of Lewis on a S by E heading, shelled by U-boat (U.30); abandoned vessel in boat but one man left behind (George E Clark). At about 4.00am trawler sunk by gunfire in position 58.54N 6.30W and after 14 hours in boat, sixteen survivors picked up by HMS ISIS (P.No.D87) directed to area by a Gladiator bi-plane. Survivors landed at North Scottish port. (Less than an hour after the sinking, U.30 had stopped the Swedish steamer HISPANIA (1337grt/1912) and asked them to pick up the survivors). 13.1.1940: Fleetwood registry closed - "Vessel sunk by enemy action".

JOHN MANN Ad.No.4246 Mersey class	888 19.03.1919 05.09.1919	324 148	138.3 23.7 12.8	C D Holmes 600 ihp 3-cyl 11.0 knots	The Admiralty, Whitehall, London

1919: Sold at auction to Frank Orlando & Owen Stooks Hellyer for £18,500 and completed as a fishing vessel. 04.10.1919: Registered at Hull as **EARL HAIG** (H87). Official No.139352. 13.10.1919: Sold to Hellyer Bros Ltd, Hull. 13.03.1934: Sold to the Admiralty. Converted to a boom defence vessel. 21.04.1934: Hull registry closed. Renamed **BARNET** (P. No.Z.100). Based Aden. 1945: Sold to the Turkish Navy. Renamed **KILYAS**. 1947: Sold to shipbreakers and broken up.

THOMAS MATTHEWS Ad.No.4246 Mersey class	889 19.03.1919 12.09.1919	324 148	138.3 23.7 12.8	C D Holmes 600 ihp 3-cyl 11.0 knots	The Admiralty, Whitehall, London

1919: Sold to Frank Orlando & Owen Stooks Hellyer Hellyer Bros Ltd, Hull, for £18,500 and completed as a fishing vessel. 04.10.1919: Registered at Hull as **EARL BEATTY** (H88). Official No.139353. 13.10.1919: Sold to Hellyer Bros Ltd, Hull. 03.1922: Sold to Viuda de Canosa-Cierto, Barcelona, Spain. 25.03.1922: Hull registry closed. Registered at Barcelona as **RAMON**. 1932: Sold to Cie Portuguesa de Pesca, Lisbon, Portugal. Barcelona registry closed. Registered at Lisbon as **ALFEITE**. 1939 - 1945: Requisitioned for war service with Portuguese Navy. 04.05.1956: Stranded at Fuerteventura, Canary Islands, broke in two and became a total loss. Lisbon registry closed.

THOMAS MALONEY Ad.No.4247 Mersey class	890 14.06.1919 23.09.1919	324 148	138.3 23.7 12.8	C D Holmes 600 ihp 3-cyl 11.0 knots	The Admiralty, Whitehall, London

1919: Sold to Thomas Hamling & Co Ltd, Hull, and completed as a fishing vessel. 15.11.1919: Registered at Hull as **ST. NEOTS** (H112). Official No.139360. Total cost with electric lights - £18,500 (payment made 23.10.1919). 18.11.1927: Sold to Henry Croft Baker, Grimsby. 26.05.1928: Sold to H Croft Baker & Sons Ltd, Grimsby. 26.04.1930: Sold to Strand Steam Fishing Co Ltd, Grimsby. 01.05.1930: In dense fog 20 miles SE of Girdleness in collision with Aberdeen trawler BEN LAWERS (A311) (176grt/1900) which foundered in three minutes. All nine crew taken aboard and landed at Aberdeen. 06.04.1934: Sold to Boston Deep Sea Fishing & Ice Co Ltd, Fleetwood. 06.1937: Sold to Towarzystwo Dalekomorskich Polowow "Pomorze" Sp.z.o.o., Gdynia. 29.07.1937: Hull registry closed. 1937: Registered at Gdynia as **ADAM** (GDY94). 09.1939: Sold to Adam Steam Fishing Co Ltd, London. 03.11.1939: Registered at Fleetwood (FD65). 12.1939: On a trip to the Faroe Islands grounds, bombed and machine gunned by German seaplanes. No damage; crew of twelve from Hull. 12.2.1940: Requisitioned for war service as a minesweeper (P.No.FY.1618); hire rate £101.5.0d per month. Based Dover with M/S Group 61. 31.05.1943: Sold to Mrs Wincenty Bartosiak, Gdynia, Poland. 01.06.1943: Fleetwood registry closed. Renamed **PODLASIE**. 14.07.1944: Returned to owner after restoration at Fleetwood. Registered at Gdynia (GDY154). 03.1946: Fishing from IJmuiden with Dutch crew. 12.1946: Returned to Poland. 05.1948: Sold to "Lawica" Rybolowstwo Dalekomorskiie i Zegluga Sp.z.o.o., Gdynia ("Lawica" Deep-Sea Fishing & Shipping Ltd). Re-registered at Gdynia (GDY124). 16.12.1949: By Order of the Ministry of Navigation the holding company and assets to be placed under control of the Polish People's Republic. 1950: Company and assets transferred to "Dalmor" Przedsiobiorstwo Polowow Dalekomorskich Sp.z.ogr.odp, Gdynia (Polish Government). 1951: Sold to "Lawica" Rybolowstwo Dalekom S.A., Gdynia. 07.1951: Re-classed and registered at Gdynia (GDY213). 04.1962: Sold for breaking up at Gdansk.

PATRICK MITCHELL Ad.No.4248 Mersey class	891 16.04.1919 24.109.1919	324 130	138.3 23.7 12.8	C D Holmes 600 ihp 3-cyl 11.0 knots	The Admiralty, Whitehall, London

1919: Sold to F & T Ross Ltd, Hull, and completed as a fishing vessel. 31.10.1919: Registered at Hull as **KELVIN** (H85). Official No.139351. 06.02.1924: On Icelandic grounds (Sk John Frederick Cant) in severe weather and snow storm, stranded at Heimaey, Vestmannaeyjar Islands. Twelve crew abandoned in boat, landed and then cared for by the local farming community. 06.03.1924: Hull registry closed - "Total loss".

PETER MAGEE Ad.No.4249 Mersey class	892 01.05.1919 30.10.1919	325 132	138.3 23.7 12.8	C D Holmes 600 ihp 3-cyl 11.0 knots	The Admiralty, Whitehall, London

1919: Sold to Pickering & Haldane's Steam Trawling Co Ltd, Hull, and completed as a fishing vessel.   07.11.1919: Registered at Hull as **LORD ERNLE** (H113). Official No.144021.   07.1929: Sold to Perihelion Steam Fishing Co Ltd, Grimsby.   24.07.1929: Hull registry closed.   25.07.1929: Registered at Grimsby (GY109).   02.03.1937: Homeward from a White Sea trip (1,200 kits) (Sk Arthur Phillipson), at about 10.00pm, in dense fog stranded at Staple Newk, Bempton Cliff, East Yorkshire. Attempted to refloat but held by rocks. Flamborough lifeboat, ELIZABETH & ALBINA WHITLEY (Cox George Leng) responded to distress and with great difficulty all fifteen crew rescued.   07.04.1937: Grimsby registry closed - "Stranded - total loss".

JAMES McLAUCHLIN FY.4250 Mersey class	893 01.05.1919 07.11.1919	324 129	138.3 23.7	C D Holmes 87 nhp 3-cyl 11.0 knots	The Admiralty, Whitehall, London

1919: Sold to Hellyer Bros Ltd, Hull, for £13,875 and completed as a fishing vessel. Total cost of £23,799.6s.6d including fitting out. 18.11.1919: Registered at Hull as **GENERAL BIRDWOOD** (H121). Official No.144023.   1928: Fish carrier for halibut fishery in the Davis Strait, Greenland. A joint venture between Hellyer's and Engvold Baldesheim of Trondheim.   24.11.1933: Sold to Fred Parkes, Blackpool, & Basil A Parkes, Cleveleys.   08.1939: Sold to the Admiralty for £6,000.   27.10.1939: Hull registry closed. Fitted out as a minesweeper (P.No.FY.724). Based Freetown with M/S Group 93.   03.1944: Fitted out as a smoke making trawler and assigned to Operation Neptune - Normandy landings.   11.06.1944: Sailed Solent for Mulberry B with Group A1 as part of Convoy ETC6. Employed smoke making.   03.07.1944: Operation Neptune ended.   05.1946: Sold to Easton Trawling Co Ltd, Swansea. Registered at Swansea as **WOODESSE** (SA23).   06.1949: Sold to John S Boyle Ltd, Glasgow.   06.1949: Swansea registry closed. 28.06.1949: Registered at Glasgow (GW6). Fishing from Granton.   1955: Sold to BISCO and allocated to Malcolm Brechin, Granton, for breaking up.   05.1955: Delivered Granton.   05.1955: Granton registry closed.

EDWARD McGUIRE Ad.No.4251 Mersey class	894 17.05.1919 03.12.1919	324 148	138.3 23.7 12.8	C D Holmes 600 ihp 3-cyl 11.0 knots	The Admiralty, Whitehall, London

1919: Sold to West Riding Steam Trawling Co Ltd, Hull, and completed as a fishing vessel.   19.01.1920: Registered at Hull as **CAPE ST. VINCENT** (H139). Official No.144032.   31.10.1928: Sold to H Croft Baker & Sons Ltd, Grimsby.   19.12.1928: Registered at Hull as **ST LOLAN** (H139).   01.10.1931: Proceeding to sea after bunkering at Blyth, at about noon in collision in South Harbour with Workington steamer GALACUM (585grt/1915). Both vessels damaged.   06.01.1932: Homeward from Norwegian coast, stranded at Storfjorden, Norway.   07.01.1932: With salvage steamer in attendance, refloated at 9.20pm with slight damage. Proceeded to Grimsby.   11.04.1934: Sold to Boston Deep Sea Fishing & Ice Co Ltd, Fleetwood.   25.05.1937: Sold to Red Funnel Trawlers Pty Ltd, Sydney, New South Wales, Australia.   26.05.1937: Hull registry closed.   16.07.1937: Registered at Sydney as **KOROWA**.   14.09.1939: Requisitioned for war service (Royal Australian Navy) as a minesweeper (P.No.FY.79).   02.1946: Returned to owner after restoration and survey at Sydney.   1955: Sold for breaking up at Sydney.   13.07.1955: Registry closed after breaking up completed.

MICHAEL McDONALD Ad.No.4252 Mersey class	895 17.05.1919 21.11.1919	324 148	138.3 23.7 12.8	C D Holmes 600 ihp 3-cyl 11.0 knots	The Admiralty, Whitehall, London

1919: Sold to East Riding Steam Fishing Co Ltd, Hull, and completed as a fishing vessel.   29.11.1919: Registered at Hull as **KANUCK** (H123). Official No.144024.   17.10.1923: Sold to Hudson Steam Fishing Co Ltd, Hull.   01.1925: Sold to H/F Græðir Flateyri, Onundarfjordur, Iceland.   28.01.1925: Registered at Flateyri as **HAFSTEIN** (IS449), but operated from Isafjordur until 1934.   19.01.1935: Sold to H/F Gnott, Flateyri.   15.03.1938: Sold to H/F Gnott, Grundarfjordur, but operated from Reykjavik. 1938: Flateyri registry closed. Registered at Reykjavik (RE156).   30.12.1939: Sold to H/F Mars, Hafnarfjordur; operating from Hafnarfjordur.   11.01.1940: Rescued crew of sixty-two from German blockade running steamer BAHIA BLANCA (8558grt/1918) which sank after striking ice in the Denmark strait.   06 - 07.12.1940: Connected to London-registered (MOWT) steamer EMPIRE THUNDER (5965grt/1940) which had suffered machinery breakdown and delivered British port.   07.1944: Sold to Olafur E Einarsson H/F, Keflavik.   22.08.1944: Registered at Keflavik (GK363); operating from Hafnarfjordur.   24.04.1945: Sold to H/F Vestri, Reykjavik; operating from Reykjavik.   27.04.1947: Sold to Dieselskip H/F, Reykjavik, and sold to Faroe Islands same day. 1947: Sold to P/F Selvik A/S, Sørvåg, Faroe Islands.   1948: Registered at Sørvåg as **HAVSTEIN** (VA16).   1953: Registered at Sørvåg as **HAFSTEIN** (VA16).   1955: Sold to H J Hansen, Denmark, for breaking up.   25.10.1955: Arrived Odense.   Sørvåg registry closed.

HENRY MARSH Ad.No.4253 Mersey class	896 31.05.1919 23.12.1919	324 148	138.3 23.7 12.8	C D Holmes 600 ihp 3-cyl 11.0 knots	The Admiralty, Whitehall, London

1919: Sold to East Riding Steam Fishing Co Ltd, Hull, and completed as a fishing vessel.   19.01.1920: Registered at Hull as **SPRINGBOK** (H137). Official No.144031.   17.10.1923: Sold to Hudson Steam Fishing Co Ltd, Hull.   12.1928: Sold to Strand Steam Fishing Co Ltd, Grimsby.   03.01.1929: Hull registry closed.   04.01.1929: Registered at Grimsby (GY494). 26.02.1930: Registered at Grimsby as **NORTH CAPE** (GY494).   06.03.1931: Sailed Grimsby for Icelandic fishing grounds. 16.03.1931: Last spoken to off the south coast of Iceland. No further contact. No survivors.   25.06.1931: Grimsby registry closed - "Total loss".

The **Thomas Maloney** *(890) in Polish ownership as* **Podlasie**.

(Authors' collection)

The **James McLauchlin** *(893) was renamed* **General Birdwood** *within days of being handed over.*

(David Slinger collection)

SIMEON MOON Ad.No.4254 Mersey class	897 31.05.1919 11.03.1920	324 148	138.3 23.7 12.8	C D Holmes 600 ihp 3-cyl 11.0 knots	The Admiralty, Whitehall, London

1919: Sold to Hellyer Bros Ltd, Hull, and completed as a fishing vessel.   10.03.1920: Registered at Hull as **GENERAL RAWLINSON** (H173). Official No.144038.   08.1924: Sold to Fiskveidahlutafelagid Vidir, Hafnarfjordur, Iceland, for £9,500.   22.08.1924: Hull registry closed. Registered Hafnarfjordur as **VER** (GK3).   04.09.1931: Sold to H/F Ver, Reykjavik. Hafnarfjordur registry closed. Registered at Reykjavik (RE32).   18.04.1936: Sold to Togarafelag Neskaupstadar H/F, Neskaupstadur. Reykjavik registry closed. Registered at Neskaupstadur as **BRIMIR** (NK75).   29.07.1939: Sold to H/F Helgafell, Reykjavik. Neskaupstadur registry closed. Registered at Reykjavik as **HELGAFELL** (RE280).   15.08.1940: Homeward having landed at Fleetwood, picked up eight men from a liferaft survivors of the Swedish steamer NILS GORTHON (1787grt/1921) (Capt E Kastman) torpedoed by U-boat (U.60) 25 miles NE of Malin Head on 13.08.1940.   19.08.1940: Landed survivors at Reykjavik.   15.06.1945: Sold to H/F Hrimfaxi & H/F Svidi, Hafnarfjord. Reykjavik registry closed.   Registered at Hafnarfjördur as **SKINFAXI** (GK3).   01.08.1947: Sold to P/F Skinfaxi A/S, Sölmundarfjordur, Faroe Islands. Hafnarfjordur registry closed. Registered at Sölmundarfjordur.   1948: Registered at Sölmundarfjordur as **MIDAFELLI**.   1952: Sold to Danish shipbreakers and broken up.   Solmundarfjord registry closed.

SAMUEL MARTIN Ad.No.4255 Mersey class	898 28.06.1919 29.03.1920	324 129	138.3 23.7 12.8	C D Holmes 600 ihp 3-cyl 11.0 knots	The Admiralty, Whitehall, London

1919: Sold to Hellyer Bros Ltd, Hull, and completed as a fishing vessel.   23.03.1920: Registered at Hull as **FIELD MARSHAL PLUMER** (H174). Official No.144040.   19.11.1924: Sold to Einar Thorgilsson, Olafur Tryggvi Einarsson & Thorgils G Einarsson, Hafnarfjordur, Iceland, for £9,500.   22.11.1924: Hull registry closed. Registered at Hafnarfjordur as **SURPRISE** (GK4).   04.11.1939: Transferred to Einar Thorgilsson & Co, Hafnarfjordurur.   16.10.1941: West of Iceland, guided by RAF aircraft, picked up twenty-three crew members, six gunners and two RAF personnel, survivors from the armed merchantman (CAM) EMPIRE WAVE (7463grt/1941) (Capt Clement P Maclay) which had been torpedoed and sunk by U-boat (U.562) 500 miles E of Cape Farewell on 02.10.1941. Survivors landed at Patreksfjordur, Iceland.   26.04.1942: Attacked and bombed by German FW200 160 miles south of Vestmannaeyjar, but bombs missed target.   17.11.1945: Sold to H/F Sæfell, Vestmannaeyjum. Hafnarfjord registry closed. Registered at Vestmannaeyjar as **HELGAFELL** (VE32).   1951: Laid up.   23.06.1952 to Oddi Helgason, Reykjavik.   1952: Sold to P & W MacLellan Ltd, Bo'ness, for breaking up.   Vestmannaeyjar registry closed.   09.07.1952: Arrived Bo'ness under tow.   08.12.1952: Breaking up commenced.

ROBERT MURRAY Ad.No.4256 Mersey class	899 28.06.1919 26.02.1920	324 148	138.3 23.8 12.8	C D Holmes 600 ihp 3-cyl 11.0 knots	The Admiralty, Whitehall, London

Completed as a fishing vessel.   05.03.1920: Delivered.   23.02.1920: Registered by the Admiralty at London as a fishing vessel (LO337). Official No.144393. Laid up.   03.1923: Sold to Irish Free State Government, Dublin.   28.03.1923: London registry closed.   03.1923: Registered at Dublin.   04.05.1923: Commissioned in the Irish Free State Coastal & Marine Service, Dublin.   31.03.1924: Decommissioned. Transferred to Commissioners of Public Works in Saorstat Eireann, Dublin.   1925: For sale.   26.01.1926: Sold to George L Young & Richard M Fleming, Culdaff, Co Donegal.   02.1926: Sold to Cygnet Steam Fishing Co Ltd, Fleetwood.   02.1926: Dublin registry closed.   11.02.1926: Registered at Fleetwood (FD90).   19.04.1927: Sailed Fleetwood for St Kilda with a survey party, mails and provisions.   14.04.1938: Sold to Thomas Cardwell & Robert H Bagshaw, Fleetwood.   26.05.1938: Registered at Fleetwood as **NORTHLYN** (FD90).   27.06.1939: Sold to Robert H. Bagshaw, Fleetwood.   07.10.1939: Requisitioned for war service as a boom defence vessel (P.No.Z.103); hire rate £105.6.0d per month. Cost of conversion £15,596.   18.11.1943: Sold to Cevic Steam Fishing Co Ltd, Fleetwood.   07.12.1943: Compulsorily acquired by Ministry of War Transport.   23.05.1944: Assigned to Operation Neptune - Normandy landings.   03.07.1944: Operation Neptune ended.   1945: Based at Portsmouth.   11.1945: Paid off, 'care and maintenance' at Rosyth.   12.01.1946: Fleetwood registry closed. Estimated cost of re-conditioning £7,500.   07.03.1947: Sold to Cevic Steam Fishing Co Ltd, Fleetwood. Re-registered at Fleetwood (FD90).   04.01.1955: Sold to Saint Andrew's Steam Fishing Co Ltd, Hull.   04.1955: Sold to Jacques Bakker en Zonen, Bruges, for breaking up.   21.04.1955: Delivered to Bruges.   04.1955: Fleetwood registry closed.

Not built	900 - 933 inclusive. Mersey class trawlers. Orders cancelled after 11.1918.				

LORD LONSDALE 147158 Steam trawler H32	934 20.05.1924 15.07.1924	338 137	138.8 23.7 13.3	C D Holmes 96 rhp 3-cyl 11.0 knots	Pickering & Haldane's Steam Trawling Co Ltd, Hull

Cost - Cochrane £8,150, CD Holmes £5,900.   07.07.1924: Registered at Hull (H32).   14.07.1938: Sold to Hellyer Bros Ltd, Hull.   02.1939: Sold to P/f Trolarafelagid Tór, Tórshavn, Faroe Islands.   07.02.1939: Hull registry closed. Registered at Tórshavn as **TOR II** (TN79).   07.09.1942: Having landed at Fleetwood, outward for fishing grounds (Sk Óli Fossaber) with twenty-one crew, at about 10.00pm when some 70 miles S of Vestmann Islands, torpedoed by U-boat (U.617) and foundered in approximate position 62.30'N 18.30'W; three survivors.   Tórshavn registry closed.

The **Ver** (897) was originally the Hull-registered **Simeon Moon**.

(Authors' collection)

Originally named **Robert Murray**, yard number 899 is seen as **Northlyn** in the colours of Cevic Steam Fishing Co Ltd.

(David Slinger collection)

PLAYMATES	964	93	86.0	Crabtree	C E Strowger &
144146 Steam drifter	25.04.1925	41	18.5	27 rhp 3-cyl	A W Wilkinson,
YH141	25.05.1925		9.0	8.5 knots	Gorleston

27.06.1925: Registered at Yarmouth (YH141).   05.10.1939: Requisitioned for war service as a minesweeper (P.No.FY.738); hire rate £37.4.0d per month. Based Dover.   20 - 26.05.1940: Evacuation from Boulogne, Calais & Dunkirk.   25.05.1940: Sailed Dover for Calais towing river launches in company with the trawlers ARLEY (P.No.FY.620) (FD44), BOTANIC (P.No.707) (see yard no.1023), BROCK (P.No.FY621) (FD47), CALVI (GY269), FYLDEA (P.No.666) (FD72) (see yard no.1072), MARETTA (P.No.FY.665) (FD45) (see yard no.1046), POLLY JOHNSON (H322) and drifter WILLING BOYS (P.No.FY.947) (LT737), also with several river launches in tow.   26.05.1940: Returned to Dover.   06.10.1945: Returned.   11.02.1946: Sold to East Briton Steam Fishing Co Ltd, Lowestoft.   28.02.1946: Yarmouth registry closed.   06.03.1946: Registered at Lowestoft (LT180).   03.1955: Fishing out of Newlyn on mackerel.   22.03.1955: Reported 40-50 miles WNE of Seven Stones Light vessel.   28.03.1955: Reported overdue. Lifebuoy found but no survivors.   28.09.1955: Lowestoft registry closed.

SHEPHERD LAD	965	100	87.0	Elliott & Garrood	John Tait, Cairnbulg,
125365 Steam drifter	1925	45	18.5	43 rhp 3-cyl	Jennie & Annie Tait,
FR123	25.06.1925		9.1	8.5 knots	Fraserburgh

29.06.1925: Registered at Fraserburgh (FR123).   1938: Sold to Gilbert & Co, Lowestoft. Fraserburgh registry closed.   31.03.1939: Registered at Lowestoft (LT7).   30.08.1939: Requisitioned for war service under naval control (P.No.FY.698); hire rate £40.0.0d per month.   04.1946: Returned.   1960: Sold to Jacques Bakker en Zonen, Bruges, for breaking up.   07.12.1960: Arrived Bruges.   09.12.1960: Lowestoft registry closed.

MARINUS	966	93	86.0	Crabtree	Seagull Steam Fishing
145826 Steam drifter	25.04.1925	42	18.5	27 nhp 3-cyl	Co Ltd,
LT240	25.05.1925		9.0	8.5 knots	Lowestoft

08.07.1925: Registered at Lowestoft (LT240). Valued at £3,000.   31.01.1929: Sold to Edmund T Capps, Lowestoft.   11.06.1929: Registered at Lowestoft as **JUSTIFIED** (LT240).   09.03.1937: Sold to E T Capps & Sons Ltd, Lowestoft.   02.12.1939: Requisitioned for war service as a minesweeping drifter; hire rate £37.4.0d per month. Based Malta as an escort vessel.   24.10.1941: Assumed minesweeping role.   16.06.1942: Mined off Malta. Three crew lost.   08.03.1947: Lowestoft registry closed.

STERNUS	967	93	86.0	Crabtree	Seagull Steam Fishing
145827 Steam drifter	09.05.1925	42	18.5	27 nhp 3-cyl	Co Ltd,
LT238	11.06.1925		9.0	8.5 knots	Lowestoft

22.07.1925: Registered at Lowestoft (LT238). Valued at £3,000.   10.10.1939: Requisitioned for war service with Naval Control of Shipping (P.No.FY.1706); hire rate £37.4.0d per month.   04.1941: Employed on port duties.   1942: Fitted out as a LL minesweeping drifter. Based Harwich.   09.1944: Employed on miscellaneous naval duties.   25.09.1945: Returned.   08.07.1954: Registered at Lowestoft as **SWIFTWING** (LT238).   15.07.1954: Surveyed following conversion to motor by Richards Ironworks Ltd, Lowestoft, and fitted with a 4-cylinder 240bhp oil engine by Ruston & Hornsby Ltd, Lincoln.   15.07.1954: Registered as a motor vessel.   20.01.1964: Sold to Lola Fishing Co Ltd, West Hartlepool.   04.02.1964: Lowestoft registry closed.   05.02.1964: Registered at Hartlepool (HL147).   1970: Sold to Hughes Bolckow Ltd, Blyth, and broken up. Hartlepool registry closed.

LUNAR 12	968	118	79.5		William H J Alexander,
Swim lighter	07.05.1925	115	22.5	N/A	London
	11.05.1925				

LUNAR 14	969	118	79.5		William H J Alexander,
Swim lighter	07.05.1925	115	22.5	N/A	London
	11.05.1925				

LUNAR 15	970	118	79.5		William H J Alexander,
Swim lighter	07.05.1925	115	22.5	N/A	London
	19.05.1925				

LUNAR 16	971	118	79.5		William H J Alexander,
Swim lighter	07.05.1925	115	22.5	N/A	London
	19.05.1925				

LUNAR 17	972	118	79.5		William H J Alexander,
Swim lighter	23.05.1925	115	22.5	N/A	London
	29.05.1925				

LUNAR 18	973	118	79.5		William H J Alexander,
Swim lighter	23.05.1925	115	22.5	N/A	London
	29.05.1925				

CAPE CROZIER	974	322	140.2	C D Holmes	Hudson Steam Fishing
149015 Steam trawler	09.07.1925	132	24.0	96 rhp 3-cyl	Co Ltd,
H213	07.09.1925		14.7	11.0 knots	Hull

07.09.1925: Registered at Hull (H213).   29.11.1932: Sold to Charleson Fishing Co Ltd, Hull.   08.10.1937: Registered at Hull as **STELLA ARGUS** (H213).   02.1938: Sold to P/f Kimbila A/S, Tórshavn, Faroe Islands.   01.03.1938: Hull registry closed. Registered at Tórshavn (TN266).   27.10.1957: Went missing whilst homeward to Tórshavn. Believed to have foundered in heavy weather. All twenty-two crew lost. Tórshavn registry closed.

Lord Barham *(955)*

(Barry Banham maritime photo collection)

Shepherd Lad *(965)*

(Barry Banham maritime photo collection)

Sternus *(967)*

(Barry Banham maritime photo collection)

*Yard number 967 was converted to a motor vessel and renamed **Swiftwing** in 1954.*

(Barry Banham maritime photo collection)

Un-named			90.0		James Murchie & Co Ltd
Water barge	1927		19.0		(for re-erection at Bangkok)
(for shipment)					

FAITHFUL STAR	998	103	90.3	Crabtree	Star Drift Fishing Co Ltd,
146197 Steam drifter	07.03.1927	44	19.0	260 ihp 3-cyl	Lowestoft
LT323	09.04.1927		9.2	9.0 knots	

19.06.1927: Registered at Lowestoft (LT323). Valued at £3900.   03.09.1939: Requisitioned for war service employed on contraband control (1-3pdr); hire rate £49.11.4d per month.   06.1941: Based Weymouth as armed patrol.   09.03.1946: Returned to owner. 21.11.1952: Surveyed following conversion to motor by L.B.S. Engineering Co Ltd, Lowestoft; fitted with a 3-cylinder 300bhp oil engine by W H Podd Ltd, Lowestoft.   14.12.1957: At night in a strong onshore wind and snow showers, got into difficulties whilst seeking shelter and stranded about 1/4 mile S of Orford Ness Lighthouse (Sk George Challis). Two crew got ashore and raised alarm, other crew members made it to shore but Sk Challis was rescued by LSA breeches buoy. Salvage arranged with Yarmouth tug RICHARD LEE BARBER (122grt/1940) but delayed due to picking up a barge which was adrift and delivering Harwich. Pushed further up the beach and damaged by heavy seas. Declared a total loss.   15.05.1958: Lowestoft registry closed.

ONE ACCORD	999	102	90.3	W Burrell & Co	G Catchpole, F E
	07.03.1927	43	19.0	260 ihp 3-cyl	Catchpole & F Mullender,
	09.04.1927		9.2	9.0 knots	Lowestoft

10.06.1927: Registered at Lowestoft (LT324). Fishing from Milford.   23.10.1929: Deckhand Edward W Read fell overboard, 2nd Engineer William Turrell (27) of Kessingland, jumped in the sea fully clothed in oilskins and seaboots, but failed to reach him before he drowned (Turrell was awarded the Royal Humane Society's Bronze Medal).   23.12.1929: Sold to George Frederick Catchpole; Francis George Gamble; Orlando Frederick Mullender, Lowestoft.   21.03.1934: Sold to George Catchpole; Frederick Ernest Catchpole & Francis George Gamble, Lowestoft.   16.11.1939: Requisitioned for war service as a minesweeping drifter (P.No.FY.983); hire rate £49.1.9d.   11.1944: Employed on miscellaneous naval duties.   21.02.1945: Sold to Frederick Ernest Catchpole; John Francis Gamble and D G Gamble; Ernest Herbert Holland and Frederick Ernest Catchpole, Lowestoft. 19.03.1945: Sold to Accord (Lowestoft) Ltd, Lowestoft.   01.1946: Returned.   18.03.1949: Sold to Gilbert & Co Ltd, Lowestoft. 18.03.1958: Sold to Anson Steam Trawler Co Ltd, Milford Haven.   17.11.1959: Sold to Picton Bros (Milford Haven) Ltd, Milford Haven.   30.08.1960: Converted to motor at Lowestoft and fitted with 5-cylinder 315bhp oil engine by Mirrlees, Bickerton & Day Ltd, Stockport. Re-measured to 111grt, 39net.   10.12.1969: Sailed Milford for fishing grounds (Sk Bill Philips); seven crew. In good visibility, 2.5 miles off the Smalls Lighthouse in collision with German motor tanker YORKSAND (500grt/1964) sustaining damage to stem and bow plating. Tanker stood by until stern trawler ROSS FAME (GY1360) (see yard no.1500) arrived in response to distress; escorted to Milford.   11.12.1969: Arrived Milford. Laid up.   02.1970: As a result of survey, considered beyond economical repair. Sold to Haulbowline Industries Ltd, Passage West, Co Cork, for breaking up.   27.06.1989: Lowestoft registry closed (mortgage discharged).

KENIA	1000	200	100.0	Crabtree & Co	William Watkins Ltd,
149891 Steam tug	05.04.1927	66	25.1	760 ihp 3-cyl	London
	10.05.1927		11.8	12.0 knots	

05.1927: Registered at London. Passenger certificate for 200 passengers.   1929: Fitted with W/T.   1939: Towed training ship VINDICATRIX from Gravesend to Sharpness, Gloucestershire.   08.1939: Requisitioned for war service on contraband control; hire rate £142.8.3d per month.   28.10.1939: Employed on miscellaneous naval duties.   26.05.1940: 'Operation Dynamo' (Dunkirk evacuation) put into effect. At Ramsgate (Capt W Hoiles) as inspection vessel.   1940: Based Harwich as rescue tug (P.No.W47). 11.11.1945: Returned.   01.02.1950: Placed under management of Ship Towage (London) Ltd, London.   12.10.1964: Whilst undocking Dutch motor vessel MAASHAVEN (5524grt/1948) from Tilbury Dock new entrance, holed in engine room and foundered. 25.10.1964: Salved by Port of London Authority and beached. Sold to Metal Recovery Ltd, Newhaven.   11.1964: Resold to Lacmots Ltd, Sheerness, for breaking up.   12.11.1964: Delivered Sheerness in tow of tug SUNNYSIDE (54grt/1944). Registry closed.

GONDIA	1001	200	100.0	Crabtree & Co	William Watkins Ltd,
149941 Steam tug	05.04.1927	66	25.1	760 ihp 3-cyl	London
	21.05.1927		11.8	12.0 knots	

05.1927: Registered at London. Passenger certificate for 200 passengers.   08.1939: Requisitioned for war service on miscellaneous naval duties; hire rate £143.11.0d per month.   01.10.1939: Employed on port duties at Dover.   20 - 26.05.1940: Evacuation from Boulogne, Calais & Dunkirk.   22.05.1940: At Boulogne (Capt C Pratt) berthing ships embarking troops.   26.05.1940: 'Operation Dynamo' (Dunkirk evacuation) put into effect. On harbour duty at Dover (Capt C Pratt) berthing and refuelling.   22.04.1942: Based at Reykjavik.   02.04.1944: Returned to UK.   21.08.1944: Returned.   01.02.1950: Placed under management of Ship Towage (London) Ltd, London.   03.1966: Laid up at Gravesend.   1966: Sold to Scrappingco S.r.l., Brussels, for breaking up by Jos de Smedt, Antwerp.   04.07.1966: Sailed Thames in tow of tug MOORCOCK (272grt/1959).   05.07.1966: Arrived Antwerp. Registry closed.

K.L.C.B. No. 6	1002	69	60.0		King's Lynn Conservancy
Gas lighter	21.03.1927	66	8.0	N/A	Board,
	03.04.1927				King's Lynn

CASTLE GALLEON	1003	852	190.4	Amos & Smith	Galleon Shipping Co Ltd,
149437 Steam cargo ship	19.05.1927	446	31.0	90 rhp 3-cyl	Newcastle
	21.07.1927		12.2	9.5 knots	

07.1927: Registered at Newcastle.   02.06.1932: On a voyage from Blyth towards Dieppe with a cargo of coal, foundered three miles E by S of Corton Lightship off Lowestoft in position 52.29.5N 01.56E.   Registry closed.

Prizeman *(981)*

(Peter Bass collection)

Neptunia *(992)*

(Authors' collection)

Kenia *(1000)*

(World Ship Photo Library)

Gondia *(1001)*

(World Ship Photo Library)

SURF FLOWER 160055 Steam trawler H363	1004 16.06.1927 30.07.1927	352 145	140.3 24.0 13.3	C D Holmes 600 ihp 3-cyl 11.0 knots	Yorkshire Steam Fishing Co Ltd, Hull

26.07.1927: Registered at Hull (H363).   09.1938: Sold to Firma Wed S I Greon, IJmuiden.   22.09.1938: Hull registry closed. Registered at IJmuiden as **EENDRACHT** (IJM183).   1938: Sold to N V Stoomvisscherij Maats "Mercurius", IJmuiden. Registered at IJmuiden as **VIKINGBANK** (IJM183).   06.1940: Requisitioned for war service by the Royal Netherlands Navy as a minesweeper (P.No.FY.1781).   31.01.1945: Returned.   12.1966: Sold to Arie Rijsdijk Boss & Zonen, Hendrik-Ido-Ambacht, for breaking up. 1967: IJmuiden registry closed.

LARUS 149202 Motor drifter LT381	1005 30.06.1927 02.04.1928	101 44	86.3 18.6 9.0	Plenty-Still 210 bhp 3-cyl semi diesel 10.0 knots	Alexander Fishing Co Ltd, Lowestoft

05.03.1928: Registered at Lowestoft (LT381). Valued at £4500.   02.06.1928: Engine trouble, towed 80 miles to Milford by drifter PLUMER (LT596) (113grt/1919).   18.07.1928: Sold to Plenty Still Oil Engines Ltd, Newbury. Further engine breakdowns. 12.12.1928: Lowestoft fishing registry closed - "Not used for fishing".   30.03.1929: Sold to Arthur G Catchpole, Kessingland. Converted to steam and fitted with 3-cylinder steam engine of 34rhp by Elliott & Garrood, Beccles. Re-measured to 94grt, 41net. 18.05.1929: Renamed **SILVER CREST**.   23.06.1929: Lowestoft registry closed as a motor vessel.   23.07.1929: Registered at Lowestoft as steam drifter **SILVER CREST** (LT46).   16.01.1930: Sold to Arthur G Catchpole & Benjamin Utting, Lowestoft. 28.07.1939: Following death of Arthur G Catchpole, sold to F E, V C & A G Catchpole Jnr and Benjamin Utting, Lowestoft. 03.10.1939: Requisitioned for war service as a minesweeping drifter (P.No.FY.733); hire rate £43.9.6d per month. Based Yarmouth. 05.04.1940: Sold to Silver Fishing Co Ltd, Lowestoft.   06.1943: Employed on miscellaneous naval duties.   26.02.1946: Laid up. 03.1946: Returned.   22.10.1956: At Lowestoft landed 215 crans of herring, £1700 gross.   1956: Joint winner of the Prunier Trophy. 1960: Sold to Jacques Bakker & Zonen, Bruges, for breaking up.   08.11.1960: Arrived Bruges.   11.11.1960: Lowestoft registry closed.

BOATMAN 160051 Steam tug	1006 18.05.1927 24.06.1927	31 2	57.0 14.2 4.8	F T Harker 125 ihp 2-cyl 9.0 knots	United Towing Co Ltd, Hull

Shallow draught tug for upriver and salvage work. Completed at a cost of £1750.   04.07.1927: Registered at Hull. 21.11.1935: Capsized in River Humber whilst working on the salvage of trawler EDGAR WALLACE (H262) (see yard no.987) beached on the river bank near Hessle and later salvaged. Master and two crew got aboard salvage lighter, engineer swept away and drowned.   21.12.1937: Re-registered on alteration of tonnage and other particulars following refurbishment and conversion to motor and twin screw; fitted with two Deutz oil engines of 230 bhp by Klöckner-Humboldt-Deutz, Köln; now 9 knots; re-measured to 33grt.   12.1963: Sold to David Cook Ltd, Saltend, en bloc with WATERMAN (see yard no.1067) and broken up at New Holland shipyard.   05.07.1965: Hull registry closed - "vessel broken up"

BANCO 149942 Steam tug	1007 30.08.1927 25.10.1927	107 -	77.7 21.6 11.0	Plenty & Sons 650 ihp 3-cyl 11.0 knots	Union Lighterage Co Ltd, London

10.1927: Registered at London.   26.11.1939: Requisitioned for war service on balloon barrage; £12.8.9d for period of service. 27.11.1939: Returned.   1966: Sold to Tsavliris (Salvage & Towage) Ltd, Piræus, Greece. London registry closed. Registered at Piræus as **NISOS KALYMNOS**.   1976: Sold to N E Vernicos Shipping Co Ltd, Piræus. Registered at Piræus as **VERNICOS KATERINA**.   1981: Sold to shipbreakers and broken up. Registry closed.

LORD ANSON 149201 Steam drifter LT344	1008 30.06.1927 28.07.1927	99 42	88.3 19.1 9.0	Pertwee & Back 43 nhp 3-cyl 10.0 knots	Lowestoft Steam Herring Drifters Co Ltd, Lowestoft

21.09.1927: Registered at Lowestoft (LT344).   30.08.1939: Requisitioned for war service under naval control; hire rate £48.2.6d per month.   21.09.1943: Sold to Saint Andrew's Steam Fishing Co Ltd, Hull.   02.1946: Sold to J C Llewellin (Trawlers) Ltd, Milford Haven.   16.02.1946: Returned.   03.1948: Sold to William Picton, Milford Haven.   04.1956: Sold to Metal Industries (Salvage) Ltd, Faslane. Lowestoft registry closed. Registered at Glasgow and used as a tug at Faslane.   1960: Sold to BISCO and allocated to W H Arnott Young & Co Ltd, Dalmuir, for breaking up.   07.11.1960: Delivered Dalmuir. Registry closed.

REGAL 160351 Steam tug	1009 09.11.1927 04.02.1928	91 40	74.5 19.5 10.6	McKie & Baxter 550 ihp 3-cyl 11.0 knots	William Cory & Son Ltd, London

02.1928: Registered at London.   1934: Owners re-styled Cory Lighterage Ltd, London.   07.1962: Sold to Thos W Ward Ltd, Sheffield, for breaking up.   06.07.1962: Arrived Grays, Essex. Registry closed.

ABEILLE No. 14 Steam tug	1010 12.10.1927 25.11.1927	126 26	80.1 22.1 11.6	C D Holmes 93 nhp 3-cyl 11.0 knots	Cie de Remorquage & de Sauvetage "Les Abeilles", Le Havre, France

11.1927: Registered at Le Havre.   03.07.1940: Seized by Royal Navy. Transferred to Ministry of War Transport, London. Registered at Southampton. Official No.167843.   07.1940: Requisitioned for war service as an auxiliary salvage tug.   05.10.1944: Transferred to War Department.   20.12.1945. Returned.   1946: Southampton registry closed. Registered at Le Havre.   1961: Registry closed. 09.1961: Broken up at Le Havre by owners.

ABEILLE No. 18 Steam tug	1011 26.03.1927 25.05.1928	126 26	80.1 22.1 11.6	C D Holmes 93 nhp 3-cyl 11.0 knots	Cie de Remorquage & de Sauvetage "Les Abeilles", Le Havre, France

05.1928: Registered at Le Havre.   1960: Registered at Le Havre as **ABEILLE No.16**.   1967: Registry closed. Broken up at Le Havre by owners.

SPRAYFLOWER 160109 Steam trawler H437	1012 21.04.1928 26.06.1928	352 145	140.3 24.0 13.3	Amos & Smith 600 ihp 3-cyl 11.0 knots	Yorkshire Steam Fishing Co Ltd, Hull

14.06.1928: Registered at Hull (H437).   20.09.1938: Sold to Boyd Line Ltd, Hull.   17.11.1938: Registered at Hull as **ARCTIC TRAPPER** (H437).   19.09.1939: Sold to Shire Trawlers Ltd, Grimsby.   02.10.1939: Hull registry closed.   05.10.1939: Registered at Grimsby (GY217).   07.06.1940: Requisitioned for war service as an auxiliary patrol vessel; hire rate £156.18.8d per month. 03.02.1941: Attacked and bombed by German aircraft ½ mile WS-W of Gull light buoy, Goodwin Sands, and foundered in position 51.19.6N 01.31.2E. Seventeen crew including the CO, Ty/Sk Louis M Harvey RNR, were lost.

CEYLON BUL-BUL 160109 Steam trawler H437	1013 08.02.1928 31.03.1928	270 98	125.7 23.5 9.8	C D Holmes 500 ihp 3-cyl 10.5 knots	Ceylon Fisheries Ltd, Columbo, Ceylon

23.03.1928: Registered at Hull (H412).   10.04.1928: Hull registry closed.   04.1928: Registered at Colombo.   09.1935: Sold to Boston Deep Sea Fishing & Ice Co Ltd, Fleetwood. Colombo registry closed.   21.11.1935: Registered at Fleetwood as **OUR MAVIS** (FD52).   03.1938: Sold to Uruguayan Government (Servicio Oceanografic y de Pesca), Montevideo.   28.03.1938: Fleetwood registry closed.   1938: Registered at Montevideo as **ANTARES**.   1940: Removed from *Lloyd's Register* - vessel's continued existence in doubt.

CAPE HATTERAS 160105 Steam trawler H423	1014 08.03.1928 24.05.1928	345 136	140.4 24.0 13.3	Amos & Smith 600 ihp 3-cyl 11.0 knots	Hudson Steam Fishing Co Ltd, Hull

17.05.1928: Registered at Hull (H423).   10.11.1933: Sold to Charleson Fishing Co Ltd, Hull.   03.06.1937: Registered at Hull as **STELLA LEONIS** (H423).   29.07.1938: Sold to Charleson-Smith Trawlers Ltd, Hull.   06.1939: Sold to the Admiralty. Fitted out as a minesweeper (1-12pdr, AA weapons) (P.No.FY.706).   28.02.1940: Hull registry closed. Based Harwich with M/S Group 4. 1944: Fitted out for dan laying and assigned to Operation Neptune - Normandy landings.   23.05.1944: Attached to the 7th Minesweeping Flotilla as a dan layer.   05.06.1940: Sailed Solent for Juno beach ahead of Assault Convoy J2. 03.07.1944: Operation Neptune ended.   1946: Sold to Royal Netherlands Government, The Hague.   05.1947: Sold to De Vem N V, IJmuiden, Netherlands. Registered at IJmuiden as **CATHARINA DUYVIS** (IJM60).   01.02.1953: At sea during the Great Storm made a distress message from a position west of IJmuiden.   11.02.1953: Posted missing; all sixteen crew lost.   IJmuiden registry closed.

JULIANA 146907 Steam trawler GY461	1015 25.02.1928 08.05.1928	324 129	138.6 23.9	Amos & Smith 96 rhp 3-cyl 11.0 knots	Perihelion Steam Fishing Co Ltd, Grimsby

04.05.1928: Registered at Grimsby (GY461).   06.10.1934: Sailed Grimsby for Icelandic grounds (Sk A E Macallan); thirteen crew total.   09.10.1934: In wireless communication but not heard of again. Vessel posted missing; no survivors.   24.12.1934: Grimsby registry closed - "Missing".

DEEPDALE WYKE 160799 Steam trawler H459	1016 22.05.1928 22.08.1928	335 134	138.8 23.8 13.3	C D Holmes 600 ihp 3-cyl 11.0 knots	West Dock Steam Fishing Co Ltd, Hull

17.08.1928: Registered at Hull (H459). Completed at a cost of £17,200.   1939: Sold to the Admiralty for £7,057.   28.06.1939: Hull registry closed. Fitted out as a boom defence vessel. Renamed **RENNET** (P.No.Z.99).   1940: At Rosyth. 1941: Mediterranean Command.   1944: Based Aden.   1946: Sold to Iago Steam Trawler Co Ltd, Fleetwood.   10.1946: Rebuilt and reclassed at Barrow; converted for burning oil fuel (first Fleetwood trawler converted to burn oil).   01.1947: Registered at London as **RED ARCHER** (LO430).   07.1958: Sold to BISCO and allocated to Thos W Ward Ltd, Sheffield, for breaking up.   17.07.1958: Delivered Barrow-in-Furness from Fleetwood under own power.   London registry closed.

JAMES BARRIE 160800 Steam trawler H460	1017 19.06.1928 23.08.1928	338 132	140.3 24.0	C D Holmes 96 rhp 3-cyl 11.0 knots	Newington Steam Trawling Ltd, Hull

17.08.1928: Registered at Hull (H460).   23.01.1940: Requisitioned for war service as a boom defence vessel (P.No.Z.110); hire rate £150.13.10d per month. Iceland Command. Based Hvalfjordur.   19.11.1945: Returned.   17.12.1945: Last landing at Hull (one trip). 27.03.1946: Sold to Pair Fishing Co Ltd, Milford Haven.   08.1947: Sold to Ytre Rollöya Fiskarsamvirke, Breivoll i Ibestad, Norway. 02.08.1947: Hull registry closed. Registered at Harstad as **NORD ROLLNES**.   1953: Registered at Hamnvik.   1967: Sold to Brodrene Anda, Stavanger, for breaking up.   17.07.1967: Arrived Stavanger. Registry closed.

LORD TRENT 160866 Steam trawler H116	1062 05.10.1929 14.11.1929	346 135	140.3 24.0 13.3	Amos & Smith 96 nhp 3-cyl 11.0 knots	Pickering & Haldane's Steam Trawling Co Ltd, Hull

12.11.1929: Registered at Hull (H116). 04.1939: Sold to the Admiralty for £7500. Converted to a "Berberis" class minesweeper (1-4" HA). 08.05.1939: Hull registry closed. Renamed **HORNBEAM** (P.No.T.53). Based Liverpool ungrouped then as A/A minesweeper/escort. 1946: Sold to P/f Rankin, Trangisvaag, Faroe Islands. 11.1946: Re-classed as a steam trawler after special survey at Leith. Registered at Trangisvaag as **RANKIN**. 1952: Sold to P/f Rankin A/S, Tveraa. Trangisvaag registry closed. Registered at Tveraa. 1955: Sold to P/F Hargafelli, Tveraa. 10.1959: Sold to Aksel Hodal Hillerod, Denmark, and broken up at Frederikssund. 1959: Tveraa registry closed.

LORD DAWSON 160871 Steam trawler H140	1063 05.10.1929 05.12.1929	346 135	140.3 24.0 13.3	Amos & Smith 96 nhp 3-cyl 11.0 knots	Pickering & Haldane's Steam Trawling Co Ltd, Hull

29.11.1929: Registered at Hull (H140). 02.1939: Sold to the Admiralty for £7500. Converted to a "Berberis" class minesweeper (1-4"). 08.05.1939: Hull registry closed. Renamed **BEECH** (P.No.T.44). Based Grimsby with M/S Group 18. 22.06.1941: Heavily damaged by German air attack off Scrabster, Caithness, and foundered. Eleven crew including CO, Ty/Lieut A P Cocks RNVR, lost.

CAPE MELVILLE 160872 Steam trawler H150	1064 21.10.1929 16.12.1929	343 136	140.4 24.0 13.3	C D Holmes 96 nhp 3-cyle 11.0 knots	Hudson Steam Fishing Co Ltd, Hull

13.12.1929: Registered at Hull (H150). 31.08.1939: Requisitioned for war service as a minesweeper (1-12pdr) (P.No.FY.651); hire rate £161.9.11d per month. Based Gt Yarmouth with M/S Group 12. 19.05.1940: Sailed Harwich (Ty/Sk J E C Wright RNR) escorted by HM Destroyer JAGUAR (Lt Cdr J F Hine RN) (P.No.F34) and HM Patrol Sloop PUFFIN (Lt Cdr Earl Beatty RN) (P.No.L52) accompanied by HM M/S trawlers, GRAMPIAN (Ch Sk A. Robb RNR) (P.No.FY.546) (H502), JAMES LAY (Sk W H Makings RNR) (P.No.FY.667) (LO333), MILFORD QUEEN (Ty/Sk F Burgess RNR) (P.No.FY.615) (M225), MILFORD PRINCESS (Ty/Sk J W Cook RNR) (P.No.FY.616) (M228) and PELTON (Sk J A Sutherland DSC RNR) (H288), engaged in Operation Quixote (to creep and cut telephone cables between Lowestoft, Bacton, Mundesley and Borkum and Norderney, Germany). 28.05.1940: Operation completed. 29.09.1945: Returned. 24.01.1945: Sold to Hudson Brothers Trawlers Ltd, Hull. 28.01.1946: Sold to Loch Fishing Co of Hull Ltd, Hull, for £16,668. 12.07.1946: Registered at Hull as **LOCH ALSH** (H150). 03.04.1956: Laid up. 05.1956: Sold to Van Heyghen Frères, Ghent, Belgium for £6,100. 24.05.1956: Hull registry closed. 25.05.1956: Delivered Ghent for breaking up.

TEWERA 161345 Steam trawler LO9	1065 02.11.1929 07.01.1930	335 130	135.4 24.9 13.7	Amos & Smith 99 rhp 3-cyl 11.7 knots	Brand & Curzon Ltd, Milford Haven

04.01.1930: Registered at London (LO9). 10.09.1937: Sold to Boston Deep Sea Fishing & Ice Co Ltd, Fleetwood. 27.08.1939: Requisitioned for war service as a minesweeper (1-12pdr) (P.No.FY.526); hire rate £166.2.1d per month. 06.1946: Returned. 10.1946: Special survey at Cardiff. Cardiff registry closed. 10.1946: Sold to Government of Poland, Warsaw (Ministry of Industry & Commerce) "Dalmor" Przedsiobiorstwo Polowow Dalekomorskich Sp.z.ogr.odn., Gdynia under the UNRRA scheme. 23.10.1946: Registered at Gdynia as **SATURNIA** (GDY91). 21.02.1966: Sold to Polish shipbreakers for breaking up at Gdansk. 02.1966: Gdynia registry closed.

TEKOURA 161352 Steam trawler LO14	1066 19.11.1929 14.01.1930	335 130	135.4 24.9 13.7	Amos & Smith 99 rhp 3-cyl 11.5 knots	Brand & Curzon Ltd, Milford Haven

09.01.1930: Registered at London (LO14). 01.09.1937: Sold to Saint Andrew's Steam Fishing Co Ltd, Hull. 1938: Lengthened by Smith's Dock Co Ltd, Middlesbrough, to 150.7 feet including new bow and stern sections. Re-measured to 368grt, 142net. 04.10.1939: Requisitioned for war service as an anti-submarine trawler (1-4", 1-20mm HA, depth charge thrower & rails) (P.No.FY.247); hire rate £191.4.7d per month. Based Scapa Flow. 31.08.1943: Sold to Heward Trawlers Ltd, London & Fleetwood. 04.1945: Paid off to reserve. 18.04.1946: Returned. 10.1948: Sold to Ocean Fisheries Ltd, Milford Haven. for £39,000. 1953: Ocean Fisheries Ltd in liquidation. 10.1953: Laid up at Milford. 25.02.1954: Sold to Dinas Steam Trawling Co Ltd, Fleetwood, for £5000. 27.02.1954: Sailed Milford for Fleetwood. London registry closed. Registered at Fleetwood (FD12). 07.1954: Sold to Van den Bossche & Co, Boom, Belgium, for breaking up. 14.10.1954: Arrived Boom from Fleetwood. Fleetwood registry closed.

WATERMAN 160881 Steam tug	1067 12.12.1929 12.02.1930	40 10	62.1 14.4 4.7	L Gardner & Sons 192 bhp 2x4-cyl 9.0 knots	United Towing Co Ltd, Hull

Shallow draught tug for upriver, barge and salvage work. 10.02.1930: Registered at Hull. Completed at a cost of £5500. 21.11.1935: Assisted in beaching BOATMAN (see yard no.1006). 12.1963: Sold to David Cook Ltd, Saltend, en bloc with BOATMAN and broken up at New Holland shipyard. 14.10.1964: Hull registry closed - "Vessel broken up".

GRANVILLE Steam cargo ship	1068 18.12.1929 05.02.1930	511 148	170.2 28.6 8.9	C D Holmes 87 nhp 3-cyl 11.3 knots	Société Havraise de Transport et de Transit, Le Havre, France

02.1930: Registered at Le Havre. 1946: Deleted from *Lloyd's Register* as a war loss.

Cape Melville (1064)

Tekoura (1066) following rebuild in 1938.

MADRUGADOR	1069	206	96.8	Plenty & Sons	The Argentine Nav Co
Oil fired steam tug	17.01.1930	-	25.1	112 nhp 3-cyl	(Nicolás Mihanovich) Ltda,
	19.03.1930		11.5	12.0 knots	Buenos Aires

03.1930: Registered at Buenos Aires.   1931: Company re-styled Cia. Argentina de Nav Mihanovich Ltda, Buenos Aires.
1943: Company re-styled Cia Argentina de Nav Dodero S.A, Buenos Aires.   1958: Company re-styled Flota Argentina de Nav de Ultramar, Buenos Aires.   1961: Vessel removed from Lloyd's Register of Shipping.

URANIA	1070	869	190.6	C D Holmes	Société Havraise du
H2229 Steam trawler	16.01.1930	333	31.1	101 nhp 3-cyl	Pêche, Le Havre,
	06.03.1930		16.4	11.5 knots	France

03.1930: Registered at Le Havre (H2229).   10.1930: Transferred to Fécamp.   09.01.1941: Bound from Saint Pierre et Miquelon towards Casablanca, stopped by the Royal Navy in approximate position 34º N 13º W; sent to Liverpool via Gibraltar.
25.01.1941: Transferred to Ministry of War Transport. Converted to an A/S trawler; on completion renamed **RETRIEVER** (P.No.FY.261). Irish Sea Escort Force.   05.09.1942: Converted to a cable ship. Far East Station.   07.1946: Reverted to **URANIA**. Restored and classified as a steam trawler.   11.1946: Returned to France.   1953: Laid up in Le Havre.   1955: Sold to B J Nijkerk SA, Belgium, and broken up at Haren.   1955: Le Havre registry closed.

DINAMAR	1071	366	140.4	Amos & Smith	Dinas Steam Trawling
162058 Steam trawler	01.02.1930	141	25.0	97 rhp 3-cyl	Co Ltd,
	18.03.1930		13.4	11.5 knots	Fleetwood

14.03.1930: Registered at Fleetwood (FD73).   1931: At Fleetwood top port landing-641 tons, highest single trip-94 tons.
10.1938: Sold to Standard Steam Fishing Co Ltd, Grimsby.   28.10.1938: Fleetwood registry closed.   01.11.1938: Registered at Grimsby (GY541).   30.01.1939: Registered at Grimsby as **SILANION** (GY541).   21.11.1939: Completed lengthening by Smith's Dock Co Ltd, Middlesbrough, to 155.7 feet including new bow and stern sections. Re-measured to 366g, 178n.
01.1940: Requisitioned for war service as a boom defence vessel (P.No.Z.116); hire rate £202.12.11d per month.
08.12.1945: Reclassed at Grimsby and returned.   1946: Transferred to Hull.   26.08.1948: Sold to White Trawlers Ltd, Hull.
08.1948: Grimsby registry closed.   26.08.1948: Registered at Hull (H577).   01.12.1948: Registered at Hull as **WHITE FLOWER** (H577).   21.12.1949: Sold to C S Taylor, MP & others, London.   01.05.1953: Laid up.   17.09.1954: Sold to Hull Merchants Amalgamated Trawlers Ltd, Hull, and sold on to Belgian shipbreakers.   05.10.1954: Arrived Liège for breaking up.
29.10.1954: Hull registry closed.

FYLDEA	1072	377	140.4	Amos & Smith	J Marr & Son Ltd,
162059 Steam trawler	15.02.1930	141	25.0	97 rhp 3-cyl	Fleetwood
FD72	29.03.1930		13.4	10.0 knots	

24.03.1930: Registered at Fleetwood (FD72).   05.11.1931: Took off crew of trawler CRISCILLA (FD23) stranded 2 miles N by E of McArthur's Head, Sound of Islay.   1934: Transferred to Hull. Crewed and operated by City Steam Fishing Co Ltd, Hull.
21.07.1936: Completed lengthening by Smith's Dock Co Ltd, Middlesbrough, to 151.5 feet including new bow and stern sections. Re-measured to 377grt, 149net.   02.09.1939: Requisitioned for war service as a minesweeper (magnetic) (P.No.FY.666); hire rate £202.12.11d per month.   20 - 26.05.1940: Evacuation from Boulogne, Calais & Dunkirk.   25.05.1940: Sailed Dover for Calais in company with the trawlers ARLEY (P.No.FY.620) (FD44), BOTANIC (P.No.FY.707) (H463) (see yard no.1023), BROCK (P.No.FY.621) (FD47), CALVI (GY269), MARETTA (P.No.FY.665) (FD45) (see yard no.1046), POLLY JOHNSON (H322) and drifters PLAYMATES (P.No.FY.738) (YH141) (see yard no.964) and WILLING BOYS (P.No.FY.947) (LT737) with several river launches in tow.
26.05.1940: At 1.40am arrived off the French coast. No evacuation order given. Returned to Dover.   26.05.1940: 'Operation Dynamo' (Dunkirk evacuation) put into effect.   01.06.1940: At Dunkirk (Sk G Whamond RNR) transported 180 troops.
30.01.1942: Based Lowestoft. Shot down German aircraft (JU88) near 54G buoy off Norfolk coast; one body recovered.
11.1945: Reclassed at Glasgow.   12.1945: Returned.   12.1945: Fleetwood registry closed.   08.12.1945: Registered at Hull (H160).
26.09.1946: Sold to Ocean Steam Trawling Co Ltd, Hull.   03.07.1947: Registered at Hull as **HOWARD** (H160).   11.1947: Sold to Iago Steam Trawler Co Ltd, Fleetwood.   12.11.1947: Hull registry closed.   01.1948: Registered at London as **RED DRAGON** (LO381).   05.02.1958: Sold to BISCO and allocated to Thos W Ward Ltd, Sheffield, for breaking up.   18.02.1958: Arrived Barrow from Fleetwood.   1958: London registry closed.

CLEVELA	1073	387	140.4	Amos & Smith	J Marr & Son Ltd,
162061 Steam trawler	15.02.1930	140	25.0	97 rhp 3-cyl	Fleetwood
FD94	10.03.1930		13.4	10.0 knots	

07.04.1930: Registered at Fleetwood (FD94).   1934: Transferred to City Steam Fishing Co Ltd, Hull, after J Marr & Son Ltd bought the company.   1938: Sold to J Marr & Son Ltd, Fleetwood. Fishing from Hull.   17.11.1938: Completed lengthening by Smith's Dock Co Ltd, Middlesbrough, to 155.5 feet including new bow and stern sections. Re-measured to 387grt, 151net.
02.09.1939: Requisitioned for war service as a minesweeper (1-12pdr) (P.No.FY.678); hire rate £202.12.11 per month.   1940: Based Grimsby with M/S Group 19.   1945: Based Grimsby with M/S Group 134.   02.1946: Sold to Trident Steam Fishing Co Ltd, Hull.
02.1946: Fleetwood registry closed.   07.02.1946: Registered at Hull (H201).   13.05.1946: Returned after survey and restoration at Liverpool.   11.12.1947: Sold to Iago Steam Trawler Co Ltd, Fleetwood.   17.06.1948: Hull registry closed.   06.1948: Registered at London as **RED PLUME** (LO419). Transferred to Fleetwood.   10.08.1955: Sold to Thos Hamling & Co Ltd, Hull, for £17,000 plus £2,269.7.1d for gear and £250 for radar.   08.1954: London registry closed.   19.08.1955: Registered at Hull (H83).
24.11.1955: Laid up.   1956: Sold to BISCO (£6,000) and allocated to J J King & Co Ltd, Gateshead, for breaking up; value of gear landed prior to sale was £984.14.5d.   26.03.1956: Delivered River Tyne under tow ; towage cost was £323.13.7d.
15.11.1956: Hull registry closed.

Madrugador (1069)

(Cochrane shipyard collection)

The **Silanion** (1071) was originally named **Dinamar**.

(Authors' collection)

Another view of the **Silanion**.

(Authors' collection)

KURD	1095	352	140.3	C D Holmes	Hellyer Bros,
162206 Steam trawler	09.10.1930	138	24.6	600 ihp 3-cyl	Hull
H344	25.11.1930		13.3	11.0 knots	

19.11.1930: Registered at Hull (H344).   08.1939: Sold to Shire Trawlers Ltd, Grimsby for £12,400.   11.08.1939: Hull registry closed. 14.08.1939: Registered at Grimsby (GY182).   05.09.1939: Requisitioned for war service as a minesweeper (1-12pdr, AA weapons) (P.No.FY.639); hire rate £174.10.8d per month. Based Grimsby with M/S Group 17 and later M/S Group 40.   10.07.1945: Sweeping British laid minefield QZX.1600 south east of Lizard Head (Ty/Act/Lt Cdr R Barrett RNR). Caught up mine in sweep and detonated when hauling, blowing off the stern; vessel sank immediately in position 49.52N 05.02W. Sixteen crew including CO lost, survivors picked up by HM Trawler ALMADINE (P.No.FY.645) (H415) (294grt/1932) and landed at Falmouth. Compensation for loss £12,400. 1945: Grimsby registry closed.

BENVOLIO	1096	352	140.3	C D Holmes	Hull Northern Fishing
162208 Steam trawler	23.10.1930	139	24.6	600 ihp 3-cyl	Co Ltd,
H347	08.12.1930		13.3	11.0 knots	Hull

05.12.1930: Registered at Hull (H347).   08.1939: Sold to Shire Trawlers Ltd, Grimsby, for £12,400.   11.08.1939: Hull registry closed.   14.08.1939: Registered at Grimsby (GY183).   05.09.1940: Requisitioned for war service as a minesweeper (1-12pdr, AA weapons) (P.No.FY.721); hire rate £174.10.8d per month.   23.02.1940: Mined off the mouth of the Humber and foundered in position 53.34N 00.10E. Ch Sk S M Aldred RNR and ten crew lost.   Compensation for loss £12,400.   1941: Grimsby registry closed.

MARSEILLAIS 3	1097	119	78.0	C D Holmes	Soc Générale de Remorq
Oil fired steam tug	07.03.1931	-	22.0	600 ihp 3-cyl	et de Travaux Maritimes,
	15.05.1931		11.5	12.0 knots	Marseilles, France

05.1931: Registered at Marseilles .   1944: Sold to T C Münakalat Vekaleti, Istanbul, Turkey.   1952: Sold to Denizcilik Bankasi T.A.O, Istanbul.   1965: Vessel removed from Lloyd's Register of Shipping.

BEACHFLOWER	1098	375	150.5	Amos & Smith	Yorkshire Steam Fishing
162210 Steam trawler	08.11.1930	145	25.5	600 ihp 3-cyl	Co Ltd,
H349	15.12.1930			11.0 knots	Hull

12.12.1930: Registered at Hull (H349).   17.04.1934: Arrested for alleged unlawful fishery inside Norwegian territorial waters (Sk Norton).   06.07.1934: In court at Vardoe, Norway, Sk Norton was found guilty and fined 5,000 kroner.   09.1935: As a result of the Abyssinian crisis and failure of British diplomacy, the Government authorised the Admiralty to procure twenty modern trawlers for conversion to minor war vessels.   11.1935: Following successful trials, sold to the Admiralty.   08.11.1935: Hull registry closed. Fitted out as a "Berberis" class minesweeper (1-4). Renamed HMS LILAC (P.No.T.26). Based Spa Flow with M/S Group 1. 23.05.1944: Assigned to Operation Neptune - Normandy landings. Assigned PLUTO (Pipe Line Under The Ocean) project. 03.07.1944: Operation Neptune ended.   1946: Sold to Great Northern Fishing Co Ltd, London & Fleetwood.   11.1946: Restored and reclassed at Fleetwood after return. Registered at London as ROBERT HEWETT (LO427).   1948: On Icelandic grounds. Connected to motor trawler ALLAN WATER (H420) disabled with engine problems. Repairs subsequently effected and tow slipped. 1955: Sold to Heward Trawlers Ltd, London & Fleetwood.   11.1960: Sold to BISCO and allocated to Thos W Ward Ltd, Sheffield, for breaking up at Preston.   18.11.1960: Sailed Fleetwood for Preston.   18.11.1960: Delivered.   1960: London registry closed.

LORD BEAVERBROOK	1099	362	150.5	Amos & Smith	Pickering & Haldane's
162212 Steam trawler	20.11.1930	141	25.5	96 rhp 3-cyl	Steam Trawling Co Ltd,
H366	31.12.1930		13.1	11.0 knots	Hull

01.01.1931: Registered at Hull (H366).   09.1935: As a result of the Abyssinian crisis and failure of British diplomacy, the Government authorised the Admiralty to procure twenty modern trawlers for conversion to minor war vessels.   12.1935: Following successful trials, sold to the Admiralty.   16.12.1935: Hull registry closed. Fitted out as a "Berberis" class minesweeper (1-4). Renamed HMS SYCAMORE (P.No.T.37). Based Scapa Flow with M/S Group 1.   1946: Sold to P/f Nevid A/S, Hvalböur, Faroe Islands. Registered at Hvalböur as DRÁTTUR.   1951: Hvalböur registry closed. Registered at Kvalbö.   1953: Sold to P/f Ranin, Kvalbö.   1958: Sold to P/F Degningur, Midvaag. Kvalbö registry closed. Registered at Midvaag as JUPITER.   07.1959: Sold to Aksel Hodal et Hillerod, Denmark, and broken up at Frederikssund. Midvaag registry closed.

MARGARET ROSE	1100	428	145.7	Amos & Smith	Boston Deep Sea Fishing
161009 Steam trawler	05.02.1931	172	25.6	98 nhp 3-cyl	Co Ltd,
GY355	12.03.1931		13.6	11.7 knots	Fleetwood

10.03.1931: Registered at Grimsby (GY355).   05.04.1931: Arrived Fleetwood (Sk Walter Holmes).   06.04.1931: Landed 3760 stone of fish, mostly hake.   05.09.1932: Sailed from Fleetwood for east coast of USA (Georges Bank) (Sk Walter Holmes) on a trial trip to exploit the supposed hake grounds a few miles offshore, the trip to take from 24 - 32 days (340 tons bunker coal, 90 tons ice, 2 tons salt and one month's provisions).   05.10.1932: Returned. Diverted to Grimsby to land 1400 boxes (mixed cod, haddock and flats); grossed £308 failed to cover a quarter of costs.   08.1933: Sold to Pêcheries de la Morinie, Boulogne.   15.08.1933: Grimsby registry closed.   08.1933: Registered at Boulogne as MARGUERITE ROSE.   08.1933: Stranded at Knott Spit Buoy when returning from trials.   18.08.1933: Sailed Fleetwood for Boulogne (with part Fleetwood crew).   10.01.1934: In North Sea, rendered assistance to Danish steamer POLLY (798grt/1911) with rudder damage sustained on passage Baltic - Dundalk with coal. Connected and delivered Aberdeen.   08.1939: Requisitioned by Marine Française as an auxiliary minesweeper (P.No.AD23).   25.05.1940: At Dunkirk 'Operation Dynamo' (Commander Flachaire Roustan) attacked by German aircraft, two bombs exploded and vessel abandoned before sinking alongside French steamer AÏN EL TURK (2508grt/1925).

Benvolio *(1096)*

(Authors' collection)

Superman *(1110)*

(World Ship Photo Library)

CAPE BARFLEUR 163960 Steam trawler H105	1127 11.09.1934 30.10.1934	457 185	161.0 26.6	C D Holmes 122 nhp 3-cyl 12.0 knots	Hudson Steam Fishing Co Ltd, Hull

23.10.1934: Registered at Hull (H105).   27.02.1939: Sold to the Admiralty (£19,260).   27.02.1939: Hull registry closed. Fitted out as a "Gem" class anti-submarine trawler (1-4", ASDIC).   1939: Renamed HMS **AMBER** (P.No.T.88). Based Port Said, Egypt, with 4th A/S/ Group.   10.1946: Sold to Eton Fishing Co Ltd, Hull.   09.1946: Remeasured to 473grt 188net after restoration and reclassification.   08.10.1946: Registered at Hull as **ETONIAN** (H333).   19.09.1950: Sold to Boyd Line, Hull.
12.10.1950: Registered at Hull as **ARCTIC CRUSADER** (H333).   19.05.1952: Sold to Eton Steam Fishing Co Ltd, Hull.
29.03.1952: Registered at Hull as **ETONIAN** (H333).   27.03.1954: Sold to J Marr & Son Ltd, Fleetwood, for £27,250.
06.04.1955: Registered at Hull as **GLENELLA** (H333).   19.12.1956: Laid up.   1957: Sold to BISCO and allocated to to J J King & Co Ltd, Gateshead.   13.05.1957: Arrived Gateshead for breaking up.   19.10.1957: Hull registry closed.

MENDIP 163952 Steam trawler H114	1128 22.09.1934 08.11.1934	412 158	152.8 25.6 13.6	C D Holmes 106 nhp 3-cyl 11.7 knots	W B Willey Sons Ltd, Hull

07.11.1934: Registered at Hull (H114).   18.07.1938: Sold to Hudson Brothers Trawlers Ltd, Hull, for £14,650.   14.11.1938: Sold to East Riding Steam Fishing Co Ltd, Hull.   09.1939: Requisitioned for war service.   11.1939: Sold to the Admiralty (£23,505). Based Harwich with 11th A/S Group.   09.12.1939: Hull registry closed. Fitted out as an anti-submarine trawler (P.No.FY.249).
09.02.1940: Renamed HMS **SPHENE**.   1946: Sold to Hull Ice Co Ltd, Hull. Restored at North Shields and classed for trawling. Remeasured to 413grt, 162net.   09.02.1946: Registered at Hull as **MENDIP** (H202).   16.11.1946: Sold to Charleson-Smith Trawlers Ltd, Hull.   18.12.1946: Registered at Hull as **STELLA DORADO** (H202).   25.03.1948: Sold to Partnership (Hull) Ltd, Hull.
22.07.1948: Registered at Hull as **HACKNESS** (H202).   04.11.1948: Sold to Saint Andrew's Steam Fishing Co Ltd, Hull.
22.06.1954: Sold to Fern Leaf Co Ltd, Fleetwood.   16.02.1955: Hull registry closed. Registered at Fleetwood (FD120).
12.11.1958: Fishing off Látrabjarg, Iceland, ordered to stop by Icelandic coastguard THOR; HMS RUSSELL (P.No.F.97) intervened and escorted outside 12 mile fishing limit.   1958: Sold to Alvis Trawlers Ltd, Fleetwood.   01.01.1959: Sold to Sun Trawling Co Ltd, Fleetwood.   24.07.1959: Sold to Jacques Bakker & Zonen, Bruges, Belgium, for breaking up.   27.07.1959: Arrived Bruges from Fleetwood under own power.   Fleetwood registry closed.

WESTELLA 163956 Steam trawler H124	1129 25.09.1934 22.11.1934	413 160	152.8 25.6 13.6	Amos & Smith 106 npt 3-cyl 11.7 knots	J Marr & Son Ltd, Fleetwood

14.11.1934: Registered at Hull (H124). Crewed and operated by City Steam Fishing Co Ltd, Hull.   31.08.1939: Sold to the Admiralty (£22,448). Converted to an anti-submarine trawler (1-4", AA weapons, ASDIC, DC) (P.No.FY.161).   15.11.1939: Hull registry closed.
1940: Based Dover with 10th A/S Group (Ch Sk A Gove RNR).   26.05.1940: 'Operation Dynamo' (Dunkirk evacuation) put into effect.   28.05.1940: On A/S patrol.   02.06.1940: On A/S patrol off Dunkirk, at 4.00pm. BLACKBURN ROVERS (P.No.FY.116) (GY102) was mined and blew up, going to her aid explosions from BLACKBURN ROVERS' depth charges almost blew her out of the water as she closed to pick up survivors; at 4.30pm also mined and disabled. All survivors picked up by HM Trawler SAON (see yard no.1111) which with GRIMSBY TOWN (P.No.FY125) set her depth charges 'safe' and sank her in position 51.19N 02.05E.
03.06.1940: Thomas M Godfrey, seaman, died of wounds.

WARWICK DEEPING 163958 Steam trawler H136	1130 11.10.1934 11.12.1934	445 182	155.8 26.1 14.0	C D Holmes 111 nhp 3-cyl 11.7 knots	Newington Steam Trawling Co Ltd, Hull

07.12.1934: Registered at Hull (H136).   11.08.1939: Sold to the Admiralty (£23,030). Converted to an anti-submarine trawler (1-4", AA weapons, ASDIC, DC) (P.No.FY.182).   19.01.1940: Hull registry closed. Based Portsmouth with 17th A/S Group.   12.10.1940: In English Channel some 25 miles SW of St Catherines Point, Isle of Wight (Sk J R Bruce RNR) in company with HM Trawler L'ISTRAC (Lt K P Pickup RNR) attacked by German torpedo boats. L'ISTRAC sunk by torpedo, WARWICK DEEPING attempted to escape but badly damaged by gunfire from the boats KONDOR and FALKE; her engine immobilised, crew abandoned to boat. Torpedo boats did not press home their attack but vessel foundered in position 50.34N 01.27W. All crew rescued.

HENDREN 162897 Steam trawler GY128	1131 11.11.1934 02.01.1935	441 191	161.0 26.6 14.2	Amos & Smith 132 nhp 3-cyl 12.0 knots	Perihelion Steam Fishing Co Ltd, Grimsby

30.01.1935: Registered at Grimsby (GY128).   05.1939: Sold to Charleson-Smith Trawlers Ltd, Hull.   10.05.1939: Grimsby registry closed.   12.05.1939: Registered at Hull (H90).   26.05.1939: Registered at Hull as **STELLA PEGASI** (H90).
01.09.1939: Requisitioned for war service as an anti-submarine trawler (P.No.FY.155). Based Iceland with 19th A/S Group.
26.11.1945: Returned.   14.09.1946: Sold to Boyd Line Ltd, Hull.   11.10.1946: Registered at Hull as **ARCTIC CRUSADER** (H90).
21.04.1947: Sold to Trawlers Grimsby Ltd, Grimsby.   24.04.1947: Hull registry closed.   04.1947: Registered at Grimsby (GY477).
09.1947: Registered at Grimsby as as **MOUNTBATTEN** (GY477).   01.1949: Stranded in Rødøy Fjord, Norway, and abandoned.
08.1949: Grimsby registry closed. Refloated and sold by salvors to Norwegian then German owners.   08.03.1951: Whilst under tow towards Hamburg for new owners in heavy weather in the Elbe estuary started to take in water, developed a list and foundered.

DRANGEY 162893 Steam trawler GY126	1132 21.11.1934 09.01.1935	434 237	156.0 25.9 14.1	Amos & Smith 110 nhp 3-cyl 12.0 knots	Rinovia Steam Fishing Co Ltd, Grimsby

02.01.1935: Registered at Grimsby (GY126).   07.1937: Sold to Drangey Steam Fishing Co Ltd, Grimsby.   08.1939: Sold to the Admiralty. Converted to an anti-submarine trawler (1-4") (P.No.FY.195).   05.01.1940: Grimsby registry closed. Based Harwich with 11th A/S Group.   06.1946: Sold to Hull Ice Co Ltd, Hull.   06.1946: Registered at Grimsby (GY280).   16.11.1946: Sold to H Croft Baker & Sons Ltd, Grimsby.   03.1947: Registered at Grimsby as **MILDENHALL** (GY280).   01.11.1948: Stranded on Laassat reef, 2 miles south-east of Cape Nyemetski, Finland. All the crew rescued.   12.1948: Grimsby registry closed.

Cape Barfleur *(1127)*

(Authors' collection)

Mendip *(1128)*

(Authors' collection)

The **Mendip** *under her later name of* **Hackness**.
Readers will notice some changes.

(Authors' collection)

Warwick Deeping *(1130)*

(Authors' collection)

CAPE CHELYUSKIN	1152	494	166.0	C D Holmes	Hudson Steam Fishing
164024 Steam trawler	08.02.1936	192	27.6	132 nhp 3-cyl	Co Ltd,
H248	23.03.1936		14.2	12.0 knots	Hull

18.03.1936: Registered at Hull (H248).   07.09.1939: Sold to the Admiralty (£27,437).   13.09.1939: Hull registry closed. Converted to an anti-submarine trawler (1-4", AA weapons, ASDIC, DC) (P.No.FY.119). Based Belfast with 12th A/S Group.   04.1940: Took part in the Norwegian campaign.   29.04.1940: In Trondheim area during evacuation (Sk H E Moran RNR), attacked by German aircraft and badly damaged; scuttled by allied forces.

CAPE ARGONA	1153	494	166.0	C D Holmes	Hudson Steam Fishing
164015 Steam trawler	24.03.1936	192	27.6	132 nhp 3-cyl	Co Ltd,
H265	04.04.1936		14.2	12.0 knots	Hull

31.03.1936: Registered at Hull (H248).   07.09.1939: Sold to the Admiralty (£27,473). Converted to an anti-submarine trawler (1-4", AA weapons, ASDIC, DC) (P.No.FY.119).   13.09.1939: Hull registry closed. Based Belfast with 12th A/S Group.   04.1940: Took part in the Norwegian campaign.   26.10.1940: Assisted in rescue of survivors from passenger liner EMPRESS OF BRITAIN (42348grt/1931), attacked and set on fire by two bombs from German FW200 bomber (Condor), 70 miles NW of Donegal Bay, Ireland.   1942: Based Iceland with 41st A/S Group.   11.1945: Sold to Hull Ice Co Ltd, Hull.   27.11.1945: Registered at Hull (H143).   16.11.1946: Sold to Hudson Brothers Trawlers Ltd, Hull.   03.05.1951: Sold to Boyd Line Ltd, Hull.   30.05.1951: Registered at Hull as **ARCTIC SCOUT** (H143).   28.05.1957: Laid up.   11.06.1957: Sold to Van Heyghen Frères, Belgium, for breaking up.   20.06.1957: Breaking up commenced at Ghent.   26.06.1957: Hull registry closed.

ADMIRAL DRAKE	1154	418	152.8	C D Holmes	C H Smith & Co (Hull) Ltd,
164919 Steam trawler	09.03.1936	162	25.6	650 ihp 3-cyl	Hull
H273	22.04.1936		13.6	11.7 knots	

20.04.1936: Registered at Hull (H273).   29.07.1938: Sold to Charleson-Smith Trawlers Ltd, Hull.   31.12.1938: Registered at Hull as **STELLA CANOPUS** (H273).   05.10.1939: Requisitioned for war service as an anti-submarine trawler (1-4", AA weapons, ASDIC, DC) (P.No.FY.248). Based Granton with 38th A/S Group.   05.1945: Operation Pledge. At Loch Eriboll with surrendered U-boats.   12.11.1945: Returned.   16.04.1946: Sold to Trawlers Grimsby Ltd, Grimsby.   16.04.1946: Hull registry closed.   25.04.1946: Registered at Grimsby (GY263).   19.06.1946: Registered at Grimsby as **CRADOCK** (GY263).   10.05.1952: Sold to Thomas Ross Ltd, Grimsby.   12.04.1954: Sold to Derwent Trawlers, Grimsby.   24.04.1954: Grimsby registry closed.   26.04.1954: Sold to Charleson-Smith Trawlers Ltd, Hull.   06.1954: Grimsby registry closed.   18.06.1954: Registered at Hull as **STELLA RIGEL** (H14).   08.1955: Sold to Derwent Trawlers Ltd, Grimsby.   15.08.1955: Hull registry closed.   16.08.1955: Registered at Grimsby as **CRADOCK** (GY11).   03.1957: Sold to T C & F Moss Ltd, Grimsby.   13.07.1960: Sold to Jacques Bakker & Zonen, Bruges, Belgium, for breaking up.   25.07.1960: Arrived Bruges.   07.1960: Grimsby registry closed.

LORD MIDDLETON	1155	464	161.3	Amos & Smith	Pickering & Haldane's
164923 Steam trawler	24.03.1936	188	26.6	112 nhp 3-cyl	Steam Trawling Co Ltd,
H282	19.05.1936		14.1	12.0 knots	Hull

07.05.1936: Registered at Hull (H282). Completed at a cost of £19,805.   09.1939: Requisitioned for war service as an anti-submarine trawler (1-4", AA weapons, ASDIC, DC) (P.No. FY.219); hire rate £301.12.0d per month.   01.1940: Based Ardrossan with 29th A/S Group.   04.1942: Murmansk convoys PQ14 to PQ17 inclusive and return QP convoys.   08.04.1942: Sailed Oban escorting convoy PQ-14 - Oban - Murmansk.   16.04.1942: In company with NORTHERN WAVE (P.No.FY153) (655grt/1936) (Ty/Lt William G Pardoe-Matthews RNR) who picked up 28 survivors, picked up 9 survivors including Master (Capt John McDonald), from MoWT steamer EMPIRE HOWARD (6985grt/1941) torpedoed by U-boat (U403) NW of North Cape (73.48 21.50E). Landed survivors at Polarnoe near Murmansk.   28.04.1942: Sailed Murmansk escorting convoy PQ-11 - Murmansk - Reykjavik.   01.05.1942: 150 miles off Bear Island picked up 14 survivors of Russian steamer TSIOLKOVSKIJ (2847g/1935) torpedoed by U-boat (U589) (71.46N 34.30E) and damaged, subsequently sunk by German destroyers Z-24 and Z-25.   04.1944: Assigned to Operation Neptune - Normandy landings.   23.05.1944: Convoy escort duties in British waters and across the Channel in support of landings.   03.07.1944: Operation Neptune ended.   12.1944: Pickering & Haldane bought by J Bennett, London.   20.06.1945: Company restyled as Lord Line Ltd, Hull.   18.03.1946: Returned.   12.1947: Converted for burning oil fuel.   17.04.1950: Sold to Associated Fisheries Trawling Co Ltd, Hull, for £20,500 (Lord Line in liquidation).   22.07.1953: Company restyled Lord Line Ltd, Hull.   21.08.1962: Sold to Wyre Trawlers Ltd, Fleetwood, for £28,304.   01.10.1962: Hull registry closed.   10.1962: Registered at Fleetwood (FD67).   05.1964: Sold to Thos W Ward Ltd, Sheffield, for breaking up.   14.05.1964: Delivered Barrow-in-Furness.   1964: Fleetwood registry closed.

LORD HOTHAM	1156	464	161.3	C D Holmes	Pickering & Haldane's
164927 Steam trawler	08.04.1936	189	26.6	114 nhp 3-cyl	Steam Trawling Co Ltd,
H309	28.05.1936		14.1	12.0 knots	Hull

26.05.1936: Registered at Hull (H309). Completed at a cost of £20,659.   09.08.1939: Landed at Hull having been recalled for war service; fishing gear removed.   01.11.1939: Sold to the Admiralty (£25,676).   15.11.1939: Hull registry closed. Fitted out as an anti-submarine trawler (1-4", AA weapons, ASDIC) (P.No.FY.133). Based Gibraltar with 7th A/S Group.   06.03.1946: Sold to Hull Ice Co Ltd, Hull, for £18,659.   16.03.1946: Registered at Hull (H231).   16.11.1946: Sold to Lord Line Ltd, Hull, for £18,659.   01.1948: Converted to burn oil fuel.   17.04.1950: Sold to Associated Fisheries Trawling Co Ltd, Hull, for £25,000 (Lord Line in liquidation).   25.11.1952: Escorted into Tromsø by Norwegian destroyer for alleged fishing in territorial waters. Sk Niels M Pedersen refused to pay a fine and elected to go to court.   28.11.1952: At a court in Tromsø, Sk. Pedersen was fined in total £4,450.   22.07.1953: Company restyled Lord Line Ltd, Hull (Thomas W Boyd, manager).   23.12.1961: Arrived Fleetwood.   04.01.1962: Sold to Wyre Trawlers Ltd, Fleetwood, for £31,501.   20.02.1962: Hull registry closed.   02.1962: Registered at Fleetwood (FD64).   1967: Sold to Scrappingco S.r.l., Brussels, Belgium, for breaking up.   19.03.1967: Sailed Fleetwood for Antwerp.   21.03.1967: Delivered Antwerp.   1967: Fleetwood registry closed.

VIVIANA 164410 Steam trawler GY233	1157 23.04.1936 12.06.1936	452 210	158.5 26.6 14.2	C D Holmes 114 nhp 3-cyl 12.0 knots	Atlas Steam Fishing Co Ltd, Grimsby

06.06.1936: Registered at Grimsby (GY233).   17.10.1939: Requisitioned for war service as an anti-submarine trawler (1-4", AA weapons, ASDIC, DC) (P.No.FY.238); hire rate £293.16.0d per month. Based Harwich with 11th A/S Group.   1942: Based N Ireland with Belfast Escort Group.   1943: Transferred to Durban, South Africa, for escort duties.   21.05.1946: Returned.   12.1962: Sold to Van Heyghen Frères, Belgium.   01.12.1962: Arrived Ghent for breaking up.   12.1962: Grimsby registry closed.

LORD ESSENDON 164934 Steam trawler H312	1158 09.05.1936 25.06.1936	464 202	161.3 26.6	C D Holmes 114 nhp 3-cyl 12.0 knots	Pickering & Haldane's Steam Trawling Co Ltd, Hull

Cost to build £20,100.   22.06.1936: Registered at Hull (H312).   30.06.1936: Sailed Hull on first trip to Greenland (Sk C Hansen). 06.1936: When in transit in Pentland Firth in thick fog, stranded on east side of Stroma. Refloated without assistance and proceeded to Aberdeen (four days).   30.08.1939: At Hull (Sk E Clarke) landed 1,104 kits grossed £871 having been recalled for war service; fishing gear removed.   09.1939: Requisitioned for war service as an anti-submarine trawler (1-4", AA weapons, ASDIC) (P.No.FY.218); hire rate £301.12.0d per month.   01.1940: Based Ardrossan with 29th A/S Group (Senior Officer, Pby/Ty/Sub Lt M R Thwaites RNVR).   1942: Based Plymouth with 20th A/S Group.   1944: Assigned to Operation Neptune - Normandy landings. 23.05.1944: Convoy escort duties in British waters and across the Channel in support of landings.   03.07.1944: Operation Neptune ended.   20.06.1945: Sold to Lord Line Ltd, Hull, for £21,100.   09.10.1945: Returned after survey and restoration at Hartlepool. 07.1947: Converted to burn oil fuel.   17.04.1950: Sold to Associated Fisheries Trawling Co Ltd, Hull, for £21,000 (Lord Line in liquidation).   22.07.1953: Company restyled Lord Line Ltd, Hull.   17.12.1962: Transferred to Fleetwood.   01.01.1963: Sold to Wyre Trawlers Ltd, Fleetwood, for £28,653.   06.01.1964: Hull registry closed.   01.1964: Registered at Fleetwood (FD75). 23.04.1966: Sold to James A White & Co Ltd, St. Davids, Fife, for breaking up.   09.07.1966: Delivered St. Davids. 1966: Fleetwood registry closed.

KIRKELLA 164937 Steam trawler H319	1159 21.05.1936 04.07.1936	435 170	157.3 26.1 14.1	Amos & Smith 750 ihp 3-cyl 11.3 knots	J Marr & Son Ltd, Hull

03.07.1936: Registered at Hull (H319). Crewed and operated by City Steam Fishing Co Ltd, Hull.   31.08.1939: Sold to the Admiralty (£25,168). Fitted out as an anti-submarine trawler (1-4", AA weapons, ASDIC) (P.No.FY.174).   19.01.1940: Hull registry closed. Based Swansea with 17th A/S Group.   17.12.1945: On completion of refit at Ellesmere Port and classification as a steam trawler, sold to Hull Ice Co Ltd, Hull.   17.12.1945: Registered at Hull (H155).   16.11.1946: Sold to J Marr & Son Ltd, Fleetwood. 17.12.1947: Sold to Dinas Steam Trawling Co Ltd, Fleetwood, for £67,500.   22.12.1948: Sold to Parkholme Trawlers Ltd, Fleetwood.   08.01.1949: Hull registry closed.   11.01.1949: Registered at Grimsby (GY592).   28.02.1949: Registered at Grimsby as **MOORSOM** (GY592).   29.03.1951: Sold to Ravendale Trawlers Ltd, Grimsby.   07.03.1952: Sold to Great Western Fishing Co Ltd, Aberdeen.   29.03.1952: Registered at Grimsby as **ST BENEDICT** (GY592).   18.09.1952: Off the west coast of Norway in heavy seas, lost fires due to water ingress. Salvage steamer DRAUGEN (207grt/1898) connected and commenced tow to Unde, east of Aalesund.   19.09.1952: Delivered Unde.   04.01.1955: Sold to Cevic Steam Fishing Co Ltd, Fleetwood.   18.09.1956: Grimsby registry closed.   09.1956: Registered at Fleetwood (FD7).   1957: Registered at Fleetwood as **RENEVA** (FD7).   1960: Sold to BISCO and allocated to Thos W Ward Ltd, Sheffield, for breaking up.   07.07.1960: Sailed Fleetwood for Preston. 08.07.1960: Delivered Preston.   11.02.1962: Fleetwood registry closed.

BRITISH GUIANA 164419 Motor trawler GY331	1160 1936 27.10.1936	146 53	101.2 21.1 10.3	Ruston & Hornsby 91 nhp 6-cyl 11.2 knots	Grimsby Motor Trawlers Ltd, Grimsby

10.1936: Registered at Grimsby (GY331).   27.11.1939: Requisitioned for war service as an anti-submarine trawler (P.No. FY.271); hire rate £118.12.6d per month. Based Holyhead with 35th A/S Group.   1942: Based Larne with 35th A/S Group.   03.1943: Sold to Frederick Ernest Catchpole, Lowestoft (Star Drift Fishing Co Ltd).   09.03.1946: Returned.   1946: Grimsby registry closed. Registered at Lowestoft as **SUNLIT WATERS** (LT93).   04.1947: Sold to Milford Steam Trawlers Ltd, Milford Haven. 30.04.1947: Registered at Milford (M176).   07.06.1947: Registered at Milford as **MILFORD KNIGHT** (M176).   26.05.1949: Sold to Claridge Trawlers Ltd, Lowestoft.   04.01.1950: Registered at Lowestoft as **BRITISH GUIANA** (LT52).   11.1968: Sold to T G Darling & Co Ltd, Oulton Broad, Lowestoft, for breaking up. Lowestoft registry closed.

ADMIRAL COLLINGWOOD 164963 Steam trawler H341	1161 19.08.1936 30.09.1936	447 181	155.0 26.6 13.9	Amos & Smith 105 nhp 3-cyl 11.0 knots	C H Smith & Co (Hull) Ltd, Hull

28.09.1936: Registered at Hull (H341).   30.12.1936: Last radio contact when homeward towards Hull on the 1330 mile passage from Bear Island grounds (Sk Frederick G. Danton); believed foundered during a storm.   05.01.1937: Boat and wreckage washed up on Ona Island, near Ålesund, west coast of Norway. All eighteen crew lost.   23.03.1937: Hull registry closed - "Total loss".

ONER 165398 Motor tug	1162 01.12.1936 11.02.1937	89 -	80.6 21.1 7.4	British Auxiliaries 101 nhp 6-cyl 11.0 knots	James Contracting Towage & Shipping Co Ltd, London

02.1937: Registered at London.   1940: Sold to Venezuelan Oil Concessions Ltd, Maracaibo, Venezuela. London registry closed. Registered at Maracaibo as **TIA JUANA**.   1958: Sold to Venezolana de Servicios Maritimos, Maracaibo. Registered at Maracaibo as **TERESA MORAN**.   1959: Sold to Compania SHELL de Venezuela, Maracaibo. Registered at Maracaibo as **TIA JUANA**. 1963: Vessel removed from Register of Shipping.

Cape Campbell *(1172)*

(Authors' collection)

Hugh Walpole *(1173)*

(Authors' collection)

Reighton Wyke *(1174)*

(Authors' collection)

ARCTIC RANGER	1175	501	166.7	C D Holmes	Boyd Line Ltd,
165007 Steam trawler	15.12.1936	190	27.6	132 nhp 3-cyl	Hull
H429	19.02.1937		14.2	12.0 knots	

16.02.1937: Registered at Hull (H429).   08.1939: Sold to the Admiralty (£28.636).   13.09.1939: Hull registry closed. Converted to an anti submarine trawler (1-4", AA weapons, ASDIC, DC) (P.No.FY.186). Based Gibraltar with 7th A/S Group.   03.1946: Sold to Hull Ice Co Ltd, Hull.   28.03.1946: Registered at Hull (H251).   16.11.1946: Sold to Boyd Line Ltd, Hull.   03.1948: Converted to oil fuel. 28.11.1951: Sold to Newington Steam Trawling Co Ltd, Hull.   29.11.1951: Registered at Hull as **CONAN DOYLE** (H251). 22.12.1965: Laid up.   1965: Sold to James A White & Co Ltd, St Davids on Forth, for breaking up.   07.01.1966: Arrived St Davids on Forth.   20.01.1966: Hull registry closed.

ARCTIC EXPLORER	1176	501	166.7	C D Holmes	Boyd Line Ltd,
165010 Steam trawler	30.12.1936	189	27.6	132 nhp 3-cyl	Hull
H445	12.03.1937		14.2	12.2 knots	

04.03.1937: Registered at Hull (H445).   08.1939: Sold to the Admiralty (£28,741).   09.12.1939: Hull registry closed. Converted to an anti-submarine trawler (1-4", AA weapons, ASDIC, DC) (P.No.FY.162). Based Belfast with Escort Group.   1942: Based Plymouth with 34th A/S Group.   25.02.1942: Loaned to United States Navy (retained RN crew).   10.1942: Returned to the Royal Navy. 1943: Transferred to South Africa station, based at Durban for convoy duties.   07.1946: Sold to Hull Ice Co Ltd, Hull for £27,600. 31.07.1946: Registered at Hull (H287).   16.11.1946: Sold to Prince Fishing Co Ltd, Hull.   22.03.1947: Sold to Northern Fishing Co (Hull) Ltd, Hull.   04.06.1947: Registered at Hull as **CAPTAIN OATES** (H287).   26.07.1948: Sold to Boyd Line Ltd, Hull. 18.09.1948: Registered at Hull as **ARCTIC EXPLORER** (H287).   07.1956: Converted to burn oil fuel.   30.12.1966: Laid up. 25.04.1967: Sold to P & W Maclellan Ltd, Bo'ness, for breaking up.   26.06.1967: Hull registry closed. Such was the affection the company had for this ship she was scrubbed clean and repainted to look her best on her final journey.

ARCTIC PIONEER	1177	501	166.7	C D Holmes	Boyd Line Ltd,
165649 Steam trawler	14.01.1937	189	27.6	132 nhp 3-cyl	Hull
H462	25.03.1937		14.2	12.0 knots	

19.03.1937: Registered at Hull (H462).   26.08.1939: Requisitioned for war service as an anti-submarine trawler (1-4", AA weapons, ASDIC, DC) (P.No.FY.164); hire rate £338.3.6d per month. Based Harwich with 11th A/S Group.   04.1940: Took part in the Norwegian campaign.   1942: Based Southampton with 26th A/S Group.   27.05.1942: In Cowes Roads (Sk George Bryan RNR) attacked and bombed by a German JU-87 Stuka aircraft, hit and sunk; seventeen crew lost.   06.12.1946: Hull registry closed. 1947: Salved and repairs carried out in Southampton. Transferred to Wm Gray & Co Ltd, West Hartlepool for restoration and re-engined with triple expansion by Amos & Smith Ltd, Hull; converted for burning oil fuel.   08.1947: Remeasured on completion to 533grt, 203net.   08.1947: Returned to Boyd Line Ltd, Hull.   26.08.1947: Registered at Hull as **ARCTIC VIKING** (H452). 27.05.1956: When some 45 miles WS-W of Bear Island, in collision with and sank trawler ST. CELESTIN (H232) (790grt/1952). Picked up all crew and landed them at Hull.   18.10.1961: Homeward to Hull in heavy seas 15 miles off Flamborough Head capsized and foundered; five crew lost. Fifteen survivors including skipper Philip Garner picked up by Polish lugger DERKACZ. 10.11.1961: Hull registry closed.

ELIZABETH COOPER	1178	227	100.0	Crossley Bros	William Cooper & Sons Ltd,
164328 Motor hopper	11.05.1937	114	26.1	116 nhp 6-cyl	Widnes
barge	30.06.1937		10.4	12.0 knots	

06.1937: Registered at Liverpool.   10.12.1963: Sank at Ince in the Manchester Ship Canal following collision with sludge vessel MANCUNIUM (1390grt/1946).   16.12.1963: Removed from the main fairway after causing disruption to the canal traffic. Sold for breaking up.   Registry closed.

MAN O'WAR	1179	517	173.2	Amos & Smith	Earl Steam Fishing Co Ltd,
164423 Steam trawler	12.02.1937	216	28.6	135 nhp 3-cyl	Grimsby
GY396	14.04.1937			12.2 knots	

09.04.1937: Registered at Grimsby (GY396).   08.1939: Sold to the Admiralty (£30,121). Converted to an anti submarine trawler (1-4", AA weapons, ASDIC, DC) (P.No.FY.104).   02.03.1940: Grimsby registry closed.   04.1940: With 21st Strike Force took part in the Norwegian campaign.   1942: Based Londonderry with Escort Group.   01.01.1946: Sold to Hull Ice Co Ltd, Hull for £16,268. 01.01.1946: Registered at Hull (H181).   16.11.1946: Sold to Hellyer Bros Ltd, Hull.   18.11.1948: Sold to Devon Fishing Co Ltd, Hull. 15.11.1952: Name of Devon Fishing Co Ltd changed to Hellyer Bros. Ltd, Hull.   07.1953: Converted to burn oil fuel. 31.05.1963: Laid up.   1963: Sold to Thos W Ward Ltd, Sheffield, for £5,145 and allocated to Inverkeithing for breaking up. 09.12.1963: Arrived Inverkeithing.   27.07.1964: Hull registry closed.

Index of vessel names following sale or transfer (and yard numbers)

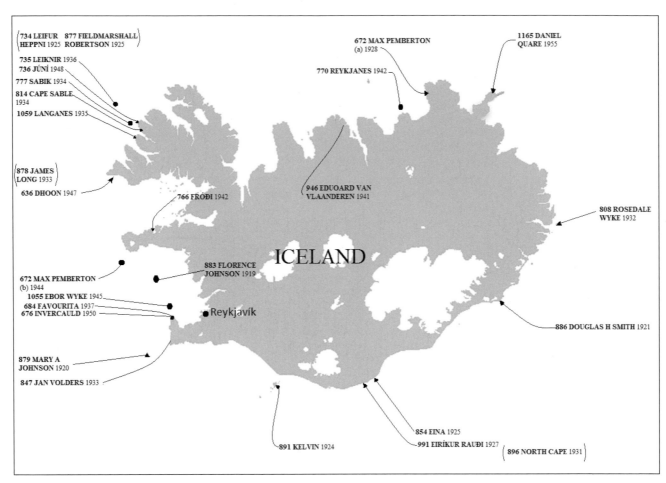

Map of Iceland showing location of all casualties in the area involving vessels mentioned in this book.

(Birgir Thorisson)